At Great Risk: Memoirs of Rescue during the Holocaust

THE AZRIELI SERIES OF HOLOCAUST SURVIVOR MEMOIRS: PUBLISHED TITLES

ENGLISH TITLES

Judy Abrams, *Tenuous Threads*/ Eva Felsenburg Marx, *One of the Lucky Ones*
Amek Adler, *Six Lost Years*
Ferenc Andai, *In the Hour of Fate and Danger*
Molly Applebaum, *Buried Words: The Diary of Molly Applebaum*
Claire Baum, *The Hidden Package*
Bronia and Joseph Beker, *Joy Runs Deeper*
Tibor Benyovits, *Unsung Heroes*
Max Bornstein, *If Home Is Not Here*
Felicia Carmelly, *Across the Rivers of Memory*
Judy Cohen, *A Cry in Unison*
Tommy Dick, *Getting Out Alive*
Marian Domanski, *Fleeing from the Hunter*
Anita Ekstein, *Always Remember Who You Are*
Leslie Fazekas, *In Dreams Together: The Diary of Leslie Fazekas*
John Freund, *Spring's End*
Susan Garfield, *Too Many Goodbyes: The Diaries of Susan Garfield*
Myrna Goldenberg (Editor), *Before All Memory Is Lost: Women's Voices from the Holocaust*
René Goldman, *A Childhood Adrift*
Elly Gotz, *Flights of Spirit*
Ibolya Grossman and Andy Réti, *Stronger Together*
Pinchas Gutter, *Memories in Focus*
Anna Molnár Hegedűs, *As the Lilacs Bloomed*
Rabbi Pinchas Hirschprung, *The Vale of Tears*
Bronia Jablon, *A Part of Me*
Helena Jockel, *We Sang in Hushed Voices*
Eddie Klein, *Inside the Walls*
Michael Kutz, *If, By Miracle*
Ferenc Laczó (Editor), *Confronting Devastation: Memoirs of Holocaust Survivors from Hungary*
Nate Leipciger, *The Weight of Freedom*
Alex Levin, *Under the Yellow and Red Stars*
Rachel Lisogurski and Chana Broder, *Daring to Hope*
Fred Mann, *A Drastic Turn of Destiny*
Michael Mason, *A Name Unbroken*
Leslie Meisels with Eva Meisels, *Suddenly the Shadow Fell*
Leslie Mezei, *A Tapestry of Survival*
Muguette Myers, *Where Courage Lives*
David Newman, *Hope's Reprise*
Arthur Ney, *W Hour*
Felix Opatowski, *Gatehouse to Hell*
Marguerite Élias Quddus, *In Hiding*
Maya Rakitova, *Behind the Red Curtain*
Henia Reinhartz, *Bits and Pieces*
Betty Rich, *Little Girl Lost*
Paul-Henri Rips, *E/96: Fate Undecided*
Margrit Rosenberg Stenge, *Silent Refuge*
Steve Rotschild, *Traces of What Was*
Judith Rubinstein, *Dignity Endures*
Martha Salcudean, *In Search of Light*
Kitty Salsberg and Ellen Foster, *Never Far Apart*
Morris Schnitzer, *Escape from the Edge*
Joseph Schwarzberg, *Dangerous Measures*
Zuzana Sermer, *Survival Kit*
Rachel Shtibel, *The Violin*/ Adam Shtibel, *A Child's Testimony*
Maxwell Smart, *Chaos to Canvas*
Gerta Solan, *My Heart Is At Ease*
Zsuzsanna Fischer Spiro, *In Fragile Moments*/ Eva Shainblum, *The Last Time*
George Stern, *Vanished Boyhood*

Willie Sterner, *The Shadows Behind Me*
Ann Szedlecki, *Album of My Life*
William Tannenzapf, *Memories from the Abyss*/ Renate Krakauer, *But I Had a Happy Childhood*
Elsa Thon, *If Only It Were Fiction*
Agnes Tomasov, *From Generation to Generation*
Joseph Tomasov, *From Loss to Liberation*
Sam Weisberg, *Carry the Torch*/ Johnny Jablon, *A Lasting Legacy*
Leslie Vertes, *Alone in the Storm*
Anka Voticky, *Knocking on Every Door*

TITRES FRANÇAIS

Judy Abrams, *Retenue par un fil*/ Eva Felsenburg Marx, *Une question de chance*
Molly Applebaum, *Les Mots enfouis: Le Journal de Molly Applebaum*
Claire Baum, *Le Colis caché*
Bronia et Joseph Beker, *Plus forts que le malheur*
Max Bornstein, *Citoyen de nulle part*
Tommy Dick, *Objectif: survivre*
Marian Domanski, *Traqué*
John Freund, *La Fin du printemps*
Myrna Goldenberg (Éditrice), *Un combat singulier: Femmes dans la tourmente de l'Holocauste*
René Goldman, *Une enfance à la dérive*
Anna Molnár Hegedűs, *Pendant la saison des lilas*
Helena Jockel, *Nous chantions en sourdine*
Michael Kutz, *Si, par miracle*
Nate Leipciger, *Le Poids de la liberté*
Alex Levin, *Étoile jaune, étoile rouge*
Fred Mann, *Un terrible revers de fortune*
Michael Mason, *Au fil d'un nom*
Leslie Meisels, *Soudain, les ténèbres*
Muguette Myers, *Les Lieux du courage*
Arthur Ney, *L'Heure W*
Felix Opatowski, *L'Antichambre de l'enfer*
Marguerite Élias Quddus, *Cachée*
Henia Reinhartz, *Fragments de ma vie*
Betty Rich, *Seule au monde*
Paul-Henri Rips, *Matricule E/96*
Steve Rotschild, *Sur les traces du passé*
Kitty Salsberg et Ellen Foster, *Unies dans l'épreuve*
Zuzana Sermer, *Trousse de survie*
Rachel Shtibel, *Le Violon*/ Adam Shtibel, *Témoignage d'un enfant*
George Stern, *Une jeunesse perdue*
Willie Sterner, *Les Ombres du passé*
Ann Szedlecki, *L'Album de ma vie*
William Tannenzapf, *Souvenirs de l'abîme*/ Renate Krakauer, *Le Bonheur de l'innocence*
Elsa Thon, *Que renaisse demain*
Agnes Tomasov, *De génération en génération*
Leslie Vertes, *Seul dans la tourmente*
Anka Voticky, *Frapper à toutes les portes*

At Great Risk: Memoirs of Rescue during the Holocaust

Eva Lang, David Korn, Fishel Goldig

FIRST EDITION

THE AZRIELI FOUNDATION · www.azrielifoundation.org

Cover design by Endpaper Studio · Book design by Mark Goldstein · Interior maps by Deborah Crowle · Endpaper maps by Martin Gilbert.

Eva Lang's memoir was translated from French by Phyllis Aronoff (2017) with the editorial assistance of Elizabeth Lasserre. Letter and speech on pages 55–58 translated by Elizabeth Lasserre. Some of Eva Lang's photos on pages 63–69 were provided by the United States Holocaust Memorial Museum and Yad Vashem (photo archive numbers 6162/1; 6162/5; 906). See the captions for specific credit information. David Korn's letters from Pastor Vladimir Kuna on pages 142–146 were translated from Slovak by Eva Brejova (2020). Photos of Fishel Goldig on pages 210–211 used with permission and courtesy of Ron Diamond. Photo of Fishel Goldig on the bottom of page 210 used by permission and courtesy of Burney Lieberman. Quotes on page 188 from *Israeli Society, the Holocaust and Its Survivors* (Vallentine Mitchell, 2008) used with permission of the author, Dina Porat.

LIBRARY AND ARCHIVES CANADA CATALOGUING IN PUBLICATION

At Great Risk: Memoirs of Rescue during the Holocaust/ Eva Lang, David Korn, Fishel Goldig.

Lang, Eva, 1930– Three stars in the sky. Korn, David, 1937– Saved by luck and devotion. Goldig, Fishel, 1933– Survival story of a six-year-old boy.

Azrieli Foundation, publisher.

Azrieli series of Holocaust survivor memoirs. Series XIII.

Includes bibliographical references and index.

Canadiana 20210169621 · ISBN 9781989719107 (softcover)

LCSH: Lang, Eva, 1930– LCSH: Korn, David, 1937– LCSH: Goldig, Fishel, 1933– LCSH: Holocaust survivors — Biography. LCSH: Holocaust, Jewish (1939–1945) — Personal narratives. LCSH: World War, 1939–1945 — Jews — Rescue. LCSH: Righteous Gentiles in the Holocaust — Biography. LCGFT: Autobiographies.

LCC D804.65.A8 2021 DDC 940.53/180922 — DC23

PRINTED IN CANADA

The Azrieli Foundation's Holocaust Survivor Memoirs Program

Contents

Series Preface: In their own words. . .

In telling these stories, the writers have liberated themselves. For so many years we did not speak about it, even when we became free people living in a free society. Now, when at last we are writing about what happened to us in this dark period of history, knowing that our stories will be read and live on, it is possible for us to feel truly free. These unique historical documents put a face on what was lost, and allow readers to grasp the enormity of what happened to six million Jews — one story at a time.

David J. Azrieli, C.M., C.Q., M.Arch
Holocaust survivor and founder, The Azrieli Foundation

Since the end of World War II, approximately 40,000 Jewish Holocaust survivors have immigrated to Canada. Who they are, where they came from, what they experienced and how they built new lives for themselves and their families are important parts of our Canadian heritage. The Azrieli Foundation's Holocaust Survivor Memoirs Program was established in 2005 to preserve and share the memoirs written by those who survived the twentieth-century Nazi genocide of the Jews of Europe and later made their way to Canada. The memoirs encourage readers to engage thoughtfully and critically with the complexities of the Holocaust and to create meaningful connections with the lives of survivors.

Millions of individual stories are lost to us forever. By preserving the stories written by survivors and making them widely available to a broad audience, the Azrieli Foundation's Holocaust Survivor Memoirs Program seeks to sustain the memory of all those who perished at the hands of hatred, abetted by indifference and apathy. The personal accounts of those who survived against all odds are as different as the people who wrote them, but all demonstrate the courage, strength, wit and luck that it took to prevail and survive in such terrible adversity. The memoirs are also moving tributes to people — strangers and friends — who risked their lives to help others, and who, through acts of kindness and decency in the darkest of moments, frequently helped the persecuted maintain faith in humanity and courage to endure. These accounts offer inspiration to all, as does the survivors' desire to share their experiences so that new generations can learn from them.

The Holocaust Survivor Memoirs Program collects, archives and publishes select survivor memoirs and makes the print editions available free of charge to educational institutions and Holocaust-education programs across Canada. They are also available for sale online to the general public. All revenues to the Azrieli Foundation from the sales of the Azrieli Series of Holocaust Survivor Memoirs go toward the publishing and educational work of the memoirs program.

~

The Azrieli Foundation would like to express appreciation to the following people for their invaluable efforts in producing this book: Phyllis Aronoff, Eva Brejova, Judith Clark, Ron Diamond, Mark Duffus (Maracle Inc.), Benjamin Frommer, Wolf Gruner, Elizabeth Lasserre, Burney Lieberman, Jane Pavanel, Dina Porat, Susan Roitman and Second Story Press.

Editorial Note

The following memoirs contain terms, concepts and historical references that may be unfamiliar to the reader. English translations of foreign-language words and terms have been added to the texts, and parentheses have been used to include the names and locations of present-day towns and cities when place names have changed. The editors of these memoirs have worked to maintain the authors' voices and stay true to the original narratives while maintaining historical accuracy. Explanatory footnotes have been added for clarification or to provide key information for understanding the text. General information on major organizations, significant historical events and people, geographical locations, religious and cultural terms, and foreign-language words and expressions that will help give context to the events described in the texts can be found in the glossary beginning on page 347.

Introduction

At Great Risk: Memoirs of Rescue during the Holocaust features the stories of three Holocaust survivors — Eva Lang, David Korn and Fishel Philip Goldig — who were helped by non-Jews in different areas of Nazi-occupied Europe during World War II and the Holocaust. Those who helped Jews were a small minority of the predominantly Christian population in Europe during those years. *At Great Risk* should cause us all to ask ourselves why some non-Jews helped Jews during the Holocaust while so many others did not. To try to understand those who helped Jews, as well as to try to understand those who did not help them, it is important to examine what was happening in pre–World War II Nazi Germany and to consider the terror that prevailed in Nazi-occupied Europe during the war and the Holocaust.

The Rise of Hitler and the Nazi Party

In the immediate aftermath of World War I (1914–1918), Germany transformed itself from a monarchy to a democracy known as the Weimar Republic. Between 1919 and 1933, the Weimar Republic had a turbulent history, with many short-lived government administrations and increasing political polarization on the left and right. One of the new right-wing extremist political groups was called the Nazi Party (the National Socialist German Workers' Party), and its popularity grew rapidly after the global economic depression started in 1929.

On January 30, 1933, a day that was probably quite ordinary for most citizens in Weimar Germany, General Paul von Hindenburg, an aging World War I military hero and president of the Weimar Republic, appointed Nazi Party leader Adolf Hitler the head of a new government, hoping that his leadership would bring some stability. That day marked the beginning of a political upheaval that would reshape the Weimar Republic into a dictatorship, as Hitler began dismantling the Weimar democracy. By August 1934, Hitler had declared himself Führer, or leader, with unlimited power to control the German Reich (empire). Through this process, he sought to purify the so-called German race — Hitler and the Nazis called it "Aryan" — by targeting for persecution groups that either opposed the authority of the regime or were seen as a threat to German racial purity, such as Jews, political dissidents, Jehovah's Witnesses, homosexuals, people with disabilities and others. The vilification of Jews and efforts to exclude them from every aspect of German life was central to Nazi ideology and policies from the outset.

Nazi antisemitism was built on a long-standing hatred of Judaism as a religion and of Jews as a people. Hostility toward the Jews is found in the early Christian scriptures (New Testament), which include the false claim that Jews were responsible for the death of Jesus Christ. The absurd myth of "the Jews" as "Christ-killers" prevailed, and in Christian Europe over succeeding centuries, additional myths and lies circulated, horrendous and outlandish falsehoods such as Jews murdering Christian children so that their blood could be used in making matzah during the Jewish holiday of Passover, or blaming Jews for the pandemic of the Black Plague in Europe. Jews were also accused of unscrupulous business practices whenever they dealt with gentiles. As a result of this deeply entrenched hatred, Jews across Europe experienced segregation and persecution that often boiled over into violence.

By the latter part of the nineteenth century, with the rise of nationalism and racial thinking, Jews were singled out as a race that threatened the survival of other races in Europe. German journalist Wilhelm Marr coined the term *antisemitism* in 1879 to refer to the hatred of Jews based on ideas of blood and race, arguing for a biological, rather than cultural or religious, difference that distinguished Jews from other Germans. During the same period, a development known as Jewish emancipation unfolded across parts of Europe, including Germany, that saw civic rights and freedoms granted to the Jewish minority and fostered their social integration. Nonetheless, theological anti-Judaism had merged with racial antisemitism, and widespread hatred of Jews in Europe persisted into the twentieth century.[1]

Hitler and his regime embedded the hatred of Jews into Nazi Germany's laws and policies. Decrees singled out Jews for exclusion from day-to-day life: Jews were removed from various professions (medical, legal, teaching and others); Jewish businesses were subjected to Aryanization;[2] German public schools began excluding Jewish students and teachers from classes and positions; and German cultural and social events were closed to Jews. The Nuremberg Laws of 1935 stripped Jews of German citizenship and forbade new marriages between Jews and non-Jews. Pressure on Germans to participate in the social isolation of German Jews, who had become well-integrated into the German population, resulted in many interpersonal dilemmas, especially for intermarried families.

The Kristallnacht pogrom of November 1938 erupted into the most dramatic expression of antisemitism yet.Violent anti-Jewish demonstrations broke out in Germany, which had recently expanded its borders with the annexation of Austria and part of Czechoslovakia. Mobs, encouraged by Nazi officials, destroyed hundreds of synagogues, burning or desecrating Jewish religious artifacts along the way. Approximately 7,500 Jewish-owned businesses, homes and schools were plundered; ninety-one Jews were murdered; and 30,000 Jewish men were arrested and sent to concentration camps. Nazi officials blamed the Jews themselves for the violence and destruction, with the result that the Jewish community was fined over a billion

Reichsmarks (equal, in 1938 rates, to about US$400 million) to pay for the damages of Kristallnacht. Photos taken during the pogrom show many German spectators simply watching as buildings — homes, businesses, synagogues and other structures — burned. Fire companies only took action to save buildings that belonged to "Aryan" Germans, doing little or nothing to save properties owned by Jews.

Stories of Germans who tried to help their Jewish neighbours during Kristallnacht are rare. After William Kahle, a student at the University of Bonn, helped a Jewish neighbour restore order to her shop following the pogrom, he was called before a Nazi-controlled disciplinary court for "thoroughly reprehensible behaviour." The court explained that their ruling — dismissal from university and the loss of a semester's credit — was lenient since William was led astray by his mother, who had helped her Jewish friends during the violence.[3] By this point, Germans faced consequences for going against the tide of the increasingly violent state-sanctioned antisemitism.

In 1933, there were approximately 500,000 Jews in Germany (representing less than 1 per cent of the total population of roughly 66,000,000 people). By the eve of World War II in 1939, about 60 per cent of German Jews had left Germany and found refuge in other countries.[4] Leaving their homeland was a difficult decision, made worse by the financial burdens imposed by the Nazi government and restrictions on immigration in most destinations. Those who remained in Germany, isolated as they were, may have believed that the situation could not get worse, but faced new horrors as Germany radicalized its persecution of Jews during the war.

World War II and the Holocaust

On September 1, 1939, Nazi Germany invaded Poland, marking the beginning of World War II. The war was part of Germany's effort to satisfy its need for more space and to provide additional resources for the pure "Aryan" German race.[5] In the years 1940 to 1941, Nazi Germany continued its efforts to expand, sending its army north and west, invading and occupying Denmark, Norway, the Netherlands, Belgium, Luxembourg and France. Only Great Britain held off the fierce attacks on their island country by the Luftwaffe (German air force). In the spring and summer of 1941, Nazi Germany moved south and east, invading and occupying Yugoslavia, Greece and part of the Soviet Union. These invaded countries, including Poland, had large Jewish populations that together far exceeded the number of Jews in Nazi Germany by several millions. The greatly expanded Jewish population under Nazi Germany's control led to more drastic measures against Jews, more drastic even than those imposed in Germany itself.

In areas under German control, Jewish populations faced immediate and increasing persecution. In Eastern Europe, ghettos were established starting in 1939. Ghettos were an area of a town or city where Jews were physically segregated and isolated from the non-Jewish population. Conditions were appalling — massive overcrowding, as well as inadequate food and medical supplies — all of which made survival for Jews more and more difficult. Ghettos served to contain, exploit, degrade and eventually deport Jews to concentration and death camps. In Western Europe, the pace and forms of persecution differed from the east and was at first effected primarily through legislation to seize Jewish wealth and exclude Jews from public life. Beginning in mid-1942, mass deportations brought Jews in the West to join those in the East in ghettos and killing sites.

By June 1941, when Nazi Germany invaded the Soviet Union, the Germans began using SS mobile killing units known as Einsatzgruppen[6] to terrorize and mass murder approximately 1.5 million Jews, as well as communists and other "undesirables" living in Eastern Europe and the occupied Soviet Union. Jews in cities, towns and villages were murdered on the spot or rounded up and taken to be murdered in forests and other rural areas by the Einsatzgruppen, then buried in mass graves.[7] Local collaborators, or helpers, often assisted in these roundups and killings, and they were carried out in view of the local populations. Pre-existing hostilities between neighbours were exploited by the Nazis, creating a climate of chaos and fear.

In mid-1941, as Jews perished in ghettos and were killed in mass shootings, a new Nazi strategy began to take shape called the "Final Solution of the Jewish Question." On January 20, 1942, in a beautiful villa in the Berlin suburb of Wannsee, the details of the "Final Solution" were concretely worked out. Building off another Nazi murder program that used poison gas to kill German civilians with mental and physical disabilities, this plan entailed constructing permanent killing centres in Poland, then bringing Jews to these centres, rather than killing them in place as they had been doing in parts of Eastern Europe and the Soviet Union. Although these sites were created specifically to kill Jews, members of other groups targeted by the Nazis were also deported to these killing centres.

Over the next three years, Jews from all across Europe were murdered in killing centres — Chelmno, Treblinka, Sobibor, Belzec, Majdanek and Auschwitz-Birkenau — all located in areas of Poland occupied and controlled by Nazi Germany, even as the Einsatzgruppen continued their work of mass murder in other parts of Eastern Europe. This context of violence is essential to understanding the issue of non-Jews trying to help, or failing to help, Jews in Nazi-occupied Europe during World War II and the Holocaust.

Rescue and Survival

The memoirs of each of the three survivors in this anthology describe very different experiences of rescue and survival in different areas of Europe. In *Three Stars in the Sky*, the first account we read, nine-year-old Eva Lang and her family flee Brussels for the South of France soon after Nazi Germany's occupation of Belgium in May 1940. France, too, was invaded and subsequently divided into the German-occupied area in the north and the unoccupied area in the south, with a new French government in the unoccupied area known as Vichy France that worked in close collaboration with the German occupiers. When Eva Lang's family reached the South of France after four days of train travel, they were not free for long — the police forced them to move from one location to another, and they were soon rounded up with other foreign Jewish refugees and sent to a camp in Agde and then to the detention camp Rivesaltes,[8] which Eva later described as "Auschwitz without the crematoria." As the conditions in the camp deteriorated, Eva's mother finally said to her daughters, "We'll have a better chance of survival if we separate.... Do your best, listen to the people who will be taking care of you, and don't forget who you are."

A short time later, Eva and her sister Raymonde were taken by members of the Œuvre de secours aux enfants (OSE, Children's Relief Agency),[9] a Jewish welfare organization that was permitted by the French authorities to remove children from camps and place them temporarily in French families or in group homes. In 1942, when mass deportations of Jews from France began, OSE developed a rescue network run by Jews and non-Jews that hid Jewish children under false identities. For the rest of the German occupation, Eva and her sister were moved from one location to another, constantly having to adjust to new sets of rules and personalities. The network of helpers varied. Some helpers were kind and protective, whereas others sent the children away as soon as they felt afraid or in danger for hiding Jewish children.

Although conditions for Jews in France were precarious and 10,000 children were caught, deported and murdered, France had a higher survival rate of Jews overall than did other nations in Nazi-occupied Europe. Approximately 330,000 French Jews and foreign Jews lived in France at the outset of the war; 80,000 were killed, and the rest managed to survive in France or by escaping to neighbouring neutral countries. Ten thousand children were saved by people working for rescue networks like OSE, who faced arrest and deportation for these resistance activities.[10]

In the second memoir, *Saved by Luck and Devotion*, we read about young David Korn, born in Brno, Czechoslovakia (now Czech Republic), in 1937. David and his family fled to relatives in Slovakia after Nazi Germany occupied the rest of Czechoslovakia in March 1939. Slovakia, a newly independent state created when Czechoslovakia dissolved in 1939, was allied with Nazi Germany. The head of Slovakia, Jozef Tiso, was both a nationalist and a Catholic priest who supported the Nazis and implemented antisemitic measures. In 1942, Slovakia, eager to be rid of its Jewish population, agreed to pay Nazi authorities to deport their Jewish citizens to death camps and concentration camps — the only unoccupied country to do so. The survival rate of Jews in Slovakia was considerably lower than in France. Out of a population of approximately 90,000 Slovak Jews, 70,000 were deported and 60,000 did not survive the war.[11]

David and his brother, Jacob, were fortunate enough to find shelter in an orphanage run by Pastor Vladimir Kuna, a minister of the Evangelical Lutheran Church. Five-year-old David even recalls having a fairly regular childhood — he was surrounded by other children whose parents were not present, which normalized his situation, and he was eventually able to go to school. However, his life was still in danger — the possibility that Pastor Kuna would be betrayed was ever-present. Kuna was especially vulnerable because Lutherans were a small Protestant minority in Catholic-dominant Slovakia, representing only about 7 per cent of the Slovakian population, but they were outspoken in their resistance to the pro-Nazi Slovak state.[12] "There were seventy children in the orphanage," explained David, "twenty-six of whom were Jewish. It was superhuman how Pastor Kuna and his staff risked their lives to save ours. If they had been found out, they would have been executed."

While Pastor Kuna and his staff were largely responsible for the rescue of David and his brother, luck and resourcefulness also played a role. When the Korns left Brno for Slovakia, they joined members of their family living in David's father's hometown. David's family members had ties to non-Jews in nearby communities and arranged for false identification papers for David and his brother. They also succeeded in communicating with the Evangelical Lutheran community, some of whom were prepared to help Jews. Rescue by non-Jews is only a part of the story of Jewish survival during the Holocaust; when Jews had the opportunity and resources, they, too, helped family members in any way they could.

The third memoir, *The Survival Story of a Six-Year-Old Boy*, is by Fishel Philip Goldig, born in 1933 in Mielnica, Poland (now Melnytsia-Podilska, Ukraine), near the border with Soviet Ukraine. At the beginning of World War II, the Soviet Union invaded and occupied the part of Poland where he and his family were living. By the summer of 1941, after the Germans broke their non-aggression pact and invaded the Soviet Union, they were under German occupation and were constantly threatened by German officials as well as by local Nazi collaborators. This part of Poland saw repeated warfare and brutal treatment of civilians by the occupation forces and the Einsatzgruppen, and this violence affected social relations within the local populations. The fate of the two million Jews living in this region was at first ghettoization and then deportation to killing centres — and those few who escaped being deported found themselves desperately relying on non-Jews to shelter them. People who aided Jews faced enormous risk of denunciation by their neighbours, many of whom expected to receive rewards such as money or goods in exchange for assisting the German occupiers as they hunted down and killed the few remaining Jews.

Fishel's memoir captures the constant fear he and his family endured during those years. As a nine-year-old, Fishel witnessed the killing of Jews, including members of his own family. In 1943, while he and his parents were living in the ghetto of Borszczów, they heard rumours that the ghetto was to be liquidated. Under threat of death or deportation, Fishel and his family managed to escape, just barely. One of his uncles, a doctor who was living in the area, knew a farmer in a small town nearby by the name of Mr. Kukurudza. This man, a good friend of the mayor, sympathized with the family's situation but could not risk taking the family in because the Nazis and their collaborators constantly checked his home. However, Kukurudza located a local potato farmer, Nikolai Kravchuk, who agreed to help the family.

The original plan was to hide the family in the farmer's attic, but when that proved too dangerous, they moved to a cave behind the potato cellar on the property. The space was quite small, and the farmer and members of the family were eventually able to enlarge the cave, which became their home for a long time. Throughout this time, Mr. Kravchuk brought supplies and food to the cave and occasionally spoke with the family about news of the war. As Fishel explains in his memoir, "Nikolai Kravchuk was a simple and good man, and he despised what was being done to the Jews…. There was nothing to stop him from killing us or calling the police and taking whatever possessions we had. But he didn't do that because he was a decent person."

Ordinary People in Difficult Times

What can we say about the people who helped Eva Lang, David Korn and Fishel Goldig? Certainly their actions were exceptional, making them unlike so many other non-Jews in Nazi-occupied Europe who fall under the broad category of "bystanders." This term describes people who stood by and chose inaction when they witnessed or became aware of atrocities against Jews and other Nazi targets. Bystanders' lack of active response stemmed from a variety of reasons, including fear of punishment, disinterest in the fate of others due to personal wartime difficulties, perceived lack of opportunity, or even support of the perpetrators' actions.

Many rescuers often say they only did what any decent person would have done in their position, and yet we know that is not true. They did what so many others did not do. As the author Cynthia Ozick writes, rescuers were "not the ordinary human article." She states:

Nothing would have been easier than for each and every one of them to have remained a bystander, like all those millions of their countrymen in the nations of Europe.... The ordinary human article does not want to be disturbed by extremes of any kind — nor by risks or adventures, or unusual responsibility.... In Europe in the most extreme decade of the twentieth century, not to be a bystander was the choice of the infinitesimal few. These few are more substantial than the multitudes from whom they distinguished themselves, and it is from these undeniably heroic and principled few that we can learn the full resonance of civilization.[13]

For decades, scholars have tried to explain the motivations and backgrounds of rescuers, but they do not agree on any generalizations about them.[14] Why? For one thing, rescuers came from different religious, educational, national, ethnic and cultural backgrounds, and their rescue activities were not always consistent. There were times when a person would not take the risk involved in trying to help Jews, even though he or she had empathy for the victims. At other times, the same person would help someone, despite the danger involved and the possibility they could be caught by the Germans and their Nazi collaborators in their "illegal" acts. We see this, for example, in the behaviour of Mr. Kukurudza in Fishel Goldig's memoir. Although unable to take the family into his home, he was willing to find someone who could help, and once he placed the family with the local farmer, Nikolai Kravchuk, Mr. Kukurudza continued to be in contact with the Goldig family, even with the distinct possibility that he might be caught.

Eva Fogelman, a child of Holocaust survivors and a psychologist who has spent decades extensively researching rescuers during the Holocaust,[15] contends that "Rescue of Jews under the Nazis was, in psychological parlance, a 'rare behavior.' From a population of 700 million in Germany and the allied occupied countries, [those] who risked their lives to save Jews and others from Nazi persecution constituted an aberration from the norm. The majority remained passive bystanders; many actively collaborated in the Final Solution."[16] As for why the few were an exception to the norm, Fogelman believes that "The diversity among rescuers of Jews during the Holocaust would dissuade any social scientist from generalizations about motivation."[17]

Other prominent Holocaust scholars, such as Martin Gilbert, Nechama Tec, Sam and Pearl Oliner, and David Gushee[18] agree that rescuers represented a cross-section of European society. Tec, a historian and sociologist who herself was saved by Christians in Poland, tried to categorize rescuers based on a variety of factors, such as social class, religious affiliation and education, and realized, "If we were part of a group of people that included altruistic rescuers, we could not distinguish these rescuers from the rest of the group. Traditional ways for placing people into certain categories are of no help."[19]

Some rescuers who were politically affiliated tended to be involved more with democratic and leftist groups than with rightest parties, but rescuers could be found all across the political spectrum. David Gushee, a theologian, examined whether or not rescuers were committed Christians while non-rescuers were not, and argues that no such claim can be sustained. Research shows that rescuers do not appear to have differed from non-rescuers on any test of religiosity, including self-identification as a Christian or in regard to any religious commitment.

Did rescuers exhibit a certain character or were they a particular personality type? These are not easy questions. Anyone who has watched the film *Schindler's List* can see that the high-living, hard-drinking, adulterous Oskar Schindler had less than a sterling character. Yet, in the moral crucible of the Holocaust, he was a man who forged a relentless commitment to helping Jews. All of which is to say that rescuers were not necessarily paragons of virtue. Philosophy professor and scholar Dr. Leonard Grob aptly wrote that "Those who saved Jews during the Holocaust were flawed human beings. They were creatures with unclean hands — finite, imperfect beings like the rest of us."[20]

Eva Fogelman argues that rescuers display an extraordinary range of personalities and motivations. There were those who identified with an altruistic parental role model and those without such strong identification, some who drifted passively and gradually into aiding Jews and others who were passionately devoted to the "underdog," ready to take up every battle on behalf of the oppressed. There were those who were fiercely anti-Nazi, those who genuinely respected Jews and even those who were actually antisemitic in attitude. Rescuers during the Holocaust were as complex as are all human beings.[21] In the most unpromising soil, human goodness took root.

There is no simple answer to the questions around who helped and why they helped. Some acted out of empathy with the victims, some out of enmity for the Nazis. Some acted to emulate their parents, others to serve God, and still others to save their self-respect. And some rescuers helped Jews simply because they were asked to do so.

The context and nature of rescue activities that Eva Lang, David Korn and Fishel Goldig describe from their own lived experiences offer a particular insight into who their rescuers were and what risks they encountered as they tried to help them survive the Nazis and their collaborators.

The Righteous Among the Nations

In 1953, the Knesset — the Israeli parliament — established Yad Vashem, the World Holocaust Remembrance Center in Jerusalem. The Knesset entrusted Yad Vashem with the task of commemorating, documenting, researching and educating the general public about the Holocaust, and in that way remembering the six million Jews murdered by the German Nazis and their collaborators. Yad Vashem also was given the task of searching out and honouring non-Jews who risked their lives to rescue Jews during the Nazi era. These gentiles are known as *Hasidei Umot HaOlam*, the Righteous Among the Nations.

To be honoured by Yad Vashem as one of the Righteous Among the Nations, a person must have accomplished a deed above and beyond the simple offer of a helping hand. That person must have risked his or her life to save a Jew, or Jews, during the Holocaust, and have been motivated by the desire to help, not for reward. The medal given to the honouree, or to their descendants if the honouree is deceased, bears a Talmudic inscription: "Whoever saves one life, it is as if he saved an entire universe." As of January 1, 2020, according to the statistics on Yad Vashem's website, 27,712 non-Jews have been honoured as Righteous Among the Nations.[22]

Eva Lang and Fishel Goldig helped to collect the necessary documentation so that the people instrumental in their survival could be honoured by Yad Vashem. David Korn's rescuer, Pastor Kuna, had been honoured as one of the Righteous in 1972. Mr. Korn took the initiative to provide financial support for Pastor Kuna in the 1990s.

Yad Vashem has an educational program for the general public so everyone who is interested can learn about these ordinary people who in extraordinary times helped Jews. They stand in stark contrast to "the mainstream of indifference and hostility that prevailed during the Holocaust."[23] As the late Elie Wiesel wrote, "we must know these good people who helped Jews during the Holocaust. We must learn from them, and in gratitude and hope, we must remember them."[24]

Dr. Carol Rittner, RSM is Distinguished Professor Emerita of Holocaust and Genocide Studies and the Dr. Marsha Raticoff Grossman Professor Emerita of Holocaust Studies at Stockton University in New Jersey. She is the author or editor of twenty-one books, including *Advancing Holocaust Studies* (New York: Routledge, 2021), as well as numerous essays about the Holocaust and other genocides of the twentieth and twenty-first centuries.

Dr. Mary Johnson is Adjunct Professor of Holocaust and Genocide Studies at Stockton University in New Jersey and a consultant for

Classrooms Without Borders in Pittsburgh, Pennsylvania. For nearly thirty years she was Senior Historian for Facing History and Ourselves, based in Brookline, Massachusetts. Dr. Johnson has written about the Armenian genocide as well as about the Holocaust. Her current area of research focuses on the atrocities and sexual violence committed by the Japanese military during the Nanjing Massacre in China (1937–1938).

NOTES

1 For an informative explanation of anti-Judaism and antisemitism, see chapters 1 and 2 in Richard L. Rubenstein and John K. Roth, *Approaches to Auschwitz: The Holocaust and Its Legacy*, rev. ed. (Louisville, KY: Westminster John Knox Press, 2003), 25–70.

2 "Aryanization" (in German, *Arisierung*) refers to the transfer of Jewish-owned property to non-Jews (known as "Aryans" in Nazi Germany) from 1933 to 1945. See further, "Aryanization," *Holocaust Encyclopedia*, United States Holocaust Memorial Museum, https://encyclopedia.ushmm.org/content/en/article/aryanization.

3 Facing History and Ourselves, *Holocaust and Human Behavior* (Brookline, MA: Facing History and Ourselves, 2018), 381–382.

4 Peter Hayes, *Why: Explaining the Holocaust* (New York and London: W.W. Norton & Company, 2017), 83.

5 Doris Bergen, *War and Genocide* (Lanham, MD: Rowman and Littlefield, 2016), 167.

6 Einsatzgruppen is a German word that is translated as "special action squads" in English. These were specially trained SS units that were assigned terror tasks for the political administration in the Nazi-occupied Soviet Union and other Eastern European territories. The Einsatzgruppen worked behind the front lines of the war, murdering Jews and political opponents (generally communists who were thought by the Nazis to all be Jews).

7 See the interview of Anna Dychkant, in Patrick Desbois, *The Holocaust by Bullets: A Priest's Journey to Uncover the Truth Behind the Murder of 1.5 Million Jews* (New York: Palgrave Macmillan, 2008), 124–125.

8 Rivesaltes was a French internment camp located in unoccupied southern France near the Spanish border, and was one of many camps administered by the French government to house foreigners or refugees before and during World War II. Rivesaltes was designated as a "family camp," and its population consisted of refugees from the Spanish Civil War, Jewish refugees and Roma; in mid-1942, foreign Jews were collected there before being deported to Nazi camps.

9 Œuvre de secours aux enfants (OSE), the Jewish children's welfare organization, according to Patrick Henry, "was founded in Russia in 1912 by a group of young doctors committed to offering sanitary protection and health benefits to poor Jews. The organization moved in 1917 to Berlin where Albert Einstein was its honorary president. In 1933, it moved to Paris, and in 1940, once again

to escape the Nazis, it moved to Montpellier in the non-occupied South of France." The organization had a number of orphanages located primarily in Vichy France. OSE helped rescue thousands of Jewish children in France during World War II and the Holocaust. See Patrick Henry, "Recognizing Jewish Rescuers of Jews During the Holocaust," *Tablet*, October 9, 2020, https://www.tabletmag.com/sections/history/articles/ose-jewish-welfare-france.

10 Renée Poznanski, *Jews in France during World War II*, trans. Nathan Bracher (Hanover, NH: University Press of New England, 2001), 554n5; Stephanie Corazza, "The Routine of Rescue: Child Welfare Workers and the Holocaust in France" (PhD diss., University of Toronto, 2017), 1–10.

11 Ivan Kamenec, *On the Trail of Tragedy: The Holocaust in Slovakia*, trans. Martin Styan (Slovak Republic: H & H, 2007), 341.

12 For more on the Protestant Churches in Slovakia during the Holocaust, see John S. Conway, "The Churches, the Slovak State and the Jews 1939–1945," *The Slavonic and East European Review* 52, no. 126 (January 1974): 85–112; Livia Rothkirchen, "The Churches and the Deportation of Jews in Slovakia," in *The Holocaust and the Christian World*, eds. Carol Rittner, Stephen D. Smith and Irena Steinfeldt, 2nd ed. (Mahwah, NJ: Paulist Press, 2019), 145–149.

13 Cynthia Ozick, prologue to *Rescuers: Portraits in Moral Courage*, by Gay Block and Malka Drucker (New York: Holmes & Meier Publishers, Inc., 1992), xvi.

14 See further, Eva Fogelman, *Conscience & Courage: Rescuers of Jews during the Holocaust* (New York: Doubleday, 1994); Ervin Staub, *The Roots of Evil: The Origins of Genocide and Other Group Violence* (Cambridge, UK: Cambridge University Press, 1989); and Nechama Tec, *When Light Pierced the Darkness: Christian Rescuers of Jews in Nazi-Occupied Poland* (New York: Oxford University Press, 1986).

15 A major example of Eva Fogelman's extensive research is Eva Fogelman, *Conscience & Courage: Rescuers of Jews During the Holocaust* (New York: Anchor Books Doubleday, 1995). Dr. Fogelman also has written many essays detailing the results of her research for various scholarly journals.

16 Eva Fogelman, "The Rescuer Self," https://www.yadvashem.org/yv/pdf-drupal/fogelman_the_rescuer_self.pdf. See further, Eva Fogelman, "The Rescuer Self," in *The Holocaust and History: The Known, the Unknown, the Disputed, and the Reexamined*, eds. Michael Berenbaum and Abraham J Peck. (Bloomington, IN: Indiana University Press, 1998), 663–676.

17 Fogelman, "The Rescuer Self."

18 See further, Eva Fogelman, *Conscience & Courage: Rescuers of Jews during the Holocaust*; Martin Gilbert, *The Righteous: The Unsung Heroes of the Holocaust*

(New York: Henry Holt and Co., 2003); David P. Gushee, *Righteous Gentiles of the Holocaust: Genocide and Moral Obligation*, 2nd ed. (St. Paul, MN: Paragon House, 2003); Samuel P. and Pearl M. Oliner, *The Altruistic Personality: Rescuers of Jews in Nazi Europe* (New York: Free Press, 1988); Carol Rittner and Sondra Myers, eds., *The Courage to Care: Rescuers of Jews during the Holocaust* (New York: New York University Press, 1986); and Nechama Tec, *When Light Pierced the Darkness: Christian Rescuers of Jews in Nazi-Occupied Poland.*

19 Nechama Tec, "A Glimmer of Light" in Rittner, Smith and Steinfeldt, *The Holocaust and the Christian World*, 200–201.

20 Leonard Grob, "Rescue During the Holocaust – and Today" (American Jewish Congress, 1997).

21 See further, Fogelman, Part II, "Motivation" in *Conscience & Courage: Rescuers of Jews during the Holocaust*, 161–270.

22 "Names of Righteous by Country," Yad Vashem, updated January 1, 2020, https://www.yadvashem.org/righteous/statistics.html.

23 See, "About the Righteous," Yad Vashem, https://www.yadvashem.org/righteous/about-the-righteous.html.

24 Elie Wiesel, foreword to *The Courage to Care: Rescuers of Jews during the Holocaust*, eds. Carol Rittner and Sondra Myers (New York: New York University Press, 1986), x.

Three Stars in the Sky

Eva Lang

WESTERN EUROPE, 1940–1945

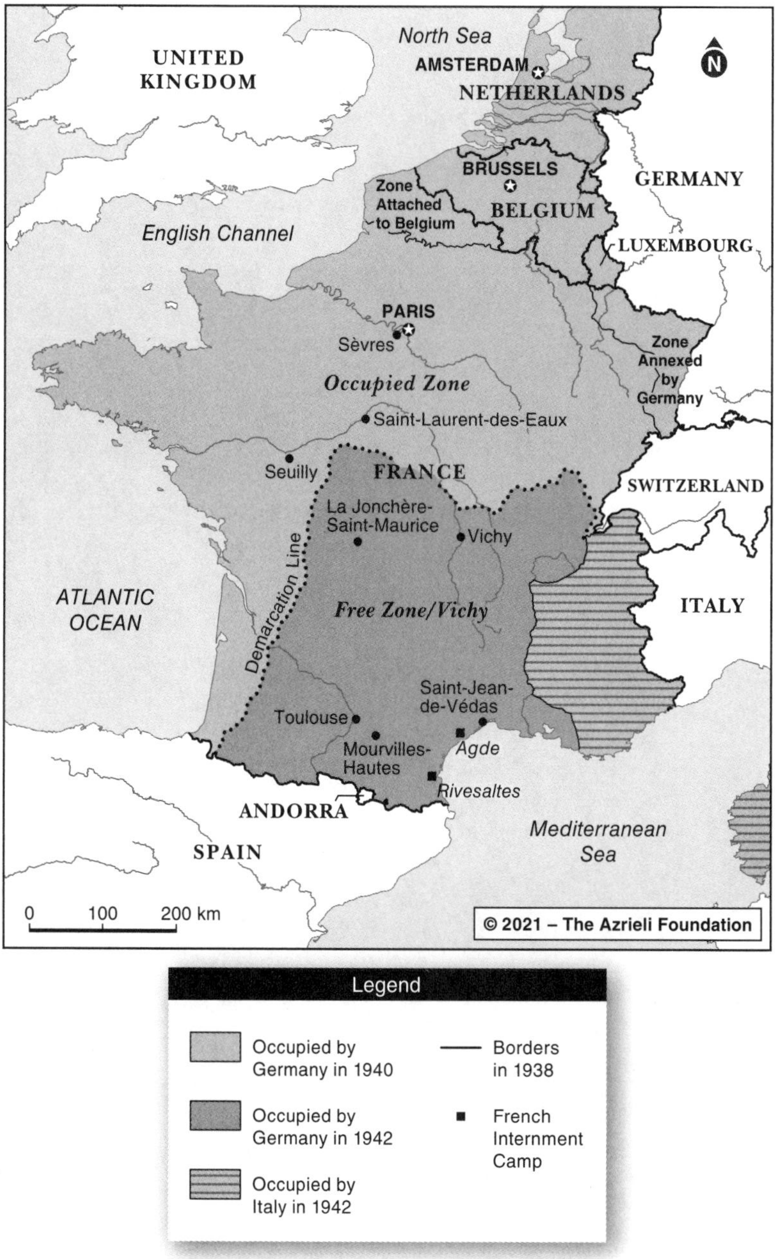

North Sea
UNITED KINGDOM
AMSTERDAM
NETHERLANDS
BRUSSELS
Zone Attached to Belgium
BELGIUM
GERMANY
LUXEMBOURG
English Channel
PARIS
Sèvres
Occupied Zone
Zone Annexed by Germany
Saint-Laurent-des-Eaux
Seuilly
FRANCE
SWITZERLAND
La Jonchère-Saint-Maurice
Vichy
Demarcation Line
ATLANTIC OCEAN
Free Zone/Vichy
ITALY
Saint-Jean-de-Védas
Toulouse
Agde
Mourvilles-Hautes
Rivesaltes
ANDORRA
SPAIN
Mediterranean Sea
0 100 200 km
© 2021 – The Azrieli Foundation
Legend
Occupied by Germany in 1940
Occupied by Germany in 1942
Occupied by Italy in 1942
Borders in 1938
French Internment Camp

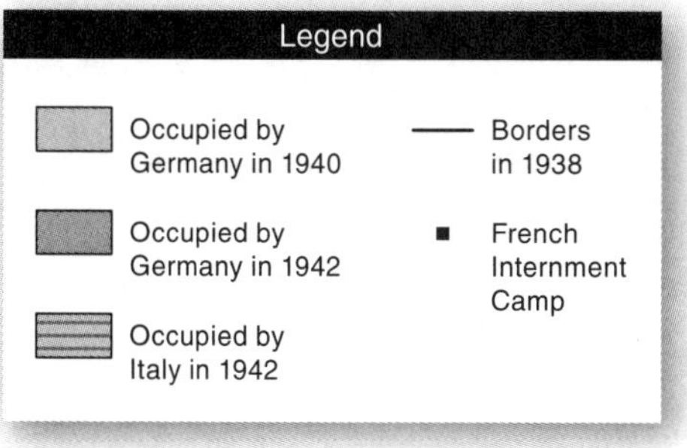

To my children, grandchildren and great-grandchildren.

The Strength of a Family

My ancestors, my grandparents and my parents belonged to the Ashkenazi Jewish community, which had lived in Central Europe since well before the Middle Ages and whose main language was Yiddish. My parents, Zacharia and Esther (née Erlich) Tuchsnajder, were from Warsaw and went to live in Belgium right after World War I.

My parents were very religious, and their lives were well ordered and respectful of tradition. They gave me and my siblings — Michel, Sarah, Raymonde and Renée — a lot of love and raised us in a protective, traditional way, so we developed in a very sheltered atmosphere. Michel and Sarah were my older siblings, born in 1922 and 1924, respectively, and Raymonde (Rivka) and Renée (Malka) were younger than me, born in 1935 and 1936. I was born on July 23, 1930, in Brussels. We mainly spoke Yiddish at home, although our native language was French.

My father had a strong personality, and my energy comes from him. We loved and respected him and would never have dared to contradict him. He was smart, emotional and very learned in Talmud. He was interested in lots of things and I'm sure he would have liked to expand his activities and his knowledge, but he was limited by lack of money and the constraints of the times. He was a leather worker and he worked hard to provide for the family. We lived modestly, but us children lacked nothing.

My mother was an exemplary homemaker. She was a talented cook, and during the week, she managed to prepare meals from practically nothing. But on Saturdays, the best dishes were served at our table and a guest was always brought home from synagogue to show that there was enough for someone less fortunate than we were. The white tablecloth, the lit candles, the warm, protective atmosphere of the family together around the table are my sweetest memories, and I will always be nostalgic for that time. I have a distinct memory of waiting for the end of Shabbat on Saturdays — my mother had always told me to wait for the three stars in the sky, a signal that Shabbat was over and that we could turn on the lights. On a rainy night in Brussels, it was hard to see the stars, and even harder to wait patiently for my father to come home from synagogue. I would always yell, "Mother! I saw three stars in the sky!"

My mother's life was focused on the family, her children and their welfare. She made everything clean and harmonious, and created an atmosphere of honesty and love in the family.

My parents placed a great deal of importance on education and respect for children and their abilities. We lived according to a strict morality and observed the Jewish religion and its laws. We belonged to the family — that was the essential thing.

My family's principles, the little jobs each of us had to do in the house and the good marks we were expected to bring home from school — everything in the way we were raised — were supposed to lead to a clearly traced future. Fate would soon decide otherwise. Later, when our lives had been irreparably turned upside-down, I often clung to these memories of my family.

From that time, I have kept deep within me something my parents taught me that has helped me all my life and given me the strength to go on in spite of everything: the idea that the world could become better and that it only depended on me to make it better. That teaching was precious to me.

I will always remember my father's horror when he told us of

Kristallnacht in November 1938. I was eight years old. Synagogues that had existed for hundreds of years were burned down in the cities and towns of Germany, and thousands of books along with them. This was just the beginning of an attempt to annihilate an entire culture.

There was a lot of German propaganda on the radio and in the newspapers. It must have had a strong influence on people, even in Belgium. At school, I liked my teacher and the principal, and they thought well of me. But the nurse decided that the Jewish children were spreading contagious diseases, and for several weeks, I had to go with my sister Sarah to a distant clinic where they sprayed our throats with an irritating solution and made us gargle with it. I felt fine and didn't understand why we couldn't go to school. One day, instead of the usual doctor, a nice young doctor examined us. He exclaimed, "But these children are in good health! What are they doing here? There's nothing wrong with them. They should go back to school." He was the first resister I met. I was happy to go back to school.

Several years later, when I went back to see my primary school on Rue du Chapeau in the Anderlecht area in Brussels, there was a plaque at the main entrance. Mme. Jeanne, the principal I had so greatly admired, had been killed by the Gestapo. A courageous resister, a great lady, she had fallen under German gunfire. The school has now been torn down.

At school, we were taught to respect books. We were never to fold down the corners of the pages and we had to cover the books with paper to protect them so that other students could use them after us. And we were told never to dirty the street by throwing paper away. Today, as I did then, I still keep any scraps of paper in my hand until I find a garbage can.

Since I didn't have any classes on Saturday, I could go and borrow books from the school. I loved to read! I didn't mind the greyness of Brussels as long as I had books to distract me. Later, during the war, I would take refuge in books to escape the painful reality around me.

Fleeing from Home

Less than a year after Germany invaded and occupied Poland, and after invading Denmark and Norway, the Germans attacked the Netherlands, Luxembourg and Belgium on May 10, 1940. I remember the roar of the planes flying over Brussels. The bombing caused panic among the residents, who began to flee the city. Very early one morning, Raymonde, Renée and I were awakened and hastily dressed. The rest of the family was already up and a few suitcases were packed.

After we left the house, my mother went back in, and a few minutes later she came out carrying a white down quilt. She was already holding a bag of sandwiches, some bottles of tea and her shiny brass candelabra. We stood silently gathered around my father, who closed the door and said a short prayer. Aware of the seriousness of this moment, none of us moved; we waited quietly, and then my father touched the mezuzah on the doorframe. He would never see his house again.

We walked to Place Bara, not far from my school, and stopped for a minute to rest. My sister Sarah and my brother, Michel, were carrying suitcases, and each of us had a little bundle as well. High in the distance, I saw the huge courthouse, its green roof standing out against the sky in the morning light. Then a familiar smell reached me from a factory nearby. It was the smell of Côte d'Or chocolate, which wafted to our school whenever the wind changed direction. These would be my last good memories of Belgium.

We were not the only ones who had come to the Midi train station; there was already a crowd there hoping to flee to France. In a matter of hours, we had all become war refugees. People were jostling and running in all directions. On the platforms, they rushed toward the trains as if they were going to take them by storm. We finally managed to board a car and find ourselves a little corner, and when night fell, my mother spread out a coat and the white quilt on the floor. My two younger sisters and I slept in that improvised bed, holding one another tight. It took us a while to get used to the noisy rhythmic movement of the train.

We travelled for four days, always heading south. The train stopped several times. We were exhausted. Fortunately, when we passed through some of the stations in France, people handed us bread and cheese through the windows, and Raymonde even got a chocolate bar. Some people on the platform seemed afraid. Others had insignia on their sleeves and were giving orders, pushing and shoving, shouting and running from group to group. The news was bad: the Germans were advancing quickly. Everyone had been taken by surprise. We were crammed together painfully in the train and we were dull with fatigue. There were repeated stops; trains ahead of ours had been bombed.

The train continued southward and stopped at Toulouse. My father took a room in a little pink hotel where even the walls of our room were papered in big pink flowers. We slept and slept for hours.

In the morning, I went with my big sister, Sarah, who was then sixteen, through the winding streets of the city to get milk. We finally met a farmer on a mule who sold us some from small cans hanging on either side of the animal. He had an open, friendly face and he was wearing baggy pants and a cap on his head. First he asked Sarah what had happened to us and requested news of the war, and then he told us that when he didn't sell all his milk at the market, what was left would be turned into butter by the beating of the cans against the mule's flanks.

I still have very clear memories of Toulouse as a pretty, old-fashioned pink city — from the colour of the bricks used for many of its buildings — sunny and smiling. We stayed there only a few days before being assigned a place in the village of Mourvilles-Hautes, forty-two kilometres southeast of Toulouse. In addition to my family, there were a lot of other people lodged in this village, including Rabbi Gertner, with whom my father used to pray in Brussels. He had a daughter my age, also called Éva, with whom I often played. The Joint Distribution Committee, an American Jewish organization, did its best to help us.

Refugees were called on to contribute to the war effort. While the women could stay at home and take care of the children, the men were sent to the North to fight the German invaders. A desperate defence was mounted at the last minute, but things were in complete disarray in France.

Then came the defeat at Dunkirk in the beginning of June, the retreat of the troops and the extraordinary evacuation of the British units in fishing boats and small craft that travelled back and forth across the Channel to England. There was a lot of talk about the rescue operation. Nearly every day a man would come back to the village and tell of the defeat, the boldness of the German advance and the first French prisoners. My father and my older brother, who had been recruited into military service, were demobilized and had to return to the village on foot. The Germans were quickly gaining ground.

We soon heard talk about Vichy, about France being cut in half. We had been in Mourvilles-Hautes a few months when the police announced that we were going to be transferred to another place. The foreign Jewish refugees were to be brought together and sent to special places by order of Vichy. The police went from village to village with trucks and buses. We waited for hours with no idea where we were going or what would become of us. It felt as though Rabbi Gertner and his family had deserted us, and I learned much later that he and his family had fled to Spain. We were left to our fate.

An Unbearable Life

In the fall of 1940, we were sent to a camp at Agde with a few families we knew from Belgium and other refugees from the Netherlands and Germany. We all shared one dismal shack. There were bunks covered with straw on each side of the room and a space in the middle just large enough for a table and benches. We weren't much better off than cows in a stable. There were rows of taps outside. It was horrible. In the morning, we got a portion of powdered milk, and at noon, Jerusalem artichokes and white beets, which was a totally inadequate diet. We were shocked and surprised by this treatment. My brother, Michel, who was quite resourceful, helped in the kitchen, and he brought us carrots and bread. With the lack of vitamins, a lot of people got skin infections. My mother and Sarah were constantly washing my little sisters and me because epidemics were prevalent. One day a delegation came to visit the camp and the women came out of the shacks and shouted, "Give the children milk!"

I saw my mother becoming thin and getting sadder and sadder. She kept saying, "This is no way to treat decent people." Many of the refugees no longer had any resistance to infections; they quickly fell ill and died prematurely. A lot of the children had impetigo. My little sister Renée, just four years old, suffered terribly with it. She had a crust covering her whole head. I went with my mother to the infirmary, where Renée received very painful treatments. That is one of the terrible memories that will always stay with me.

One day, the big shed that was used as a kitchen suddenly caught fire and burned to the ground. That provided an opportunity for the men — the fathers and brothers, who were in a separate camp from the women — to force the gate open. There was complete panic. A few people escaped and others were caught.

In mid-January 1941, we were sent to another camp, Rivesaltes, the worst place in the world to me. In the eastern Pyrenees, at the foot of the most beautiful white mountains, the wind blew constantly, raising an unbearable dust. In the camp there were still some refugees from the Spanish Civil War, Spanish soldiers and Roma (then called Gypsies). The women and children were separated from the men and crammed together on two rows of wooden platforms that served as bunks. There were taps outside, and latrines. Food was more and more scarce, and we were terribly hungry. There was barbed wire all around, with watchtowers every few metres. Everything was grey, gloomy and unpleasant, and all day long, the wind whistled around the barracks. When it rained, we walked in mud scattered with stones, and then, as time passed, through a scorching dry heat. I don't remember seeing any vegetation. In the distance, we could see those white mountains that appeared so near and seemed to be looking scornfully down at us with all our misfortune. Later, I would compare Rivesaltes to an Auschwitz without the crematoria. Along with Gurs, Rivesaltes was the worst internment camp for civilians in France.

The guards of the camp and the representatives of Vichy saw the horrible conditions and did nothing. People died. There's a cemetery in the town of Rivesaltes, where Jewish internees were buried, that bears witness to that time. I still have the scar on my upper calf from an enormous pus-filled abscess I had while there. I was ten and I went to the infirmary all by myself to stand in line in the hope that someone would be good enough to clean the sore with alcohol for me. Yet my mother and big sister were doing everything in their power to maintain good hygiene.

We had no school and no books, but I learned a lot because I observed and listened. When the wind gave us a bit of respite, we would sit outside in the sun. Or we'd go to the barracks of the Roma women. They were dark-skinned, often barefoot, and wore brightly-coloured dresses. In the evenings, sometimes the women would sing and dance around a fire. It was thrilling to see them. My sister Raymonde tried to imitate them, and she did pretty well. Even some of the camp guards would go to see these women, especially one of them who was very beautiful, with sparkling eyes full of passion. It was rumoured that she wore a hundred curlers at night because her hair was so thick.

I saw a lot of things in the camp; I watched, I took note and I kept quiet. I saw my mother wasting away in front of my eyes while courageously trying to keep up some kind of normal life, and like her, I said to myself, *They have no right to do this to us.*

One day in early May, my father came with a man who belonged to a delegation from a charitable organization, and pointed Raymonde and me out to him. A few days later, we were given a good wash, dressed in clean clothes and taken with some other children for a medical examination. After that visit, we were chosen to be part of a group of some thirty girls and boys who would leave the camp. When I was in front of the doctor, I heard a little boy behind me who had a harsh cough. He was separated from the group of children selected and his poor mother was crying and asking them to take him for pity's sake, to save him. I'll never forget that scene!

Our First Refuge

A few days later, some people from OSE — Œuvre de secours aux enfants (Children's Relief Agency) — came and escorted us out of the camp. When we were leaving, my mother explained, "We'll have a better chance of surviving if we separate. Take care of your sister Raymonde. One day we'll be together again. Do your best, listen to the people who will be taking care of you and don't forget who you are." I heard her say to the woman beside her, "I'm talking to my daughter Eva as if she were a grown-up, and she's still just a kid."

The big gate bristling with barbed wire opened. I can still picture the grey barracks disappearing in the dust as we left Rivesaltes, that camp full of horror, shame and misery. We arrived in Montpellier very tired and were taken to a place with desks. We were seated at a long table and given bowls of milk.

Once again, we went through a selection process. Mme. Sabine Zlatin, a social worker who was dressed all in blue, chose my sister Raymonde and me to go to Saint-Jean-de-Védas, a village surrounded by vineyards located just over five kilometres from Montpellier in the department of Hérault. We were sent to live with Mlle. Emma Blanc and her elderly mother, Marie, a laundress. They lived in an old house across from the square, the priest's house and the monument to the dead. At the end of the street was the school where Emma, who we were to refer to as our godmother, took care of the youngest children.

Shortly after our arrival, we took our smocks and schoolbags and went to school, I to Mlle. Rudin's class and Raymonde to Mlle. Wéber's. The teachers were very nice; they were quite old (to my child's eyes) and wore long grey skirts and white blouses. They later made some clothes for us out of their old dresses. We quickly made friends at school. I read books from the library, and I still remember a passage I learned by heart from a story called "The Old Folks," in *Letters from My Windmill.* I had a good memory and I easily learned the multiplication tables. I was what they called a good student. On Sundays, I would read all the Bécassine stories, which a neighbour loaned me, while Grandmother Marie took Raymonde to church. My sister learned all the religious songs, including one I, too, still remember:

> Virgin Mary, I give you
> My heart here below.
> Take the crown I offer you.
> In heaven, you'll return it, I know.

In the morning at school when the flag was raised, we sang, "Marshal, here we are! Before you, the saviour of France!" Lines from a song commonly sung by children at the time, it was dedicated to Pétain, the head of Vichy France.

After school, we would help with the housework, polishing the furniture and doing other chores. We would go to the river with Grandmother Marie, helping her push the handcart filled with bags of washing, and then I would help her spread the sheets on the grass to dry. We also had to bring in wood and branches of vines for the fireplace where Grandmother Marie cooked down resinated wine in copper cauldrons. In the fall, after the grape harvest, we went into the vineyards and gathered the bunches of grapes left behind by the peasants.

While we were living in Saint-Jean-de-Védas, OSE sent us to Palavas-les-Flots to an OSE children's home near the beach for two weeks. There I saw friends from the camp at Rivesaltes. Later, Mme. Zlatin and her husband, Miron, who were part of the OSE underground network, took care of those children. When the situation became more dangerous, they looked for another safe place, and with the help of an old village priest, they found a house for rent in the village of Izieu.

We spent the winter months in Saint-Jean-de-Védas. We now spoke with a strong Midi accent. I thought often of my parents, and of my brother and sisters who had remained in Rivesaltes in the cold and rain. And then one night, without any notice, we had visits from my father, then my mother, and then my sister Sarah, one after the other. Renée was not with them. They had managed to escape from the camp at Rivesaltes by bribing one of the French guards. They were going to hide in the Var region, they said, and they would come back one day and get us and we would all live together as before. But nothing would be as before. It was the last time we saw them.

The separation was heartbreaking, especially for my mother. I will never forget seeing her face: she had aged so much and she seemed so frail. I will always remember the pain of seeing her so weakened and I will never forgive those who did that to her. Years later, in records found and made public by the lawyer and historian Serge Klarsfeld, I found the number of the convoy and the list of people on it — including my father, my mother and my sister Sarah — deported via Drancy to Auschwitz. They had been arrested in the Var region in September 1942. They never returned.

Emma Blanc and her mother, Marie, finally became frightened and refused to keep us in their house, even though they had been well paid by OSE. We were returned to OSE, and Mme. Zlatin had to find us a new refuge. We were supposed to join the children in Palavas-les-Flots and then Izieu, but on the form my father had filled out for us, he had written, “If possible, place them in an observant Jewish children’s home.” And so we were sent to Le Couret. Mme. Zlatin said to me, “Eva, you’re a big girl now.” (I wasn’t even twelve yet.) “I’ll put you on the train with your sister Raymonde. Take good care of her. After a night of travelling, you’ll arrive in Limoges. There, someone I know will recognize you from your white capes and will take you to the children’s home at Couret.”

Le Couret

My sister and I boarded the train and settled ourselves as best we could in a corner of the car with our little bundles, a few sandwiches and a bottle of water. The train was full of German soldiers as well as civilians, and even the corridor was crammed with people. For reasons of safety, we were forbidden to answer if anyone asked us any questions. I had to avoid showing the fear I felt travelling without an adult and being responsible for Raymonde. Luckily, we slept most of the way, and we got to Limoges without any mishaps.

We got off the train with the other passengers, who gradually dispersed until we were almost the only ones left on the platform. We waited and waited, and I was starting to tremble with panic when, out of nowhere, a woman came over to us and told us to come with her, quickly. Later she told me, "I saw you get off the train, but I wanted to be sure the coast was clear and that there were no plainclothes agents before I came over to you." Years later when I remembered this, I wondered what would have happened to us if the Gestapo had picked us up, two little girls left alone in the Limoges railway station.

During the war, our fate often depended on circumstances and luck. The most striking example of this is the fact that we were sent to Le Couret children's home instead of to Izieu. Who could have foreseen that on April 6, 1944, just two months before the Allies' landing in Normandy, everyone at the children's home in Izieu — staff, children and the director, Miron Zlatin, Mme. Zlatin's husband — would all be caught in a terrible raid and deported on the orders of Klaus Barbie? Some of the adults would be shot at the prison in Lyon, and others, including the children, sent to Drancy and then eventually to Auschwitz. After the war, I visited Sabine Zlatin several times on Madame Street in Paris and we would spend hours talking about those events and that period.

We reached the village of La Jonchère-Saint-Maurice, in Haute-Vienne, in the late afternoon, and two older girls took us by the hand to go to Le Couret. Raymonde and I were exhausted and we didn't say anything to them. Bertie and Erika were fifteen years old. Erika, who was stout, put Raymonde on her shoulders, and Bertie carried our bundles, while I followed behind them for several kilometres. I vaguely recall a grand entry with huge trees and a lake on the right surrounded by a lawn with a rose garden. Finally, the grand home of Le Couret appeared. Once we got settled, we ate and slept, which we needed badly!

We had to quickly get used to the life and the discipline in this children's home, which housed girls from four to eighteen years of age. The director, Mme. Krakowsky, taught classes and ran the prayer services on Friday evening and Saturday morning. I learned the German and central European style and music of the prayers and the blessing at meals. Most of the girls in the home were from Austria, Hungary, Romania, Germany, Belgium and France. Many had come from the Rivesaltes camp, and even more from the one at Gurs, and much later we met some who had been through the Vélodrome d'Hiver roundup in Paris. Others had come from Germany in 1939 and had spent several months at the Château de La Guette children's home, which belonged to the Rothschild family of France.

Mme. Krakowsky and Esther, the supervisor, took care of the house. We polished the wood floors, and we peeled potatoes and washed the dishes in the basement, where the kitchen and dining room were located. The big girls took care of the little ones and learned to do sewing and secretarial work. Some of them were preparing for their certificate of studies in the neighbouring village, and others were taught at the home. Every week I went to the pond with some other girls and washed my clothes and my sister's. We had to keep our eyes on them while they dried because the peasants would steal them from us otherwise. That happened to Raymonde and me; two of our dresses disappeared — the ones Mlle. Rudin and Mlle. Wéber in Saint-Jean-de-Védas had sewn for us out of theirs and that we really loved.

We were in an area of kaolin quarries (kaolin clay was used in making Sèvres porcelain) and we would often get kaolin powder and play at making vases, inkpots and little statues, drying them in the sun. Since we didn't get enough food, we would gather chestnuts and, when the farmers let us, apples. We would find blackberries and wild strawberries in the woods.

For a while, I shared a room with two very nice girls. One of them, Marianne, was very neat; her bed was always made perfectly and she won a prize for cleanliness. The other one's name was Berthe; she was about sixteen, she already had large breasts, and her hair was blond. One night when we were in bed, Berthe told me her father was a German Jew and her mother a German Catholic. She had a choice between the two religions, and because the Nazis had arrested her parents, she decided to remain Jewish. "I'll be a pious observant Jew just to show those Nazi pigs," she said in German. That had a strong impact on us.

Sometimes we would go up to the attic by way of a narrow staircase near our room, which had most likely been a maid's room. The attic was filled with treasures covered in dust and we liked to explore it. There was old furniture, shelves of medical and other books, chamber pots, some with flowers on them, fancy beds, big armchairs, dishes, and especially, toys. The home was like a château to me, and must once have been a marvellous residence.

In the late summer of 1942, the police raided the home one night and took the girls over sixteen away with them. We never got any news of them, and none of them came back after the war. A little later, the Krakowsky family disappeared from the home — we learned later that they had gone to Switzerland — and we found ourselves alone with an elderly cook for a few days. We were very frightened.

Finally, the Garel network sent someone to take charge. She was a Girl Guide leader and, following the scouting tradition, we called her Chief Cabri, because her totemic animal was a young goat.

By early 1943, French Jews were in great danger, as were war refugees. The Vichy government had previously targeted Jews with foreign citizenship, but now they were arresting old and young, babies and sick people, without any distinctions regarding nationality. The Vichy representatives bent over backwards to collaborate with the Germans. The situation was becoming impossible. To get us away from the home, Chief Cabri (whose real name was Suzanne Clément) took us into the woods on hikes and expeditions like the scouts. She tried to make a game of it, but we understood the reason for the outings and we were afraid.

One day, my little sister Renée came to join Raymonde and me at Le Couret! It was a very happy reunion and we were glad to be together again. Renée had spent months being shunted from hospital to hospital and had finally been sent to a convent where some of the nuns were sick. At six years old, she would have to get up in the night to care for an asthmatic nun who mistreated her. After that, she was sent to a children's home in Savoie and then, finally, to be with us.

I was the big sister and Renée followed me everywhere. She felt protected, and it was good for her. As for Raymonde, she found a wonderful pastime. Dr. Levy, who came to see the children at the home from time to time, sometimes played the piano for us, and simply by watching him, Raymonde learned to play all by herself. You'd find her sitting at the piano from morning to night, and to this day, she plays the piano without having been taught a single note.

One day, Marcel Marceau, who was then a young man of twenty with curly hair, came to Le Couret with a few companions. In addition to doing mime, he smuggled Jewish children for OSE, helping find safe places where they could be hidden and taking them from shelter to shelter. That night, he entertained us by performing part of Molière's *The Miser* and telling a lot of little stories in mime.

Renée got sick again, probably from lack of vitamins — lack of everything, really. She had to go to the hospital in Limoges. When she started getting better, Marcel Marceau smuggled her from the hospital to a children's home in Sèvres, near Paris, where he himself was a staff member.

The separation from Renée, her tears and pleading when they tore her away from me to take her to the hospital, were too much for me. After that, I began to have nightmares. I trembled at night and I trembled during the day, and I suffered from cramps. I didn't want to admit to myself that it was fear because I was ashamed of this weakness. I didn't speak of it to anyone until one morning I reached the breaking point and couldn't get out of bed.

I was sharing a large bedroom, a former sitting room, with some older girls. Chief Cabri had the room next door. She sat down beside my bed, listened to my chest, looked deep into my eyes and said, "My courageous Eva, there's nothing wrong with you, you're in good health physically, but you have a serious disease — the disease of fear. I know the symptoms because all of us here have that disease — but we manage to control it. From now on, you'll do that too because you don't have any choice. Stay in bed as long as you have these cramps. They'll go away. I know you, and they'll go away."

Her saying that I was afraid was as if she had slapped me. It took away the fear that had been gripping me. All of a sudden, I wasn't trembling anymore — not at all. I couldn't believe it. I was breathing more easily. I fell asleep, and when I woke up, I was fine, and I went back to work like the others. I only hoped she wouldn't tell anyone about it; I would have been so ashamed.

A little bit later, in one of our Girl Guides activities, she made me the leader of a group that had to find a hidden path through the woods, following chalk marks on the trees. I felt very honoured to be given this responsibility, which placed me in charge of a dozen other girls, some of them older than me. I was just thirteen years old.

A month later, my companions and I would be separated again. The children's homes were becoming targets of the Vichy authorities, so OSE decided to try a more radical way to hide French Jewish children. They would change their identities. They would make the children accept that — although it was totally incomprehensible — they would have to become someone else until the end of the war. We were little girls, but we were expected to become grown-ups. We had to play a double game, to completely adopt this new personality and to act normal in spite of everything. The leaders of OSE made us promise never to reveal our true identities, and I never heard of anyone inadvertently revealing their real identity, even though there were little girls in our group who were barely five years old.

I wish I could meet the administrative geniuses who came up with the brilliant idea of hiding the Jewish children in the government's own children's homes run by the Entr'aide d'hiver du maréchal, the "Marshal's Winter Mutual Aid Society!" Life in these homes was not necessarily simple, and after the war some of my friends told me that they had been very unhappy there. A certain number of children were not taken to these hiding places. Some girls were smuggled into Switzerland, some became domestics in private homes and others were sent to convents or farms. Thanks to a few good people, innocent children were saved from the Germans' clutches.

One evening, Chief Cabri told me, "Starting tomorrow morning at dawn, your name will be Yvonne Drapier, and your sister's, Raymonde Drapier. You'll be part of a group of big sisters with little sisters under your protection. Here's a short history of your family: Your father was born in Ménilmontant. He drank a lot and didn't remember anything. He was inducted into the army and taken prisoner in Germany. No one knows where your mother is at the moment. She left you and your sister, and you were found in the streets and taken into the government children's homes. Say nothing, absolutely nothing, unless somebody asks, and try not to attract notice."

Château des Basses-Fontaines

Some smugglers came and picked us up in a truck. There were about twenty of us, some with younger sisters. In addition to me and my sister, now referred to as Yvonne and Raymonde Drapier, there were Raymonde Gerlier (whose real name was Geller), Fanny Lambert (Lamberger), Léo and René Canart (Cohen), Léa and Jacqueline Simard (Szmekanowsky), Irène and Monique Burin (Burenstein) and France, Fortunée and Huguette Colin (Cohen), among others. From now on, we would have to keep quiet and observe, to try to forget what once had been and live in the immediate present, while being careful not to draw attention from counsellors or students. What a terrible time!

We crammed into the smugglers' truck and headed toward Tours. Driving along the beautiful Loire River, we could see châteaux in the distance. After Beaugency, our truck took a different road, heading toward the village of Saint-Laurent-des-Eaux, our destination. We were in the Sologne, a particularly beautiful region with its farms and fields, its nature. The truck made a right turn and we saw the entrance to an estate. It was the Château des Basses-Fontaines, our future home. To the left of the gate stood some little houses and a building we would soon learn to call the chalet; to the right were the big empty cages of a kennel; and in front of us, surrounded by a beautiful lawn, towered the château with its turrets, its little chapel, its pond with ducks swimming in it, and best of all, its woods nearby.

I think that the director, Mme. Henriette Chautard, was the only one who knew our true identities. She greeted us and immediately ordered the staff to assign us beds in the dormitory, have us shower, cut our hair very short and issue us the uniform of the home. There too, the staff followed the scouting practice of using totemic names. Mme. Chautard was called Gazelle, and the supervisor, a lively woman, was known as Periwinkle. The residents were also divided into groups named after animals. I belonged to the Tree Frogs.

At the château, the large sitting rooms and bedrooms had been turned into dormitories. Each little iron bed was separated from the next by a night table. The counsellor slept in the same dormitory, but her bed was separated from ours by a curtain. A lot of the girls had fathers who were prisoners of war in German camps. Others had been picked up in the slums or the streets of Paris. We quickly became friends with the girls from Paris. They were very vivacious and spoke Parisian French mixed with slang. They told us stories of the neighbourhoods of Paris and taught us popular songs. Who would have imagined that the girls in the home would be so different from each other? My Jewish companions and I quickly adopted the gentile Parisians' ways of behaving and expressing themselves, and from the outside, the group looked completely homogeneous. Which means we hid our traumas well.

In the washroom in the morning, we would stand bare-chested side by side, washing with cold water, passing a single bar of soap back and forth. Sometimes we would compare our budding thirteen-year-old bosoms. We already felt grown up. There was Henriette Jacques, who had the bed next to mine, whom I liked a lot and who personified the Paris street urchin with a quick tongue. It was Henriette who introduced me to the real Paris of the working people, the Paris of songs and movies. Lise Hallet was like the grey sparrows in the trees in the park, always in good humour despite the sad stories of her family. There was Andrée Moeslin, who was not the least bit embarrassed to tell us that her father did business with the Germans, that he was a collaborator and made a lot of money. Christiane Caussin and Hélène Félix were fast runners and good in gymnastics. They taught me to do a handstand against the front wall of the château and not to worry about showing my underpants. It was touching to see these little girls at bedtime in their long white nightshirts kneeling and saying a prayer to the good Lord to bring their fathers back. Naturally, there were quarrels, hypocrisy, meanness and jealousies, but the Jewish girls hidden among those who were not Jewish would always give in to buy peace — we did everything we could to avoid notice.

I observed what went on around me attentively, and above all, I listened. The girls would mimic the cook when she had drunk too much wine and didn't know what she was saying, and they would laugh at her red nose. That was when I would hear the working-class speech they had learned from their parents in the poor neighbourhoods of Paris.

Every morning, we would line up in our teams in front of the steps of the château to salute the flag. We would sing while two of the girls unfolded and raised the flag of France. Gazelle and Periwinkle would announce the day's activities. We went on a lot of hikes in the woods of Sologne, which were wonderful. We would find wild blackberries, little strawberries and hazelnuts, which we ate on the spot because we were always hungry. It was wartime and our rations were meagre. We would play on the lawn in front of the statue of Joan of Arc. In the winter, we had a few classes, but nothing that would seriously prepare us for school. Luckily, we had free access to a little library in one of the turrets. It was the ideal spot for me because I loved to read. There were books for my age group but also a lot of old ones left behind by the owner. I would hide up there between the shelves reading whatever I came across, until I heard the bell ring. One day, I found an old Larousse dictionary, which became my secret friend. Many years later, I wrote an article for a paper in Jerusalem describing this library and some episodes from my life during the war. Here is part of the article, which I called "The Secret of the Dictionary:"

I would go there every recreation period, usually alone, to rummage around in the dusty books. I loved doing this. I had found a world of my own. One day I discovered an old Larousse dictionary there, and, leafing through it, I found two pages filled with little flags, the emblems of countries all over the world. With great emotion, I found the little blue-and-white flag of Palestine with a yellow Magen David — the Star of David. At first, I quickly closed the dictionary and instinctively looked around me. No! I must have been dreaming! I opened it again, and tears came to my eyes and clouded my vision.

That place existed! And I had discovered something that was crying out within me. A feeling that, for the longest time, I'd had to stifle, forget, deny, but that, with the sight of the flag, had been reawakened. This feeling that came from the depths of my being had to remain secret, I had to smother it, to bury it for as long as necessary.

For now, I had to put the dictionary back in its place, safe on the highest shelf in the darkest corner. I only had to raise my eyes each time I came to the library to find my friend there in the shadows hiding a beautiful secret.

One day, a problem arose with a new counsellor who had been hired to work with a group of young children. We soon noticed that when she took care of our group, she would take us to an open field dotted with grain stacks, beyond which was a German airfield. Blond, very short and chubby, this counsellor was no beauty. She would leave us in the field and go on a little further and lie down beside a grain stack in the arms of a German soldier she had arranged to meet. My Parisian companions had quite a few thoughts about this, and inevitably, the other counsellors heard about it, and then the supervisor, Periwinkle, and finally, the director, Gazelle. But Gazelle didn't know what to do, given the circumstances and the fact that the Germans were in control.

A little while before that, a young man had arrived at the château totally exhausted and had asked to be given shelter for two or three nights to regain his strength before continuing on his way. He was the brother of one of the girls who was in hiding with me. She was so happy to see her brother Jean! He soon left in search of other hiding places, and I believe he ended up joining the Resistance. He had left some family papers and documents with Gazelle, and she, in her naivety, had hidden them — along with all of the true identity documents of the Jewish children in her care — in the safe in her office in the chalet, opposite the château. Somebody informed on the young man's visit to the château. Gazelle suspected everyone, but especially the chubby blond counsellor. But she knew she was under surveillance and she didn't know what to do. The police came and searched the chalet and they wanted to see what was in the safe. As luck would have it, the lock of the safe was stuck and nobody was able to open it. The police finally gave up and said they would come back another time.

After they left, Gazelle managed to find a locksmith to open the safe. She took out the papers and put them in a box, which she buried. Because I was one of the older girls in hiding under her protection, she had me come to the chalet and told me of the decision she had made. She explained that she would have to send us to another children's home for a little while. During our conversation, she admitted she was afraid and that she could see herself lined up against a wall and shot.

Château du Coudray-Montpensier

Very early in the morning, in total secrecy, we were taken in a pickup truck to a new shelter, the Château du Coudray-Montpensier. Agathe, one of the counsellors, was let in on the secret and came with us to our destination. She had taught me how to sew a little, especially how to do buttonholes; she also took care of the infirmary. The truck took the back roads and we passed a lot of beautiful châteaux when we drove along the Loire.

The Château du Coudray-Montpensier was located near the village of Seuilly (not far from Chinon) in Indre-et-Loire. It was a medieval château with drawbridge, towers, moat, crenellations, huge halls, long exposed beams, enormous fireplaces, a secret room and passages leading to underground tunnels. No place could have been better suited to my fertile imagination. After the village of Seuilly, we drove up a hill to the château, which towered over the woods, fields and farms of the area. We were later told that Joan of Arc had slept in the room that was our dormitory before she went to Vienne to meet with the Dauphin Charles (the future King Charles VII) in Chinon.

After crossing the drawbridge, we entered a large square courtyard. It was there that all the girls would assemble with the counsellors in the morning to await the arrival of the director, Mme. Podge. Once she got there, we would sing the anthems of the flag-raising ceremony. The Château du Coudray was run by the government as part of the Marshal's social assistance program.

Mme. Podge was an extraordinarily beautiful blond, and sometimes handsome men in high boots and luxurious cars would come to visit her. Her husband was quite old — or perhaps he just appeared old to my eyes. He had been gassed in the trenches in World War I and was very weak. He was a gentleman, reserved and basically good.

The director's eldest daughter was our counsellor for a while because she needed to show the authorities she had a job or she risked being sent to do forced labour in Germany. She showed us the impressive paintings she had done on subjects from the Middle Ages. She wore a cape and had her brown hair tied back in a snood, which made her look like a princess. Rather slight, she looked a lot like her father. She explained many things to us and told us witty stories about Paris and stories about the château, especially the secret room, where it was rumoured that a number of peasants had met their deaths. One day, she showed it to us: it was a very deep, dark hole in the middle of a tiled floor in a small oval room, covered by a trap door made of wood.

Unfortunately, the daughter left us to study at the Sorbonne, and another counsellor came to replace her. The new counsellor was called Wagtail, and she quickly won us over because she was so nice. But life wasn't easy. We got very little food, and it was cold in the big dormitories where we slept in bunk beds. We had to do a lot of work, especially sorting potatoes. We would spend hours working in the sheds, where there were rats and rot. The counsellors weren't spared either. Sometimes they would read us stories or do sewing with us. As for studies, there was practically nothing.

One day, Wagtail took us on a walk to Chinon to see the ruins of an old château. As we were going through the lanes to the upper town, we saw Germans sitting in the cafés and on the terraces with French girls on their laps. They were shouting and swearing in German, and tipping the girls back and kissing them. Wagtail must have regretted taking us there. Luckily, with our gloomy grey capes, clogs and short hair, we didn't look at all appealing, and we were allowed to pass in peace. We walked back to Le Coudray by way of the Vienne, our clogs tied together over our shoulders. The weather was nice that day, which helped dispel the bad feeling the cafés had left us with.

A few of the counsellors organized a staging of the old song "Le Roi Renaud." We built a tower with crenellations out of chairs and benches covered with grey blankets. Léa Simard played the lead role, and other girls played grand ladies. Léa sang the song with so much feeling that I saw some of the counsellors weeping. The song tells of a defeat of some crusaders in the Middle Ages and the gloomy impression it created suited the time we were living in.

We sometimes got permission to lie in the grass that grew by the moat; in spite of our fears of the snakes that lived there, we would occasionally sunbathe there. All summer long, we would go into the nearby woods and eat blackberries and strawberries. Food was scarce, and this supplement to our diet was good for us. We also found lots of beautiful violets. I don't recall being close to any of the girls. We were newcomers and it wasn't easy for us to blend in with the "old-timers." Besides, I found them very cruel to the younger girls. On the other hand, the counsellors did their best — one of them, a pretty girl from Paris, even gave me a photograph of herself, which I still have. She, too, needed to have a job in France so as not to have to go and work in Germany.

After two or three months, in the winter of 1943 to 1944, half of our little group returned to the Château des Basses-Fontaines, while the other half stayed at the Château du Coudray. In addition to my sister and me, the Colin, Simard, Burin and Canart sisters and a few other girls went back to Les Basses-Fontaines. When I much later met some of the girls who had stayed behind, they told me that they mainly remembered the punishments constantly meted out to them, especially by the cook, and that they had been very glad to be taken back to Paris after liberation.

Back to Les Basses

When we returned to the Château des Basses-Fontaines, our group found that there had been some changes. To start with, the chubby little blond counsellor who flirted with the Germans at the airfield was gone. Gazelle also seemed calmer. Her son, Henri Chautard, had joined her. We called him Hummingbird, and after the war, he married the supervisor, Periwinkle (whose real name was Marie-Cécile). A whole group of new girls had come from a children's home that had been bombed and had to be evacuated.

That winter, air defence searchlights scoured the sky for British planes coming to bomb the factories between Orléans and Blois. Unfortunately for us, the château was located on the path to the target zone. I still have a clear memory of an incident that occurred one day when a few of us went with a counsellor to the village of Saint-Laurent-des-Eaux. We were just passing in front of the last houses when, from out of nowhere, a dozen planes appeared in the sky. They came down in a dive and climbed back up in an arc, and then dived down again toward their target, which was located around Beaugency, bombing it in an infernal racket. The operation lasted about ten minutes, and then they disappeared the way they had come. With the first bombs, we huddled together, trembling all over. Never will I forget this blitz the Allies carried out with such precision and speed. We all returned to Les Basses-Fontaines shaken by the air attack. After that, Gazelle made a decision not to allow walks outside the grounds of the château. But we would soon experience even more difficult times.

That winter was particularly cold, with snow and a lot of wind. Tension in the house intensified and rumours were rampant. A few counsellors left and were replaced by others. Among the new people were a nurse we called Major (perhaps that was her rank during World War I) and her daughter, who was a counsellor.

Measures had been taken to provide some education for us, but they weren't carried out seriously. We were taught a lot of songs, which we would sing in the big hall. Periwinkle decorated a Christmas tree; there weren't any presents other than those we made ourselves from scraps of fabric or paper. It was wartime, with all its restrictions. But we each received a little bar of chocolate filled with a white jelly, a treat we hadn't tasted for a long time. I don't recall going to the dentist a single time during those four years of war. We didn't eat sugar, so we didn't have toothaches.

One day, some other girls and I were punished for disobeying a counsellor. She made us go outside in the snow and run around the grounds without our capes, holding our hands at the back of our necks. She must have forgotten us because after a very long time, we were still walking, chilled to the bone, when someone who was very angry with the counsellor told us to come back inside.

But it was too late; I caught an acute case of pneumonia and had to stay in bed for a long time. After weeks of suffering, I got better thanks to Major, who cared for me harshly but effectively. In those days, we didn't yet have penicillin, and Major would put mustard plasters on my chest and back. It was horrible, unbearable, and I could hardly breathe, but Major was determined, and she saved my life. I was still very weak, but finally, when spring came, the famous spring of 1944, I was getting better.

The mother of Irène and Monique Burin came to see her daughters, but they had to call her Auntie because they were supposed to be orphans. Their mother was hiding in the area around Grenoble, but she took the risk of coming to see her children for two days. She whispered in my ear, "Eva, in three months, the war will be over and we'll finally be free." I hadn't shed a tear for years, but when I heard those words, I couldn't stop crying.

During these months, the bombing intensified and sometimes the windows shook. They must have been bombing in the region of Blois, because we could hear the air defence responding. The planes that flew over us were carrying heavy loads, as we could hear from the sound of their engines. The searchlights pierced the blackness of the sky; sometimes a plane was hit and fell into the fields.

Then came the night of June 5 to 6, a date I will always remember. It was only later that we learned it was D-Day, the day of the Allied landing. We were abruptly awakened by incredible noise above our heads. There were two terribly powerful explosions and the château shook on its foundations, while broken glass rained down on us in our beds. We heard what sounded like a mountain rising up and falling again with a loud thud, followed by the deafening roar of a plane going down in a clearing nearby.

The violence of the explosions made us scream with terror in our rooms, and we rushed to the doors onto the corridor, but we couldn't get out. There were no adults with us. In the panic, the girls ran in all directions, pushing and trampling each other. Some fell to their knees, praying to God for help, shouting and raising their arms to the heavens. I repeated to myself the only Hebrew words I could remember: "Shema Yisrael…."

Finally, we all huddled together not daring to move. My sister Raymonde curled up against me, but in a minute, she fell asleep again. A little while later, Hummingbird came to reassure us, "You can go back to your beds after you clean up the broken glass. There's nothing to fear now." But we were paralyzed with fear.

Henriette exclaimed with exasperation, "I've had enough of this! Come what may, I'm going back to bed." That made me almost want to smile, and I followed her. I always admired her charming cheekiness. She was a real little Paris urchin. She had good common sense and was very decisive.

The bombing went on all night in the distance, until we thought it would never end. We didn't yet know that the Allies were landing and thousands of soldiers were dying to liberate France.

Dawn finally came. We had been dressed for hours, and we went outside and discovered the damage caused by the two explosions. We couldn't believe our eyes. Just a few metres from the château, between it and the cabin where four women who worked as domestics lived, there were two huge, deep craters. Two yawning holes. And all around them, in the flowerbeds, the lawns and the road, there were clods of earth scattered by the two big bombs. An Allied plane had been hit and had dropped the bombs before crashing to the ground in the clearing behind the château. By an amazing stroke of luck, a true miracle, the bombs had fallen between the château and the cabin. The good old château had held out! It had been shaken, but it had proven to be a fortress. Apart from some bruises as a result of the broken windows and a few knocks and palpitations, everyone came out of it unharmed. The explosions also broke the windows of the houses in Saint-Laurent-des-Eaux.

From then on, things happened quickly. Government people in high boots came to record the damage — some of them took photographs, others talked to the girls and kissed the little ones. But these well-dressed men had a certain hesitant, fearful manner. The government would surely change, and what would become of them? I would soon turn fourteen, and I watched and tried to read the emotions their faces betrayed.

We had had another surprise visit a few days before. A whole group of German soldiers, our neighbours from the airfield, had showed up at our flag-raising ceremony while we were singing. They stayed for a while and then went away, their packs on their backs.

A few days later, I had yet another surprise, a wonderful one. An open jeep full of American GIs arrived in the courtyard of the château — and my brother, Michel, was with them! He was wearing the uniform of the French army and an armband with the letters FFI

(French Forces of the Interior). Gazelle and Periwinkle were beside themselves. The staff from the chalet, the women from the cabin, the counsellors, the girls, the cook — everyone wanted to see these first liberators of France and cheer them.

First of all, the GIs were tall, and they weren't wearing high boots. There was nothing I hated more than the sound of the Germans' boots clicking, the heels rising and falling as they walked in their aggressive, authoritarian way. The GIs wore their helmets cocked to the side and they always had their mouths full of something called chewing gum, which they shared with us. They were smiling and seemed very relaxed, with legs dangling casually out the door of their Jeep. They were like a breath of free air that rose all the way up to the clouds in the blue sky. It was a marvellous new feeling. They spoke English, and they seemed powerful and easygoing at the same time. They were so new, so different!

Michel had a three-day leave to spend with us. After escaping from Rivesaltes, he worked on farms and then joined a group of French Jews taking care of a farm in Agen, in Lot-et-Garonne. Then he and his friends went underground and joined the Resistance, and they were enlisted in the French army under the command of General de Lattre de Tassigny. In his military record, I found the army corps Michel had belonged to: 1st Armoured Division, 3rd Regiment of Dragoons, 2nd Squadron, Cavalry. I have a book that contains a photograph of Michel and his friends entering the town of Belfort in a truck with the victorious French army and being cheered by the crowd.

Michel had to go back to the army, but before leaving, he made plans for us to reunite with our little sister, Renée, who was still at Sèvres, near Paris. The other girls were already receiving news of their families, and trucks were beginning to come and pick them up to take them back to Paris.

Planes were constantly passing over our heads and we would go to the clearings and pick up pieces of parachutes left by the Allies.

They were white silk and we would make placemats from them. I'll never forget the time we saw a burned plane that had crashed in a clearing nearby. The huge skeleton of the plane was all black, and the burned body of the pilot was still in it, clutching the wheel. It was said he was English. He hadn't had time to parachute from the plane and had crashed on French soil. It was horrible and morbid. Branches of trees that had been damaged in the airplane's fall were strewn on the ground. There was an awful smell in the air.

After that, I had a frightening dream that I had wings and was gliding through the air above the rooftops, and that people were walking around on the ground. Their faces were hidden by hoods and they were each carrying a lifeless human body in their arms. One of them approached me and I caught a glimpse of what he was carrying: it was my mother, dead. I awoke with a start. The whole dormitory was asleep, but the moon was shining through a broken pane of glass and its rays came through the clouds and fell on my face. Maybe the images in my dream came from an association I made with the movement of the clouds in front of the moon. I never again had that dream, but I have often thought of it.

Our discipline had been relaxed slightly since the Allied landing, and every day brought more news. The Germans were fleeing, burning houses, stealing and leaving destruction in their wake. Planes flew over the fields looking for Germans trying to get away. Fortunately, our château and the surrounding area were spared. One day, Henriette got the idea of going rowing on the pond among the reeds. There was an old, half-rotten boat that had been left hidden in the grass; nobody ever touched it. Henriette managed to convince me to get into it with her. There we were, almost in the middle of the pond, when we heard the buzzing of an airplane engine. The plane suddenly dived toward us, traced an arc in the air and then rose again and disappeared in the clouds. It must have been a fighter plane looking for fleeing Germans — at least, that's what we were told later, after a good scolding. When the plane came toward us, Henriette and I were so scared, we rowed as fast as we could to try to reach the reeds and hide among them. I imagine the pilot was amused to see us panic like that. But since they'd shoot at anything suspect in those days, we were very lucky we were not harmed.

The war was coming to an end and the Germans were retreating to eastern France. We all felt an intense joy, a feeling that we were finally coming back to life. People came out of their shelters, out of the holes where they had lived during four years of humiliation — and they were the lucky ones. We, the girls in hiding, remained silent and suspicious, and although we were glad, we were still afraid in spite of ourselves. We sensed the hypocrisy of the adults who had suddenly changed their attitude toward us. I was fourteen years old, and I was extremely mistrustful. I was very watchful and I would amuse myself by observing the adults' expressions and trying to tell what they really thought. I was a bit of a wild child, always on my guard under a quiet, timid exterior. I still remember when Gazelle was visited by people from the Marshal's Mutual Aid Society after the bombing at the château: she had pointed to several of the girls in hiding, and a man in high boots came over and questioned me and wanted to kiss me, but I wouldn't let him. What if he had been a collaborator who was changing sides and was trying to gain sympathy? Before, they had acted as if the Germans were our friends, but now it was General de Gaulle who was our true friend.

Reunion at Sèvres

One day, I received a letter from my little sister, Renée, from the children's home in Sèvres: "Come here quickly with Raymonde. It's so nice here! On Sundays, we eat fried potatoes." Fried potatoes! I hardly remembered what they were! The German surrender, Paris, fried potatoes — all these changes happening every day, so quickly, it was too much at one time.

The road to Paris was now free, and it was decided that Raymonde and I would finally go join Renée. We were first sent to Neuilly-sur-Seine, to a triage house, and from there, we took the metro (a first for me) to the Pont de Sèvres station. The counsellor who had come with us explained how to get to the Sèvres children's home, our destination. We crossed the Seine and continued walking, passing the Sèvres porcelain factory, a bistro and Parc Saint-Cloud. Then we took La Grande Rue, with its many stores, to the intersection where, almost hidden by the angle of the houses, there was a strange stairway up to Rue de la Croix Bosset. At the top was the gate to the Sèvres children's home.

The home was a former convent. It had a high wall and was surrounded by beautiful trees. The site was ideal — out of the way, very private, hidden from view. After going through the gate, we climbed some stairs bordered by shrubs and flowers. A separate but very lively community lived there, thanks to Mme. Yvonne Hagnauer, a wonderfully active woman called Seagull. I looked around me and I liked everything I saw, but I couldn't explain why. What a feeling! I didn't know it yet, but this place, with Seagull in charge of it, would change my whole way of thinking and have a major effect on the rest of my life.

When we arrived in the entrance hall of the home, there were boys and girls between four and sixteen years of age going in and out of the backyard. They were all dressed in checkered smocks and were wearing slippers, which they changed for clogs before going outside. A cleaning woman who was polishing the stairs was scolding the children who wanted to pass. Intimidated, Raymonde and I examined the children's craft work displayed in glass cases along the wall. There were ceramics, drawings and embroidery, all very beautiful.

Suddenly there was a lot of noise from upstairs and a rather excited lady rushed down the stairs. She was wearing a smock like everyone else. With her eyes blazing, she got into a discussion with the counsellor who was with us. There was an issue about the capes and the clogs not being in the right places. Then she turned to us and said, "So! You're Renée's sisters! You, go upstairs here, and you, go over there." And she disappeared like a whirlwind.

When we arrived at Sèvres, Renée was in the infirmary because she had dislocated her arm. We went to visit her and play with her every day. She was small and thin, and much later, she suffered from osteoporosis, which was undoubtedly a result of the lack of food and vitamins and also her illnesses and hospitalizations.

Though Seagull at first seemed severe, we very quickly realized that she was also profoundly human. She was unlike the other directors, who relied on the supervisors to carry out the everyday tasks. Seagull worked directly with the teachers, the counsellors, the nurse, the cook, the manager and the cleaning women, and she often replaced one or another of them. The home was her life! She was capable of working constantly, and she expected the same of others.

There was a print shop, and in the home's newspaper, *Voile au vent* (*Sail in the Wind*), I found some articles by counsellors saying they had come to the home just to work with Seagull and had stayed for twenty years or more. Seagull would say, "You're my brave soldiers," and these women would give themselves completely to their jobs, working longer hours than they had to or were paid to.

On the second floor, there was a long corridor lined on both sides with small rooms (which must originally have been the nuns' bedrooms) with three or four beds side by side, each one with a little chest for the week's clothes and some books. That was all. Every week, we handed in our underwear and stockings to be washed. We would leave our little bundles in front of our door, and in their place, we would receive the ones we had left there the week before. A counsellor saw to it that everything was done properly. I shared my room with Claude Aaron and Jeanine Smith, and we were very good friends.

After getting washed in the bathroom, we would go back up to our rooms to make our beds. We all had chores to carry out before breakfast, such as feeding the birds in the cage on the patio, tidying the coat racks and the clogs, helping the younger children wash and dress, setting the table and other small tasks. We had breakfast in the big hall. The manager, Victor Gambau, whose bedroom was nearby, gave us the news from the radio. The manager was a Freemason, but he hid it because of the Vichy government's blacklist.

German V-1 rockets were flying over Paris to cross the Channel and bomb England. The liberation of Paris was taking place and we could hear gunfire in the streets. Several nights, we heard sirens and had to rush to the shelters. But happily, this was the end of the Germans in Paris. They hadn't damaged the national monuments, and a little while later, we went to the Saint-Cloud woods and saw the illuminated monuments of Paris from the esplanade. After the years of darkness, the humiliations, suffering and hunger, Paris was again lit up. It was beautiful and heartwarming! It was good and grand! I will never forget our cries of joy.

Seagull was already caring for a lot of Jewish children who were there under false names. I saw two of my old companions from Le

Couret, Alice Menkes and Trautchen Feith. I also met others, such as Esther, Claudine and Henri Weiss, who were among the youngest children. There were also a few Jewish teachers who had found refuge with Seagull. In particular, I recall Cicada, who played the piano very well and took care of the smaller children.

Our classes took place in the attic, which was set up for them and was protected from the neighbours' view. A little below, in a small bedroom apart from the others, was the clothing room. Two women worked together there mending our stockings and other clothes. One of them was mute, and we communicated with her by making signs with our hands, but after liberation, to everyone's surprise, the lady began to speak. It turned out that she was Jewish and spoke only Yiddish. Seagull had agreed to give her room and board on the condition that she never reveal that she couldn't speak French.

Marcel Marceau often visited Seagull at Sèvres, frequently bringing hidden children with him. He had friends in the art world and the theatre. Our drama teacher, Éliane Guyon, whom we called Dragonfly, was a close friend of his. She brought in Jean-Louis Barrault, a tall, thin man who had just finished shooting the famous film *Les Enfants du Paradis* (*Children of Paradise*). Éliane taught us mime, the art of expressing yourself through movement without using speech.

In the fall of 1944, Roger Hagnauer, Seagull's husband, whom we called Penguin, came to Sèvres and became our French teacher. He had been hiding in a sanatorium run by a Dr. Lefèbvre. Penguin was from an Alsatian Jewish background, but he had been born in Paris the year after the metro was built, as he liked to remind us.

One day, Seagull asked me for a list of the girls who had stayed at Les Basses-Fontaines and Le Coudray. I gave her the names and ages of those who were alone and those who had sisters, and she brought them to Sèvres. So I was able to see Fanny Lambert, Raymonde Gerlier and Léa and Jacqueline Simard again, and France, Fortunée and Huguette Colin and a lot of others too. These were happy reunions. Some of the girls discovered that they still had family and went to join their relatives, and I never saw them again. Trautchen Feith went to join her mother in England, and eventually Esther, Claudine and Henri Weiss were reunited with their parents, who had hidden on a farm. When the three of them left Sèvres, we wished them the best for the future, but we were terribly envious.

Seagull was an admirer of the educational approach of the Belgian Dr. Ovide Decroly, and her teaching at Sèvres was based on it. As this method recommended, we were always learning. We had to observe and question everything, absolutely everything, and record it all in a notebook. "Take notes," she would say constantly, "take notes." I still do it today, automatically. "And then, using your notes and your questions, describe, develop and explain your impressions. Do it individually or in groups, it doesn't matter! What's important is to always be active."

In the Sèvres children's home, we were occupied from morning to night — with classes in dance, drama and Greek art, which involved reciting a text while creating theatrical poses and figures, learning to play various musical instruments, singing in the choir, painting, drawing, ceramics, weaving, working with leaded glass, gardening, as well as cooking and pastry-making for the older girls. That was where I learned the secret of making perfect puff pastry. There were also activities involving printing and everything related to it, such as colours and lithography. *Voile au vent*, our newspaper, was sent to a lot of important people in Sèvres and Paris, such as the mayors and prefects, and was distributed in the schools.

Notebooks in hand, we went to visit the Sèvres porcelain factory because one student, Gisèle Debain, worked there. We started to do embroidery and weaving after visiting the Gobelins tapestry company. Jean-Louis Barrault invited us to hear him read Victor Hugo's poetry at the Palais de Chaillot theatre, where he stood alone on stage wearing a white jacket, in front of an audience of students. If we were working on transportation, we would go to an airfield and learn about it firsthand. We learned everything about the artist Jean-

Baptiste-Camille Corot and his paintings by going for walks to his ponds, which were at the end of our street. Seagull brought us copies of documents in old French to decipher and rewrite; she must have cleaned out the basement of the Sèvres city hall. She also taught us English, and we learned the name Shakespeare, so long and difficult for us to pronounce. At the end of the day, in the little library, Seagull would read us a chapter of *Gone with the Wind*. We were fascinated by history, and were studying the Civil War at that time. I made a clay statuette of a woman wearing a long dress from the period, and I called her Mélanie.

One day, Penguin took us to Meudon to visit a very old little house where Georges Sand and Frédéric Chopin had lived. After that outing, we memorized Lamartine's poem "Le Lac." Wagtail had arrived, and she taught us math and fractions. We made our own costumes for the story of Renart and learned all about the history of the Middle Ages when we put on a play for Christmas in 1944. Some talented girls painted the scenery and designed the costumes. In our classroom, Penguin put up a "question box," in which we would put scraps of paper with our questions on them. It was to answer one of those questions that he gave a class on the difference between socialism and communism, which was a subject Penguin knew a lot about. We adored our stimulating life at Sèvres, and I could go on endlessly about it.

Many years later, when Seagull was no longer my director or I her student, when we were two adult women who had become friends, she told me, "When you came to Sèvres, you were starved for knowledge and you were ideal material for a teacher. You gobbled everything up. And the best was that we almost never had to go back to a lesson. You learned quickly and retained what you learned. I really enjoyed teaching you!" I was visiting Seagull and Penguin at their home in Meudon, and Seagull also told me she had done everything possible to keep us occupied and without free time, so that we wouldn't be able to think about anything else, because the news from outside was terrifying.

In spite of all her efforts at that time, we suffered, though Seagull didn't know how much. The war continued in Germany, but survivors were already coming back from the concentration camps. Some still wore a striped uniform and they looked so confused, gaunt and skeletal, that they barely seemed human to me. They were put up at the Lutetia Hotel, which was being run by Mme. Zlatin at the request of General de Gaulle. One day, our classmate Paule Aaron brought back a newspaper she had bought in town and we were so horrified by the photographs of the concentration camps and crematoria that we cried and dreamed about them all night. We still had a faint hope of seeing our parents again, but every week that passed brought information that made it less and less probable. We couldn't understand… there was nothing to understand.

Epilogue

We remained at the home, orphans who had lost everything, alone in our suffering. "Why are we alive and not they?" we wondered. "Did they die for nothing? Why?" For years, we buried our memories of the war, we didn't dare speak, we pretended to forget, but all that time, we carried with us a heavy burden that crushed our hearts. We were forced to grow up too quickly. We lost our youth and our dreams forever. I could write a great deal more, and perhaps, one day, I will.

Seagull, Mme. Yvonne Hagnauer, helped prepare us to live fulfilling lives as adults. She was our director, our teacher, our friend, and we were her daughters. It was a privilege to know her. I kept in touch with Seagull after my siblings and I left France for British Mandate Palestine in the fall of 1945. Here is part of a letter, translated from French, that I wrote in 1949:

Dear Goéland [Seagull] *and Pingouin* [Penguin],

After all these years of silence and all the adventures that have happened since we last parted, I finally dare sending you a letter and apologize to you for this very long wait [sic]. *Since I have left Sèvres, I have not had (to put it nicely) the opportunity to really think about and really feel all the kindness you showered upon us when we lived in Sèvres.*

From the time I finished school and started working, I have more than once remarked upon the difference between your methods and those used here and your kind and intelligent way of always trying to understand us. I wish to remain in touch with you and the Maison de Sèvres because I have always loved France and my only dream is to be able to go back and visit with you. There are times when my sisters and I speak the whole day long about the good times we had under your care. I so miss our French lessons today! I read a lot but I do feel from time to time that the words don't come so easily and I often have to think before writing a word. I hope you will forgive me if you see mistakes in my letter and you will help me correct them. When I spoke to Renée and Raymonde, they urged me to resume writing to the Maison de Sèvres, even after such a lengthy wait [sic]. *I hope you will not be angry with us for not having written earlier but, if you are willing, we will remain faithful to you and to our friends. I don't know if after so much time, there are still* [former boarders] *with you but I know that I can always turn to you for help. I dearly hope that I can still get letters from my former friends (Lucie, Raymonde G., Fanny L., Sabine C., etc.). I thought about sending you a picture of us but I would prefer to get an answer back from you first to be certain that my letter has not been lost.*

We have changed a lot in the last three years. Renée is becoming a young lady, who is now nearly fourteen and a half, but she still has the sweet, shy disposition of her younger self. She is still very loving and everyone here adores her, the way Goéland used to. Raymonde […] *is still the dark, young and secretive girl she used to be. She learns very quickly and is now in her fourth year of high school, with the intention to go on to university. This desire to learn came on quite suddenly and we hope it will last until she reaches her goal. As for me, I had to interrupt my studies one year before my exams because of the war, this hard-fought and difficult battle where our soldiers were so heroic. On this topic, I have so much to write to you about in my next letter, in particular about our life during the few months in Jerusalem when we couldn't get any outside reinforcements during the occupation of the city. I have changed a lot. I see it mainly in the way I dress, I behave, I think. I will be nineteen soon, and for a young woman, every new year brings changes and new habits.*

I hope you have not forgotten us and I look forward to some news from you soon.

Raymonde and Renée wish you the best of health and send you their love.

With my deepest feelings,
Eva

I nominated Seagull for the title of Righteous Among the Nations, bestowed by the State of Israel. She was awarded the title in 1974 and presented with it on May 27, 1975, at the Israeli embassy in Paris. Her medal is now in my possession. The inscription in Hebrew on it is from the Talmud. It says, "Whoever saves one life, it is as if he saved an entire universe." These words are inscribed on the tombstone of Seagull and Penguin.

In the year 2000, along with three other former pupils of Les Basses, I gave testimony to Yad Vashem in the hopes that the late Gazelle, Henriette Chautard, would also be awarded the well-deserved honour of Righteous Among the Nations. She was successfully recognized in 2001, and in 2003, the medal and certificate were granted posthumously, with the award accepted on her behalf by her daughter-in-law, Marie-Cécile, our former supervisor Periwinkle. This is part of the speech I gave at that ceremonial event:

This is a very emotional moment for me! After many trials and tribulations, we are finally gathered here [Voiron] *today with Madame Marie-Cécile Chautard, our dearest Pervenche* [Periwinkle], *your children and grandchildren, Mathieu, David, Delphine, George, and the former counsellors and their charges of the Château, the "little girls," much older today of course, who have all come to bestow a very special honour on Madame Henriette Chautard, our dear Gazelle, headmistress of the home for young girls at the Château Basses-Fontaines, located in Saint-Laurent-des-Eaux (Loir-et-Cher).*

We are gathered here to award her grandchildren the very prestigious medal of the Righteous Among the Nations, bestowed by Yad Vashem in the holy city of Jerusalem.

We thank you, Gazelle, for the courage and fearlessness you displayed when you sheltered twenty or so girls during the war of 1940–1945, gave them pseudonyms and took personal responsibility for their care.

At that time, France was in the middle of a war. The country was living under the terrible tyranny of a cruel and brutal enemy. However, a few French men and women resisted. Following their conscience, they decided to save, preserve and respect the values they had been taught. This required intelligence, quick thinking, decisiveness, all qualities that defined Gazelle. One phone call is all it took for her to answer: "You can count on me. Send me these girls and I will take care of them under assumed names and false identities." When I was a little girl staying at the Château, Gazelle impressed me tremendously and later, much later, I thought a lot about what she had done, in all its simplicity and without expecting anything in return. Thank you, Gazelle. You are a remarkable woman!

It is people like Gazelle and Seagull who make France great. But how many of them were there during the war? All too few! As I get older and think back to this period in our lives, I've lost the discomfort that prevented me from talking about it. People have to know what happened to us and learn from it, so that it doesn't happen again. The real danger is indifference.

We, too, grow older: for the hidden children of the Shoah

The autumn is mild and golden. Sitting in my flowering garden, I smell the fragrant air. And then the silence, this marvellous silence. Tonight I am a little melancholy; now that I'm getting older, that happens sometimes.

In spite of all the sufferings you, my friends, had to endure during the war and the consequences you still endure, you are still here. The earth will turn and turn and turn, even after we are gone, but you, specifically you, you are miraculously different.

In spite of the heavy responsibility of our lives, our memories, this heavy burden, an oppressive suffering that will not let us go, we journey on. We moan with the oppressed, with those who should be here, with us. A year passes, and another one, and we are no longer children, the children of the Shoah. We will soon be old.

And yet, we have continued living, and we have preserved a little sun for us, but also for the others, for those who should have been here with us but who left us at the edge of youth. Those other children who, like us, ought to have lived, ought to have grown up and become adults, ought to have built their homes and seen their children grow. We are attached to them, we are their memory, we are there, we represent them.

Perhaps all is not lost! We take time as it comes, we are outside of time and for the little time that remains for us, you are part of us, you are inside us, and we love you. Yes, it is difficult to write about this but we try our best, by writing poems or songs to try and express what has been, what has happened, because there is no way to explain it all. We remain without words even if we write books, even if we continue to write more and more and more, even if we recite it in poems and songs, recite this cruel and inhumane reality, it will not be spoken, will not be sung. Even tears will never suffice.

No, nothing, nothing except a profound and afflicted silence. We have been meeting now for many years. We are beginning to mark time, to grow older. Our hair has turned white, even for those who, at that accursed time, were still delicate, little children. We were good, and we will continue to be good, super-good for eternity and always in silence. We are the Silent Ones. That is the fate of the children of the Shoah! We were young and innocent, we didn't understand, we suffered and lived and still live in silence until the end of time.

Eva Lang, 2010

Photographs

1 Eva's mother, Esther, in her youth. Place and date unknown.

2 Eva (in front) with her father, Zacharia, and her two older siblings, Michel (left) and Sarah (right) before the war. Brussels, Belgium, 1935.

3 & 4 Eva's parents, Zacharia and Esther Tuchsnajder. France, date unknown. Yad Vashem Photo Archive, Jerusalem.

1

2

3

1 Eva (front row, second from the left) in a class photo from the Hebrew school at Synagogue D'Anderlecht. Eva's sister Sarah is in the back row, third from the left. Brussels, Belgium, 1938.

2 Eva's siblings Michel and Sarah. France, date unknown.

3 Eva's mother, Esther (centre), with Michel and Sarah. France, date unknown. United States Holocaust Memorial Museum, courtesy of Eva Tuchsnajder Lang.

1

2

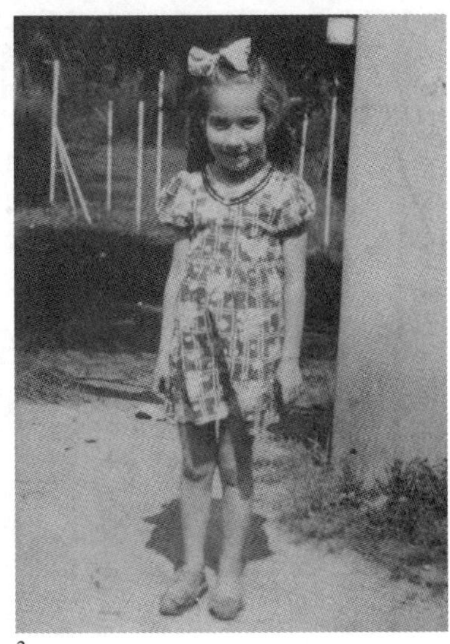

3

1 Eva (right) with her sister Raymonde and their caregiver Emma Blanc in Saint-Jean-de-Védas, where they were taken after their release from the Rivesaltes internment camp. France, circa 1941.

2 Eva and her younger sister Raymonde outside the home in St. Jean-de-Vedas. France, circa 1941.

3 Eva's youngest sister, Renée, at a children's home during the war. Savoie, France, circa 1942.

Photos from the U.S. Holocaust Memorial Museum, courtesy of Eva Tuchsnajder Lang.

1

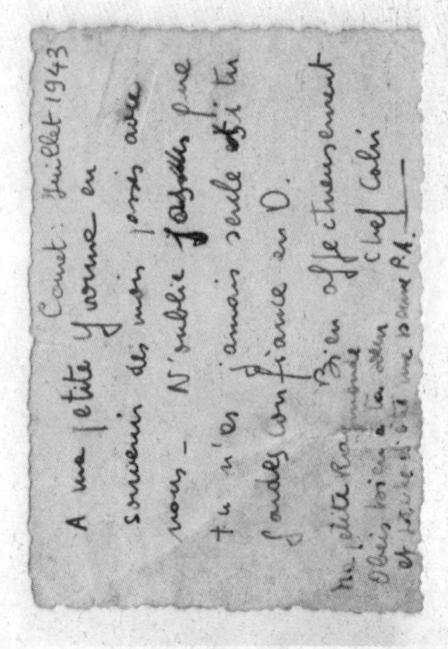

Couret : Juillet 1943
A ma petite Yvonne en
souvenir des mois passés avec
nous – N'oublie que
tu n'es jamais seule si tu
gardes confiance en D.
Bien affectueusement
Chef Cabri
Ma petite Raymonde
Obéis bien à ta sœur
et sois une bonne P.A.

2

3

1 Eva (fourth from the left) with friends and Chief Cabri (Suzanne Clément), their mentor at Le Couret. La Jonchère-Saint-Maurice, France, circa 1942–1943.

2 The reverse side of the photo reads, "For my little Yvonne as a memento of the months spent with us — Don't forget that you are never alone when you keep your faith in G [God]. Affectionately, Chief Cabri." In the left corner is written, "My little Raymonde remember to obey your sister and to be a good P. A." [Petite Aile — Little Wing, a scouting branch of Girl Guides.]

3 Group portrait of the Jewish children at the Œuvre de secours aux enfants (OSE) children's home Le Couret. La Jonchère-Saint-Maurice, circa 1942–1943. United States Holocaust Memorial Museum, courtesy of Eva Tuchsnajder Lang.

1

2

1 Eva (second row, third from the left) with friends at Le Couret. La Jonchère-Saint-Maurice, circa 1942–1943.

2 Eva (back row, third from the left) with a group of girls at the Château du Coudray-Montpensier. Seuilly, France, circa 1943.

Photos from the U.S. Holocaust Memorial Museum, courtesy of Eva Tuchsnajder Lang.

1

2

1 & 2 Group photos of youth at Les Basses-Fontaines children's home, where Eva, her sister and many other Jewish girls were hidden under false identities during the war. In the top photo, Eva's sister Raymonde is in the second row, at the far right. Yad Vashem Photo Archive, Jerusalem. In the bottom photo, Eva is in the first row, third from the left. Saint-Laurent-des-Eaux, France, 1944. U.S. Holocaust Memorial Museum, courtesy of Eva Tuchsnajder Lang.

1

2

1 Children at the OSE home in Sèvres, France, where Eva and Raymonde eventually joined their sister Renée, who was in hiding there. Renée is in the front row, far right; Marcel Marceau is pictured at top. 1944. U.S. Holocaust Memorial Museum, courtesy of Eva Tuchsnajder Lang.

2 Staff at the children's home in Sèvres. Seagull (Yvonne Hagnauer) is in the back row, second from the right; manager Victor Gambau is at far right; Marcel Marceau is standing behind the group. 1944. Yad Vashem Photo Archive, Jerusalem.

The Tuchsnajder family after the liberation of Paris. From left to right: Eva, Raymonde, Renée and Michel, wearing his uniform from the French Forces of the Interior. Sèvres, 1945.

1 Eva, age twenty. Israel, 1950.

2 Eva's brother, Michel. 1950.

3 Eva (left) with her sisters Malka (Renée, centre) and Rivka (Raymonde). Israel, 1965.

4 Eva visiting her brother, Michel. New York, 2016.

1

2

3

תעודת כבוד
ATTESTATION

Le présent Diplôme atteste qu'en sa séance du 10 Septembre 1974 la Commission des Justes près l'Institut Commémoratif des Martyrs et des Héros Yad Vashem a décidé, sur foi de témoignages recueillis par elle, de rendre homage à

איבון הגנאר YVONNE HAGNAUER

qui au péril de sa vie a sauvé des Juifs pendant l'époque d'extermination, de lui décerner la Médaille des Justes et de l'autoriser à planter un arbre en son nom dans l'Allée des Justes sur le Mont du Souvenir à Jérusalem.

Fait à Jérusalem, Israël, le 2 Février 1975

4

1 Eva (right) with Sabine Zlatin, who was part of the OSE network during the war and helped Eva and many other Jewish children find refuge, most notably by founding the children's home in Izieu. Paris, France, circa 1970s.

2 Henriette Chautard (Gazelle), director of the children's home at Château des Basses-Fontaines during the war. Date and place unknown.

3 Eva (centre) with Roger and Yvonne Hagnauer (Penguin and Seagull) on one of her many visits to see them after the war. Paris, circa 1970s.

4 The Yad Vashem certificate of honour naming Yvonne Hagnauer as Righteous Among the Nations in 1974.

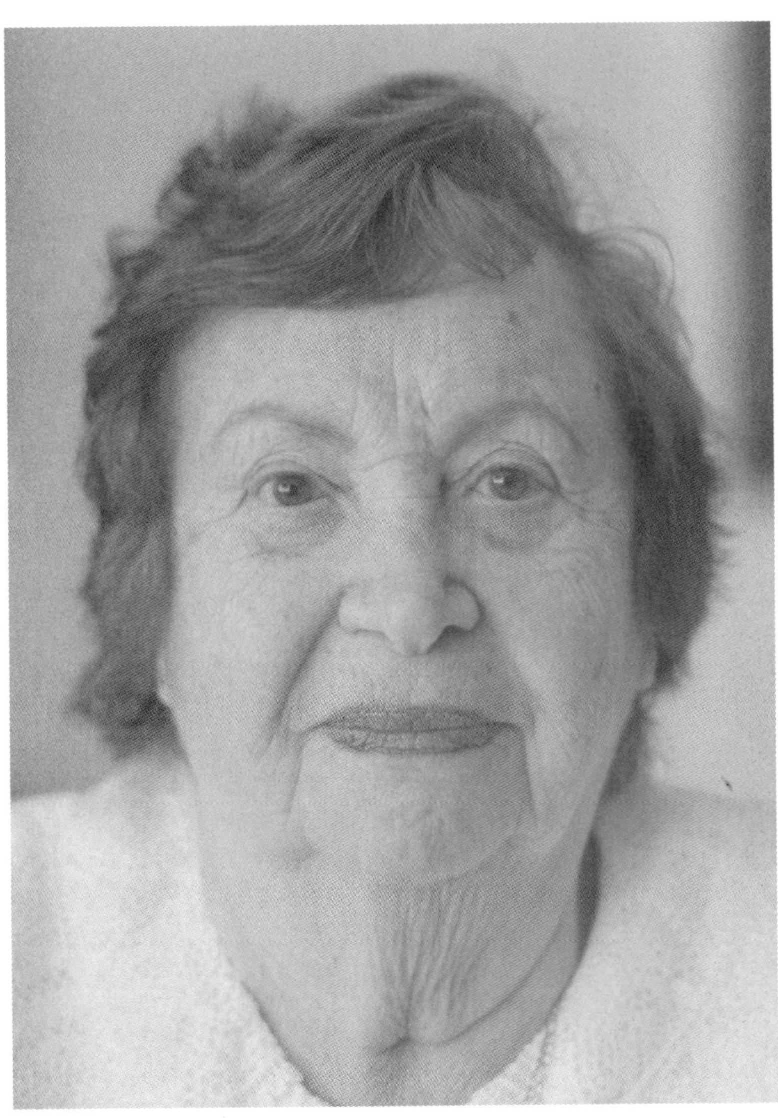

Eva Lang, 2020.

Saved by Luck and Devotion

David Korn

CZECHOSLOVAKIA/SLOVAKIA, 1938–1945

Legend
Borders in 1938
Annexed by Germany in 1938
Annexed/ occupied by Germany in 1939
Occupied by Germany in 1944
Acquired by Hungary in 1938-1941

GERMANY
POLAND
Elbe
Oder
Vistula
PRAGUE
Protectorate of Bohemia and Moravia 1939–1945
CZECHOSLOVAKIA
Brno
Spišská Stará Ves
Stará Ľubovňa
Ružomberok
Liptovský Svätý Mikuláš
Banská Bystrica
Slovakia 1939–1945
BRATISLAVA
Danube
AUSTRIA
HUNGARY
Lake Balaton
0 50 100 km

The biggest expression of bravery is when a person endangers their own life to serve the supreme purpose of saving the lives of other human beings. My brother, Jacob, and I owe our survival to many dedicated individuals: our parents, Abraham and Miriam Korn, for their resourcefulness and wisdom, and Pastor Vladimir Kuna, Sister Maria, Uncle Martin Korn, Aunt Libusa Frish (née Korn), Aunt Malka Taub (née Korn) and Uncle Joseph Taub, for their care and assistance. I would also like to acknowledge the many people who helped me to recover and build my life after the war: Lia Korn (née Schwartz), Feri Frish, Mr. Hausner from the OSE, my teachers from Kfar Batya — Haim Enoch, Chaim Ziegler, David Eliach, Shmuel Rosenbaum — and, in Canada, Morris Treitel and Jack Hahn. I would also like to thank the Azrieli Foundation for their work on my story.

No Peace for Our Time

In 1938, when British Prime Minister Neville Chamberlain boasted to the world that he had secured "peace for our time," I was just one year old, and my brother, Jacob, was two years old. We were born to our mother, Miriam (née Steiner), and father, Abraham Korn, in Brno, the second-largest city in Czechoslovakia. My father owned a textile factory, and we lived well.

In spite of the peace treaty that Chamberlain had assumed, Germany invaded Czechoslovakia in March 1939, and about six months later, World War II started. Once Germany took over Czechoslovakia, they were able to control the weapons factory in Brno — at the time, the Škoda Works was one of the largest armament factories in Europe.

During the first year Brno was invaded by the German army, the new masters rounded up many Jewish men and ordered them to come up to the Spielberg (Špilberk) Castle, located in the centre of Brno, where they were to be given instructions. My father went up there while me and my brother, Jacob, stayed with our mother.

The German army administration made all the men wait there because at the time, the Germans' policy toward the treatment of Jewish people in Czechoslovakia was unclear. After one week had passed, the Germans told the men that if they left the country within a given time frame, nothing would happen to them and their families.

I later found out that my parents were indeed trying to get out of the country, from letters I saw to their friend in Massachusetts, Mr. Naparstek. He was like family, and they asked him for help. But it didn't come.

So my father decided to move our family to Spišská Stará Ves in Slovakia, where he was born. My father's younger brother, Martin, and his younger sisters, Libusa, Malka and Chaya, still lived there and owned a textile store. Their mother, my paternal grandmother, Rosa Korn (née Kalfus), lived there as well. My paternal grandfather, Jacob, had been a soldier in World War I and was killed fighting for the Germans — Slovakia, then an ally of the Germans, had been part of the Austro-Hungarian empire.

My grandmother Rosa was of German origin. She was a real *eshet chayil*, a woman of valour. She managed to raise her family by herself brilliantly, insisting on her children's education. She spoke to her kids in German, and my father, the eldest, was sent to a yeshiva. She was very gentle, and I have a memory of her feeding me, scraping a kohlrabi and giving me one portion while she ate the next.

Spišská Stará Ves is a small town near both the Pieniny Mountains and lower Tatra Mountains, on the border with Poland. Many of the town's inhabitants were descendants of fifteenth-century German settlers, and the languages spoken in the local school were Slovak and German. Relations between the gentile population and the small Jewish population were mutually beneficial, however, they were not without incident. My uncle Martin had many non-Jewish friends, like the young Roman Catholic priest who told him that "the Jews are like salt. In small quantities the salt improves the soup; in large quantities it spoils it."

We lived near the Červený kláštor monastery. In our backyard was a small river that powered a nearby flourmill. At three years old, I remember us bathing in this river before the Sabbath. I went to the cheder, the Jewish religious school, and life felt normal for us kids. But my father had to find work, and I remember him being very nervous about it. He didn't know what our lives would look like here. My father started selling cloth to stores in the region and he was rarely home. We didn't have any toys, so one day I took his cloth samples and played with them. But I almost destroyed them. When he came back home I got spanked, but looking back, I think he should have provided us with toys, and then I wouldn't have taken his samples to play with.

Deportations Begin

On January 20, 1942, a conference was convened in Wannsee, a suburb of Berlin, during which German officials decided to annihilate the Jewish people. By February 1942, the Slovak government, which was headed by the Catholic priest Jozef Tiso, had begun to arrange for the first deportation of Jews from Slovakia, and Tiso's government agreed to pay Nazi Germany five hundred Reichsmarks for each person that they took — apparently for resettlement purposes. This is the only government in all of Europe that paid Germany to take its citizens. Prior to this, anti-Jewish laws in Slovakia had allowed for the Slovak government to confiscate Jewish properties and businesses, and gentile Slovak citizens known as *arizátori* took ownership and controlled them. After the deportations, the government would also be able to take the residences where Jews had lived, along with their possessions and their bank accounts. Between March and October 1942, approximately 60,000 Jewish citizens were deported from Slovakia to work camps and collection points, and then to the Nazi camps of Auschwitz-Birkenau, Majdanek and Sobibor.

One day in March 1942, a police officer came to our textile store on Main Street with officers from the Hlinka Guard, Nazi collaborators, and ordered my grandmother Rosa and Aunt Libusa to be at the railway station in the larger town of Kežmarok the next morning, which was just under forty kilometres away. My aunts Chaya and

Malka did not live with us anymore — both had married and moved to different towns. My grandmother and Libusa were told that they would be taken to the cities of Poprad and then to Žilina, and that from there, when the train was full of one thousand people, it would travel to the north to a work camp in Poland.

When they went to the station the next morning, my father brought them flowers. About a week later, we got a postcard from Grandmother. She wrote that she was working in a kitchen, peeling potatoes, and that she was okay. In reality, as we later found out, it was all a deception — they had been shipped to Auschwitz-Birkenau.

About a week later, policemen came to the store and ordered Uncle Martin to come with them to the police station. My uncle asked, "What am I charged with, what did I do?" To one policeman he said, "Remember when we were in the same school and we played soccer together? We are good friends and you know that I am a respectable man and a law-abiding person. Why are you taking me to the police station?" The policeman looked at him and said, "Okay, if you disappear, I will go back to the station and say I didn't find you." So Uncle Martin took all the money from the cash register and he left through the back door and disappeared into the woods.

My father had commercial ties with people in Zakopane, one of the neighbouring Polish towns. People there soon told him that the "work camps" were killing centres. This information was a well-guarded secret and spreading it was punishable by death, for spreading "false rumours." None of the deportee victims in Slovakia knew the real meaning of their destination, the so-called work camp.

My parents realized that it would soon be their turn to be deported, so they started to look for a place to hide. One day, I was walking on the street and I saw the policeman in charge of our neighbourhood. He was a friend of our family, and wanting to show him how smart I was, I told him that we were going to leave. He approached my mother and said, "Your boy is telling me that you have a plan to leave." My parents gave him money to shut him up. After that, any time they discussed a hiding place, they put my brother and me in a different room and closed the door. My brother remembers seeing them burn all the family photographs, probably because they had a plan to hide us separately from them, and if they were found out as Jewish and a family photo were found, the police would be able to say that me and my brother were also Jewish. Up until recently, I did not even have a photograph of my father; I had only a photograph of my mother. Miraculously, in the summer of 2020, a relative in New Jersey found my parents' wedding photo and sent it to me.

On the Move

Not too long after the incident with Uncle Martin, we left Spišská Stará Ves in the middle of the night. We went to live on a farm in a nearby village. We would spend the whole day inside the farmer's house, only allowed to go out during the dark evenings when we were sure we could not be seen by anyone who might betray us. After about a month, the farmer told my parents that it was too dangerous for him to hide us any longer; sheltering a Jew was punishable by death, and we had to leave.

But we had been extremely lucky to have left our town when we did. On May 26, 1942, all the remaining Jews from our town and the nearby villages were ordered by the local police to come to the synagogue. Men, woman, children and the elderly were rounded up and loaded on trains with the enthusiastic support of the Hlinka Guard. Their final destination was one of the Nazi death camps.

When we left the farm, my parents took us to the nearby town of Stará Ľubovňa, where my aunt Malka lived. She had married Joseph Taub, who was from there, in 1941, in a wedding ceremony I still remember so well, even though I was only four years old then.

Through the Taubs, who we stayed with for some time, we had a connection with the local Lutheran Evangelical priest, who was sympathetic to Jews. This priest issued my brother and me false identity documents that stated we had been born as gentiles in a village near

Stará Ľubovňa: Jacob was given the name Kubo, and mine stated that my name was Šano Alexander. After receiving these documents, I remember walking past a sign in the entrance to a garden that read "Jews and dogs not allowed," and saying, "Now we are allowed to enter the garden." I was five years old.

Eventually, the priest from Stará Ľubovňa communicated with an orphanage that the Lutheran Evangelicals operated in Liptovský Svätý Mikuláš, a town about a hundred kilometres away. We arrived at the orphanage on October 2, 1942, and my parents asked the pastor, Vladimir Kuna, who managed the orphanage, to take in their two Jewish kids and keep them until the end of the war. They must have been thinking that if something happened to them and they did not make it, at least we, their children, would survive. Otherwise, all of us would perish. In hindsight, it must have been an agonizing decision for our parents to let their children be in a different place, separate from them. But the decision proved to be the smart one, the right one. My parents were very resourceful, and we were very lucky.

A Fortunate Decision

Our admission to the orphanage at that time was very fortunate — there were thousands of parents looking for places to hide their children. During the height of the deportations from Slovakia, many Slovak Jews tried to cross the border and escape into Hungary because the Hungarian government, although allied with the Germans, didn't deport its Jewish population — until after the German occupation of Hungary in March 1944. After the war, we assumed that our parents were among those who had escaped into Hungary. We didn't learn of their true fate until much later.

We entered the orphanage through a corridor and went into a reception room where my brother and I were given toys to play with. My parents went to the next room to talk to the pastor. Evening came and our parents had not come to pick us up. A woman named Sister Maria came in and said, "You will stay here for the night; I will show you your beds." When you are five years old, you do what you are told, and we were quite tired so we went to sleep there. We expected that our parents would come get us the next day, or at least when it was safe to do so. I think that both my brother and I assumed our parents were hiding somewhere else due to the dangers of war. The situation was somehow normalized for us, probably because the other children did not have their parents with them either; we knew that we should behave, and we did not cry.

The next day, Sister Maria woke us up and told us that she would take us to school. It was about a twenty-minute walk. At the school the teachers said I was too young to be a pupil in first grade, so while all the other children went to school, I stayed by myself in a room in the orphanage for the next few months.

The orphanage had a pig farm, and as Christmas approached, one big fat pig was slaughtered for Christmas dinner in the courtyard outside the building. I was there in a room, by myself, while someone was slaughtering the pig. Hearing the pig screaming and squealing was so traumatic for me. At Christmas dinner, when I was given a piece of pork, I knew that I was not allowed to eat it because Jews did not eat pork. But seeing that piece of meat also brought back the horrible shrieking and screaming of the pig. Even though the orphanage had meat only once a year, on Christmas, I wouldn't eat it. Normally, our food consisted of a piece of bread in the morning, and potato and cabbage in the evening.

As a Jewish boy, I didn't know much about Christmas. This was my first one, and I saw a tall tree being erected and decorated with sweets. I even remember my dream before Christmas, because people had been talking about the holiday so much. I was in heaven and I saw angels walking. It was the most amazing dream I ever had in my life.

When I turned six years old, life really felt more normal because I was admitted to the school. The teacher was always dressed in black, and I later realized that she was in mourning because her husband had been killed in the war. My brother, Jacob, was apparently the smartest pupil in school, and it was a privilege for me to be known as his brother.

In the orphanage, many children got sick, and when one kid got a disease, it was passed on to everyone. The state-of-the-art treatment for healing measles in those days was having sulphur spread all over your body and then, with a strong bristled brush, having it brushed into your skin until you bled. This was terrible and extremely painful.

I think Sister Maria, in her civilian life, was probably a nurse because she knew a lot about illnesses.

Sister Maria was really the only person who always looked after us. For me, this was such a different feeling, because in my childhood in Spišská Stará Ves, my brother and I had been raised by three women — our mother, our aunt and our grandmother. I remember once being bitten by a bee, and Maria comforting me. (Much later in my life, I was to become a beekeeper for a short time, and I was once hospitalized after being stung thirty times!)

At some point the lack of proper food, heat and winter clothing caused me to catch pneumonia. Pneumonia is a dangerous disease for both young and old, especially when no medications are available, not even an aspirin. Admission to the hospital was out of the question, as any admission was to be reported to the local agency, which then had to relate the information to the fascist authorities. On a previous occasion, a little Jewish girl from our orphanage had been sick. Pastor Kuna sent her to the hospital and asked the hospital administration *not* to report the admission to the authorities, but his request was ignored.

After the war, I read an article that described how the Pastor was asked to explain to the town secretary the circumstances of the little girl's admission to the hospital. Pastor Kuna asked him, "Do you have children? If a child is sick, would you do anything you could to heal the child?" The secretary said, "I do have children and yes, of course I would do anything to keep them well." Pastor Kuna replied that he was glad to hear it, and that all seventy children in the orphanage were his children and that he was doing his fatherly duty. The secretary looked the Pastor in the eyes and said, "This is the last time I will let you get away with it." His response meant that he must have known that the girl was Jewish. So when I became sick, the healing had to be done in house. Sister Maria placed a cold towel on my hot body, and kept replacing it every hour, day and night.

Pastor Kuna was able to communicate with my uncle Martin in

case of an emergency. Uncle Martin was hiding in the nearby woods in a bunker shared with a family by the name of Wintner. It was extremely difficult to find shelter or a hiding place at this time, and I think it is likely that the Wintner family allowed my uncle to hide with them because he did not look stereotypically Jewish — with his blond hair, he could more easily "pass" as gentile, and thus go into the nearby village to get groceries. My uncle also told the Wintners where Jacob and I were in hiding, and suggested that their three children could possibly hide there as well. Indeed, in time, their children, Yeta, Tomy and Yehudit, joined us in the orphanage.

Pastor Kuna would deliver a message to my uncle by sending a letter to a certain house in the village; from time to time, my uncle would come there in the evenings, once the German patrols had left the area, to check for messages and buy some groceries. One evening, Uncle Martin got a message that I was dying and that if he wanted to see me before I died, he should come immediately. Seeing a member of my family made me feel so much better, and I'm sure it helped me overcome my sickness.

In 1943, for a reason unknown to me, Jacob and I were sent to have a photograph taken. This is the only picture that we have of our early childhood, and as the only one, it would prove to be a very important photo. Later, Uncle Martin told me that he had asked for this photo to be taken because he realized that otherwise, were I to die, there would be no evidence of my existence.

The possibility of betrayal was a constant reality. When a stranger came into the dining room, the Jewish children were instructed to keep quiet and look out the window. The war was all around us. On our way to school, we would see a convoy of German trucks on the highway moving in the direction of the Soviet front. On Sundays when we went to the forest with Sister Maria, we would see heavy trains loaded with German soldiers travelling to the Eastern Front. We knew that there was a war even at the ages of only five and six years old. We knew words like *front* and *enemy* and we knew that the Germans were the enemy and that the Russians were the good guys. One day on the way to school, a large gun was being towed by a truck. One of the kids said, "You know, this gun could shoot down the moon." I was seven years old by then and I said, "If the moon is still there, it means they can't shoot it."

One day, I showed my report card from school to Sister Maria; suddenly, she was quite upset. It was almost all A's. Why was she was so upset? The report card listed my name as David Korn, but my nom de guerre was Šano Alexander Korn. In Slovakia, the name David was given only to Jewish children. This was the first time that I had been called David during my time in hiding. I did not even realize until then that my name was David because my parents had always called me by my middle name, Salomon. After the war, my name was confirmed via my birth certificate.

The Tide of War

By 1944, the Soviets were advancing westward and the Germans were retreating. In the spring of 1944, two prisoners escaped from Auschwitz and reported on the horrific events in the death camp; by June, parts of their account had reached Switzerland, Pope Pius XII, and the British and American Allies. In the summer and fall of 1944, we would look up to the skies and often we saw clusters of hundreds of Allied airplanes. They looked like pieces of aluminum. They were flying from northern Italy to the Soviet Union as they executed bombing raids against the retreating German forces, disrupting German communication, railways and so on. After the war, the Allies were asked why they didn't bomb Auschwitz. One reason given was that it was out of their range. But almost daily in August 1944, we saw hundreds of American and British airplanes over our town. We were located less than fifteen minutes by air from Auschwitz. They could have bombed the concentration camp if they had wanted to! It was not out of their range! It was out of their range in 1942 and 1943, but it was not out of their range in 1944, and they had already bombed nearby factories. Had the Allies bombed Auschwitz, I believe that many lives would have been saved.

At the end of August, in the nearby city of Banská Bystrica, there was a rebellion by the Slovak partisans. This was the historically well-known Slovak National Uprising against the collaborationist regime in Slovakia and the imminent German occupation of the country. Banská Bystrica was central to the fighting, and when it was controlled by the Slovak partisans, many people, like my uncle who had been hiding in the woods, came to the city. Everybody thought that Banská Bystrica had been permanently liberated. My uncle soon sent a partisan to our orphanage to take us out. When I was asked if I wanted to go, I said yes, but when they asked my brother, he said, "The war is not over yet and I am not leaving the orphanage." I wouldn't leave without my brother.

In just two short months, Banská Bystrica was re-occupied by the Germans. Over the course of the uprising and in its aftermath, thousands of Jews were caught and transported to Auschwitz, Theresienstadt and other Nazi camps, and many Jews and partisans were killed. During this time, my uncle, a young man, was able to run back to the forest. But later he told us that we were lucky that we didn't leave the orphanage because after the rebellion, the conditions became much worse. The Germans discovered the bunker they were hiding in, and the elderly Wintners, who had not been able to escape, were taken by the Germans. In the area, the German patrols increased from once a week to daily.

In November 1944, Pastor Kuna and another priest were accused of helping the Slovak partisans and the Jewish people. Apparently, Kuna was a Slovak nationalist and had offered some funds to the uprising. They were taken to Bratislava for interrogation, and I heard that the other priest died of torture. When the Germans interrogated Pastor Kuna, one of the questions they asked him was if he knew of a General Kuna; he was the leader of a contingent of Slovak soldiers in the resistance. Pastor Kuna admitted that this was his brother. I think that the Germans realized, by then, that they were losing the war, and I believe that they did not want to be charged with killing the brother of a Slovak hero. They let him go in January 1945, but they watched Pastor Kuna much more carefully after that.

The Soviets were still advancing and the Germans decided that Liptovský Svätý Mikuláš would be a stronghold to be defended at any cost. The town had been occupied and re-occupied several times. There were huge mountains near the town and the German army had set up guns on one side of a mountain while the Soviet and Czechoslovak armies had guns on the other side of the mountain. We were situated in a valley between them and could hear the constant shooting. One morning, I was on the third floor of the building brushing my teeth when a volley of shots flew over the orphanage. I quickly ran downstairs to the basement, where I fainted! When I woke up, I went to the dining room and ate my breakfast. Nobody knew about this episode.

The intensity of the fighting in March and April 1945 are now manifested through a commemorative area and war memorial located on a ridge over the town, renamed Liptovský Mikuláš in 1952, where there are graves of the approximately 1,400 soldiers from the 1st Czechoslovak Army Corps.

Eventually, the authorities decided that during a lull in the fighting they would have to evacuate us. One day, they put us on trucks and tried to find a place for us, but there was nothing vacant so we ended up in the basement of the local jail, because this was the only place with any room. The next day, we were trucked to a nearby town called Ružomberok — where the Slovak nationalist Andrej Hlinka became a priest in the early 1900s — and were lodged in a local school.

One morning during Easter of 1945, we woke up and we saw trucks filled with Russian soldiers. We knew we were liberated. The first thing that the Russians said to everybody they met was "davay chasy," which meant "give me your watch." When an officer or soldier took a watch he would open up his sleeve and his entire arm would be filled up to the elbow with watches! The Russian soldiers were actually very brutal — they wanted alcohol and women, and they didn't care whether your country was a friend or an enemy. They knew that the next day, they might be dead. All the young girls and women, including Maria, hid because it was dangerous for them to be outside.

We were soon driven back to the orphanage in Liptovský Svätý Mikuláš. In the backyard there were hidden stores of food, including sugar. As the workers carried sacks of sugar on their backs to the house, the sugar seeped out of holes in the sacks, and us kids saw the trails of it. We had not seen sugar for many years so we scooped it from the ground to eat it.

The next morning, I told Sister Maria that the lower right side of my stomach was hurting. She told me to go back to bed, but after everybody went to school, she took me in a children's carriage all the way to the hospital, as there was no other transportation. The hospital was three kilometres away! There, the doctors diagnosed me with appendicitis and took me to the emergency operating room, which was still in war mode and located in the basement. On both sides of the corridor in the basement, there were beds lined up, mainly with soldiers in them who were missing one leg, waiting for their operations. The soldiers were crying for their mothers. It was a frightening sight for a young boy to witness. The doctors rushed me in because if an appendix bursts it can be fatal.

When I was on the operating table, I heard one nurse say, "Oh look, a Jewish boy." I was crying but when I heard her, I stopped. For some reason the doctors didn't put me to sleep at first, probably because anesthetic was in short supply. I think they wanted to operate on me with a local anesthetic. I started to cry again, and I remember hearing the doctor say, "Make him go to sleep." So they put me out and I woke up several hours later in the basement.

I was in the hospital for a few weeks, and I became friends with another boy there. He had lost his hand after playing with some ammunition that exploded while he was holding it. At this point, all three floors of the hospital were full and operational. We were on the third floor and everybody was singing a song called "Mamma," a well-known and popular song because the wounded soldiers all wanted their mamas close to them. My friend and I went from one bed to another singing the patients' favourite songs. In return, they gave us chocolates, candies or some coins. After seventeen days I left to go back to the orphanage, but I still had to stay in bed.

On May 8, 1945, there was a long, loud siren. During the war, when the planes came, the tone of the siren was usually high and low. This siren was one straight even sound. I asked Sister Maria what it meant. "The war is over," she said.

The Fate of My Family

By the end of June 1945, the parents and relatives of many of the kids had come to pick them up. Nobody had come for us yet. In July, Aunt Libusa arrived with a woman named Mila. Our aunt brought a picture with her — of me and my brother, Jacob. It was the very same photo that had been taken of us shortly after we arrived at the orphanage. She must have met up with my uncle Martin before coming to the orphanage, who had given her the photo. She brought it as proof that she knew who we were, and she told Pastor Kuna — although I didn't see him at that time — that she was my aunt and wanted to take us with her. He gave permission for us to leave with her.

It is important to note that in many cases, people who hid children during the war wouldn't let the children go when family came to claim them. In 2005, a letter surfaced from the time when rescuers of Jewish children in Catholic institutions had asked the Pope what to do with the Jewish children who were baptized during the war. The answer was that if they were baptized, they should not be returned to parents or relatives. So Pastor Kuna was extremely virtuous in letting us go. We were the last of the Jewish children to be released.

Aunt Libusa's friend Mila was a non-Jewish woman from Slovenia. She had probably been a political prisoner in Auschwitz, and she had saved my aunt. When my aunt and grandmother had arrived at the camp, the Germans lined them up with many others. My grandmother and Libusa were holding hands until a selection officer pointed my grandmother to the left side. Older people and children were directed to the left and younger people who could work, to the right. My aunt was still holding her mother's hand; she didn't want to let her go but eventually, she had to. All her life she regretted letting go of her mother's hand. The people on my grandmother's side went straight to the gas chambers, while Libusa was given a bed in a barracks. The Germans tattooed a number on her arm: 7922. I will remember seeing those numbers for the rest of my life.

After her mother had been taken from her, my aunt Libusa was shaky and unable to stand exactly in line, and one of the kapos — a foreman in charge of prisoners — beat her up badly and left her lying in the mud. It was then that she met Mila, who helped her up and took her to get cleaned up. Mila was working in the registry office of the camp, and she told the man in charge of the office that she had found a woman with very neat handwriting who spoke German and could be of help to her. So the officer gave her permission to bring Libusa into the office. Her knowledge of German was probably how she survived Auschwitz for almost three years. But she was still subject to the daily selection. If prisoners were sick or too weak to work, they were taken to the gas chambers.

Mila saved Libusa's life a second time during the death marches from Auschwitz in January 1945. When Libusa, exhausted, stopped walking, Mila insisted that she get up and continue. Libusa mentioned to me that she had been carrying a heavy book in which the names of the arriving Jews were written, and that, although these names were so important to her — for records, evidence, memorialization — she had to abandon the book because it was too heavy.

Libusa had nightmares, for her entire life, about being in line with her mother in the camp and letting go of her mother's hand, letting her be selected to go to the gas chambers. She never talked about the past, or of any family members who perished. For Libusa, the world did not exist prior to 1945.

My aunt Chaya, my aunt Malka and my uncle Joseph were all

murdered in the Holocaust. Aunt Libusa did not tell us the fate of our parents. And we didn't ask. We assumed they had been caught in Hungary, and it wasn't until the mid-1950s, just before my brother and I went with her for an interview at a reparations office to apply for money from the German government, that she turned to us and said, "Your parents died in Auschwitz." And that was all. My brother and I never really spoke about our parents either, and my brother never wanted to speak about our experiences during the war. He is a very private person.

Aunt Libusa brought us to our uncle Martin, who was living in Košice, Slovakia, and we stayed with him. It was difficult to get an apartment after the war, so he shared the apartment with a woman who was a professional pianist. She had a beautiful piano and she played it constantly. I developed an ear for piano music and I like it to this day.

On our first day of true freedom, we were given a glass of lemonade. Oh, was it ever good! I kept dipping my spoon into the lemonade and licking it so that it took me half a day to empty half of that glass of lemonade. And then I drank the rest. Obviously, we were not used to life outside of wartime rations. Even shoes were rationed after the war. The ration got you one pair of shoes per person for the whole year. So we often walked barefoot. My brother and I walked along the streets collecting cigarette butts to make new cigarettes out of them; then we went to the washroom to smoke. We became so sick that it was the last time in our lives we smoked cigarettes! Another day, I got money for ice cream from Uncle Martin. On the street, I came across a vegetable stall where I saw a large cucumber and I asked the vendor, "Do I have enough money to buy it?" He said yes, so I bought it and I ate the whole cucumber! I came home and my uncle asked, "How was the ice cream?" I said, "Well, I had a cucumber instead!" "Cucumber??!" We had yet to get used to ordinary life.

One day we went for a walk with a family friend by the name of Bienestock and he said, "Look, David, you are young and can do anything you want in your future." I responded, "Yes, but you cannot get to the moon." This was 1945. He said, "You're right, this you cannot do."

It was remarkable how swiftly Jewish life was re-established in Košice after the war. Synagogues were refurbished and renovated, rabbis hired, daily prayers and *minyans* and Hebrew school for the children restarted, and even a kosher restaurant was opened. Matzot were baked for Passover. A renowned cantor, Sholom Katz, was hired and we had a choir for the High Holidays. My love for cantorial music dates to this time. Several of the youth movements were also re-established. We went to Bnei Akiva and we went to cheder, learning Hebrew by translating it to Yiddish. One day, I skipped cheder because I was not prepared for a test. The next day when I arrived at cheder, I told the teacher I had been at violin class. The teacher started to ask me questions from the test, and if I did not know the answer, he whipped me. He yelled at me, "Torah is more important than violin!" It was very traumatizing, and I was afraid to tell my uncle what had happened.

We also started going to public school, where there were lessons in religion, one hour for Jewish students and separately during the same hour, for non-Jews. Adjusting back to normalcy was difficult for us, so my uncle Martin called Pastor Kuna for help. He sent Sister Maria, who reassured us that because the war was over, we didn't have to be afraid of being Jewish.

Uncle Martin told me that he and Maria had a friendship and that she had suggested he marry her so that Jacob and I would have parents. My uncle told her that he was sorry, but he already had a girlfriend. She left, and we never saw her again.

Uncle Martin soon married that girlfriend, Lia Schwartz. She was seventeen and a half and he was thirty-six years old. He had met Lia at the home of the Wintner family, the very same family that he had shared a bunker with in the forest. She came from a prosperous family and we spent a lot of time with them and shared meals with them, though Jacob and I now lived in an apartment just ten minutes away with our aunt Libusa, who had married Dr. Frantisek (Feri) Frish.

My uncle Feri, too, was a survivor, from Hungary. During the war, he was forced into the Hungarian labour service and sent into the Soviet Union to be slave labour for the Hungarian army. He wrote a book in Hebrew about his experiences; in English, the title translates to *Forced Labour Division 1940–1945*. In one story he related, one day while they were digging ditches, a Hungarian officer was walking by and told them that if they didn't work, they would not get food. Feri couldn't take it anymore, so he said, in very refined Hungarian, "Sir, we don't work because we want food, we work because we are your slaves." The officer stared at him, and then told him to come to his home after work. My uncle Feri thought that the officer was going to shoot him, so he gave all of his belongings away to his friends. That evening, the officer asked him what he did before the war and Feri explained that he was a student and had just finished studying in Prague to become a lawyer. The officer then offered him work as his personal servant, and my uncle didn't have to work as hard. He only had to clean the house and make sure that he brought food from the central kitchen for both of them. He also did the officer's accounting work and wrote his reports. So, he survived by taking this job.

Uncle Martin and Lia had moved to a big apartment that was owned by Lia's family. In the back garden grew all sorts of fruits, like cherries, as well as chestnuts. Lia's father, who had planted them, perished during the war. They lived in one of the best neighbourhoods in Košice, with a river nearby. We went to the Tatra Mountains for summer vacations and later Jacob and I went to Jewish summer camps. A note on one summer report card mentioned that I excelled in singing.

Lia was a teenager and suddenly she had to help look after two boys not much younger than her. She obviously lacked motherly skills. One day she prepared potatoes, filled a plate with them and told me to eat. I told her I wasn't hungry, but she insisted that I eat the whole plate. When she left the kitchen, I filled my pockets with the potatoes and emptied them in the washroom. When she came back to the kitchen and saw that my plate was empty, she declared, "You see, I knew you were hungry!"

Uncle Martin arranged for us to have private English lessons and music lessons. I studied violin. When it was time for me to practise, Lia sent me to a room and locked the door from the outside until an hour had passed. Martin, however, was good-natured, a gentleman, and we loved him like a father. Sometimes I wondered if I could ever go back to my biological father, if he happened to reappear.

A New Life

In early 1948, the Communist Party seized complete power in Czechoslovakia and Uncle Martin decided that we would have to leave. That spring, we left Košice for Paris, France. When the State of Israel was born in May 1948, we were still in Paris. Soon after, we were sent to a Jewish-sponsored OSE (Œuvre de secours aux enfants) orphanage called Château de Vaucelles, located in Taverny, twenty kilometres from Paris. In the fall we went to school, where the principal, Mr. Hausner, was a wonderful teacher. The school was an excellent experience; we played a lot of soccer and we learned French quickly since it was the only language spoken in the orphanage. I recently learned that the late Nobel Prize-winning Elie Wiesel was a pupil in this school and had left the year before we arrived. The children's home was later renamed in his honour.

We were in the orphanage for nine months — it was better for us than staying in a hotel with our uncle and Lia. In April 1949, after the War of Independence in Israel, my uncle Martin and his wife, Lia, and Jacob and I boarded a ship in Marseilles called *Negba* and we eventually landed in Haifa, Israel. The following year, my aunt Libusa and uncle Feri joined us with their young daughter, Chava, and their family soon grew with the birth of their next daughter, Naomi.

Many members of our family from Grandmother Rosa's side —

the Hausmans, the Basses, the Steils and the Chunes — lived in Israel. They were German Jews who had been expelled from Germany in the 1930s and settled in the Land of Israel. After the war, my cousin Natan Bass had come to visit us in Košice, wearing a British army uniform. He had been recruited by the British army because he could speak German and translate documents for them. He told us about our family in Israel — then called British Mandate Palestine — and we told him who from our family had survived the Holocaust. By that point, I understood that my parents were not alive, that they were not coming back.

We chose to live in Haifa because most of our relatives lived there. The Hausmans had a home outside of Haifa, in Kiryat Haroshet, on the Kishon River. We stayed with them for a while until my uncle arranged for us to be accepted into a boarding school run by Youth Aliyah.

Before going to the school, though, we were sent to a transit camp in Pardes Hanna-Karkur. We were only supposed to be there a short time, but Youth Aliyah didn't have a place for us yet, so we stayed there more than half a year. It was a bad situation for us because we didn't get any schooling in Karkur. All we did the entire day was swim. It had previously been a British camp and had two swimming pools; the water was very dirty and I got all kinds of boils.

In December 1949, Mr. Haim Enoch took us to Kfar Batya, a children's village and school, where he was the principal. It was one of the best Youth Aliyah schools in all of Israel and was under the auspices of the Mizrachi Women's Organization of America. When important personalities like Eleanor Roosevelt wanted to see how Israel treated new young immigrants, they would be brought to Kfar Batya. People from my class actually showed her around. Once, Cantor Sholom Katz, who had been in Košice, came to visit. I didn't know if Cantor Katz recognized me or not, but I recognized him immediately.

The principal, Mr. Enoch, was considered one of the greatest pedagogues in Israel. Originally from Germany, he insisted on strong discipline, cleanliness and attending school and work. He was a highly regarded teacher and never accepted any excuses, always saying, "It is easier to provide an excuse than do what was asked of you." For example, we had to read the local paper every day, and if a student passed Mr. Enoch in the hall, he would ask, "What did you read in the paper today?" I would always have an article ready so that if he stopped me, I was prepared with an answer.

In Kfar Batya there were children from many countries: Morocco, Tunisia, Syria, Iran, Romania, Hungary, Belgium, France, Czechoslovakia and others. In 1952, the first boys from Ethiopia came. Everybody was treated the same — it didn't matter where you came from. To make sure that we all spoke only in Hebrew, each room was made up of children from different countries.

Those of us who were survivors never talked about our experiences during the Holocaust. All our minds went to the future and not to the past. We all became good friends and during Wednesday afternoons, when we had a half-day off, sometimes we went to Ra'anana, the city nearby.

We had to be in bed at nine o'clock at night and we had to get up at five-thirty in the morning to do exercises. By 6:00 a.m., we had to be in the synagogue; 6:30 was breakfast; at 7:30, we had half an hour to clean our rooms; and by 8:00 we were in school and remained there for about four or five hours a day. Then, in the afternoon, we had to work for three hours. At first, I was a shoemaker; I didn't like it. After that, I did carpentry, but the teacher was very strict, which I also didn't like. So they shifted me to the farm, where I was in charge of the chicken coop. Later I worked in the vineyard, the apple orchards and then tried beekeeping. I learned a lot about agriculture. Eventually, I got to drive a tractor, which was the highest level one could achieve.

While plowing on my tractor, I was conscious about wasting time, so I had a Hebrew/English dictionary with me and I began learning English while plowing. We were not supposed to do work outside of what we were assigned at Kfar Batya, but we often went to the farmers nearby to earn some money. Usually they gave us the job of pulling out weeds by hand. Mr. Enoch didn't approve of this but he wanted us to be independent, so he looked the other way.

We had excellent teachers, like Chaim Ziegler, who later became a university professor. I remember almost everything he taught me. Shmuel (Samuel) Rosenbaum, a teacher from the United States, later became a professor at Bar-Ilan University. Mr. Michlin, a retired teacher from Montreal, Canada, hardly knew any Hebrew, yet he taught us Hebrew literature. He was very dedicated, though — for each hour that he taught us, he had to study at least three hours at home. He had to write down his lessons in advance because it was so difficult for him to express himself in Hebrew. Another teacher was David Eliach, who came from Jerusalem. He ended up marrying a student named Yaffa and they later moved to New York. Yaffa Eliach was talented and clever; she became a professor, established a centre for Holocaust studies and was a member of President Carter's Commission on the Holocaust.

Mr. Enoch wanted us to learn by ourselves. He constantly emphasized that what we studied in school was only a small part of all the knowledge that we had to have in life. Independent learning is an important principle. Mr. Enoch used a pedagogical system developed by Pestalozzi, a prominent Swiss educator. We elected our own classmates to be on a student committee, and they would communicate instructions to us instead of our teachers. It was a democratic education, a very advanced educational methodology, and we admired him for it.

The only criticism I have of Haim Enoch is that he was not the right role model for us. Although he was dedicated, he often humiliated the girls at school, giving preferential treatment to the young boys instead. We were children who didn't have parents and we needed a father figure; we didn't need a disciplinarian.

But we were all lucky to get a high school education, and we were the first class from Kfar Batya to graduate high school. I had even skipped two grades — Grade 5 and Grade 10 — because when I came to Kfar Batya, I was two grade levels below where I should have been for my age. When I reached eighteen, I would have to leave school to go into the army, so in order to graduate I had to learn the curriculum for all those classes during the summers. My brother and some friends were able to help teach me.

I think it's important to note that everyone in my class continued on to university and became successful professionally. Many of my classmates later became teachers and professors, or doctors in agronomy. One of my friends, Rami Atia from Syria, is the largest builder of high-rises in Panama City. Both my brother and I became engineers. So, Mr. Enoch gave us a very good education.

~

In the summer of 1955, when I was eighteen and just after I graduated from high school, I went straight into the army. I was in the army for two and a half years. Army service, especially the first five months, was extremely hard, mentally and physically. Mentally because not only had I recently survived a war, but also, in high school we had studied literature and history, and I had thought I would be working to reform the world for the better. Suddenly I found myself learning to be a soldier. Also, physically, although I thought I was in good shape, the exercises were extremely demanding and in the first five months (called Tironut) the army set out to change you from someone who thinks to someone who takes orders without thinking. You do what you are told; this was army discipline. Later, the system was changed to be less harsh.

After five months of Tironut training, we were sent to Sde Eliyahu, a kibbutz in the Beit She'an valley, where the weather was extremely hot. I worked driving a tractor during harvest time. The work in the kibbutz was much easier than the army training; although we worked eight hours during the day, there was little training in the evening.

After nine months, we began additional army training that was much more advanced and included training to be a paratrooper. I had to jump from an airplane five times, and on the fifth one, I had to jump during the night, which felt like falling into a deep hole.

Before the Sinai War broke out in the fall of 1956, I was chosen to attend an agriculture machinery course. For some reason that I never understood, the course was not cancelled, so I did not take part in the war. However, I was sent to the Gaza Strip for the Israeli evacuation in March 1957, and stationed in the city of Deir al-Balah. After this task, my entire group relocated to a kibbutz called Sa'ad near Gaza, on the Israeli side where, once again, I worked on a tractor.

I didn't like the army so much, and the army didn't like me, but the experience made me resilient, helping me to overcome many future challenges in my studies and my work.

The Rocky Path to My Career

I was honourably discharged from the army in February 1958. I wanted to study at the Technion — Israel Institute of Technology, and the academic year began in October, so I had over a half a year to earn money for tuition. I didn't really have anywhere to go. My uncle Martin had a small apartment and a growing family — he and Lia now had two children, Ruty and Yigal — and my aunt Libusa and uncle Feri were raising their two children, Chava and Naomi, so I went back to Kfar Batya, where I had received my high school education. I met with the director, who was then a Dutchman by the name of Mr. Dasberg, a fatherly figure with a long beard. I told him my story and mentioned that I would like to be an assistant teacher at the school until the term for engineering began at the Technion. He offered me the job on the spot! (I was relieved, because after serving in the army for two and a half years, I had the equivalent of about twenty dollars in my pocket!)

When I began studying at the Technion in Haifa, I became acquainted with Mr. Gome, an older man who had served in the War of Independence in 1948, until he was wounded badly on the Jerusalem front. He usually invited me over on Friday nights, and we would listen to his large collection of operas. I couldn't believe how Maria Callas could sing so beautifully. This began my introduction to the operatic world.

In 1958, at a Chanukah Ball, I met a beautiful seventeen-year-old girl. I fell in love with her and we dated for more than a year. But then, her parents intervened: they did not want her dating a poor orphan like me. They wanted to make a *shidduch*, to find her a match, with someone who was wealthy. This was not the only time I was looked down on for being a Holocaust survivor. I was often given the impression that I was not a suitable match. This was extremely difficult for me.

In the summer of 1959, I applied for work on a construction project to drain the Hula Valley swamp in the Northern Galilee. I thought tractor drivers were what was needed, but it turned out they needed welders. I mentioned to the employer that I had taken a course in welding, so I was given two pieces of steel and told to prove that I could weld. I went to a metal shop, asked a welder to do it for me, and brought them back. I was hired, and after three months I became the best welder in the shop! After eight hours of working at my welding job, I would have something to eat and then go to work a second shift for another eight hours at a peanut sorting facility.

During my second year at the Technion, I didn't have enough money to finish my academic studies. Fortunately, a certain lawyer from New York came to the Technion to give a stipend to a student from Czechoslovakia. At first, he couldn't find anyone and then somebody told him about the Korn/Koren brothers (Jacob now went by Koren for the spelling of his last name). We applied for that stipend and Jacob got it because he was already in his third year. He generously gave me half of his share, which is how I finished my studies that year.

In those days, if you needed money you were paid for donating blood to the hospital. Several times, when I was at the end of my rope, I donated blood to make some money to tide me over.

By the time I was in my third year, I qualified for the restitution payments that Germany was making to Holocaust survivors through the Conference on Jewish Material Claims Against Germany, and this additional money helped me greatly.

In 1960, the director Otto Preminger was filming *Exodus* in Haifa. It was Passover vacation, and I signed up to work as an extra with the famous actor Paul Newman. I still have a picture that was taken with him, and he gave me his autograph. During another summer, I enjoyed being a cultural guide in some resort villages. I performed by singing and playing my guitar, and I invited other singers — even opera singers — and performers to some of the cultural events.

I finally graduated from the Technion in 1964 and became an engineer. My studies had been quite difficult, and I am grateful that I made it through. I wanted to continue studying for my master's degree, so I applied to the University of Guelph in Ontario, Canada. I was told they would accept me on the condition that I passed an English exam. In the meantime, I went on a student exchange between Israel and the Netherlands, where I worked for three months on the polders. During that same time, I went for the English test. I learned later that I didn't pass, but since I already had a visa and landed immigrant papers, I came to Canada anyway.

I arrived in Halifax by boat on the morning of February 18, 1965, and took a train to Montreal later that day. I had hoped to find a job with a certain company I had corresponded with, but it didn't work out; another place I applied to told me to come back in a few days. I went to look elsewhere. My uncle Martin had a friend in Montreal, Mr. Treitel. I told him I was looking for work. The next day, a friend of Mr. Treitel, Mr. Frankel, called me and directed me to SNC (Surveyor, Nenninger and Chênevert). I went there for an interview with Jack Hahn and was accepted. Often in my life, whatever my options were, something else always came up, and it usually turned out much better. By hiring me, Mr. Hahn opened up an engineering career for me with vast potential, and I thank him for that.

It was the middle of the winter in Montreal and I still didn't have a coat. As I walked down the street or waited for a bus, people would ask me if I was cold. But I never was because I had a trick — if I had to walk somewhere, I would go into every tenth store on the street to warm up.

It was two years before Expo 67, the famous international exhibition marking Canada's 100th birthday. Montreal had never needed so many engineers, not only for Expo but also for several hydro electrical projects in Northern Quebec. SNC, where I was employed, was designing the biggest dam of its kind in the world: Manicouagan 5 (Manic-5, now known as the Daniel-Johnson dam). I worked for them in a French-speaking office for three years.

I was working in Montreal when I met my future wife, Yona. We were married in Israel in 1966. In 1967, we went to Expo almost every weekend for the whole summer. I had been in Montreal for three years when the FLQ (Front de libération du Québec) escalated their campaign of bombing and violence in the name of sovereignty for Quebec, and I decided I hadn't come to Canada to be in a place where there was war. So we moved to Ottawa. I had been working there for about eight months for a private structural engineering firm when the federal government hired me and sent me to Halifax to work in the federal Department of Fisheries. I worked on dams and fishways and then I progressed and was promoted from one department to another until I was working for Public Works Canada. During those years, my daughter, Miriam, and son, Gil, were born in Halifax. In 1975, my brother, Jacob, and his family — his wife, Bracha, and their children, Avi, Hila and Sharon — joined us in Canada.

When it was announced that the Halifax Citadel was going to be restored, I applied to be Chief of Engineering for the restoration. I got the job. I was lucky to be the right guy in the right place. Restoration of the Citadel began in 1977, and I worked there until the summer of 1985. In 1981, I had been sent to Venice on a two-month course sponsored by UNESCO to study state-of-the-art historic restoration engineering. Very few people from Canada were chosen to take this course. With all my experience from the Citadel, and the course in Venice, I became an expert in historic masonry stonewall restoration. When the Mulroney government decided to stop the restoration of the Citadel, my crew of seventy-five restoration professionals was dismissed. I remain proud that not one was injured while working on masonry walls that were twenty-five feet high.

I continued to work with Parks Canada on different national historic sites, and then in September 1994, I was assigned a position working on the Centre Block Parliament Buildings in Ottawa. At the time, I was probably the most experienced restoration engineer in Canada due to my experience with the Halifax Citadel and my studies in Venice. I was originally seconded for only six months. I was assigned the riskiest work on the building — riskiest because the solutions were quite unconventional, and there was a chance that they might not succeed, so I had to be very careful. There were many problems with the stone and masonry; some stones were falling off and a tower in the back of the building was leaning badly. It was assumed that it would have to be dismantled, which would be expensive. We were able to restore the tower *in situ*, without dismantling it, using an advanced stone reinforcement system devised to stabilize the affected tower.

It was such an honour to work on the Parliament Buildings. It was really the pinnacle of my career as a Restoration Engineer to work on this building. I did other projects on The Hill, including the preliminary restoration studies for the Library of Parliament. Eventually, it cost 120 million dollars to restore the library, which I think is the most beautiful architectural building in Canada.

The original six-month secondment lasted close to three years, and I worked in Ottawa until February 1997, when I retired and came back to Halifax. In my retirement, I have been busy doing different things. I worked part-time as a consulting architect on masonry work; I am a regular speaker at events dedicated to Holocaust education; and I was a cantor in Yarmouth, Nova Scotia, for approximately eight years for the High Holy Days. I am sure that my late father, Abraham, would be both proud and surprised at hearing me sing the Kol Nidre, and perhaps, he was even looking down on me from heaven as I sang.

In October 1998, I was asked to come back to Ottawa to be recognized for my work there, for my contributions to Canada in general and for my dedication to Holocaust education, as I had been speaking about my survival experience in high schools in the Maritimes. At that special ceremony in Ottawa, which commemorated the fiftieth anniversary of the Universal Declaration of Human Rights, there were fifty other Holocaust survivors from across Canada who were being honoured for their contributions to Canadian society and their work in Holocaust education.

Reconnecting to My Past

In the summer of 1991, I read in a newspaper that there was going to be a gathering in New York of hidden child survivors from World War II. My wartime experiences qualified me to attend the conference, so Yona and I went. Until this conference, I had not looked back. What happened, happened. I had to look ahead to the future. I had married, had two children, Miriam and Gil, and was raising my family.

At this conference, all the people had similar backgrounds to mine. There were about 1,500 participants from all over the world. To me it felt as though each of the participants represented 1,000 Jewish children who had been murdered — one and a half million children had been killed in the Holocaust. A keynote speaker was Yaffa Eliach, my classmate from Kfar Batya! She was one of the main organizers of the conference.

During the conference, I met a representative from Yad Vashem, Mordecai Paldiel. I told him my story of survival and that I wanted Pastor Kuna to be given recognition by Yad Vashem. He said that the name sounded familiar to him, but that he would have to check his records back in Israel to determine whether there was already a file on Kuna. In the meantime, he said, I should write him my testimony.

After the conference, Yona and I went to Czechoslovakia. I hoped to find Sister Maria, so Yona and I went to Liptovský Mikuláš, and I located the orphanage. I knocked on the door where Pastor Kuna used to live in a special home on the orphanage grounds. A woman answered and introduced herself as Mrs. Ticho. She had been the organist in the local church, where we used to go every Sunday from the orphanage. Although I hadn't prayed much then, I remember that I always sat close to the organ and listened to the music. This was one of the pleasant memories from my time at the orphanage. I introduced my wife and myself and told Mrs. Ticho that I had been there during the war, at the orphanage. I told her that I was looking for Maria. She informed me that Maria had disappeared after the war, and that she assumed she was no longer alive.

Mrs. Ticho continued by telling me that Pastor Kuna lived not far away. I was surprised that he was still alive, since after the Gestapo took him away, I didn't remember seeing him again. After Kuna returned from the prison in January 1945, he kept a very low profile, so the only people who saw him were the staff, or later, the children's relatives who came for them after the war.

So off we went to see Pastor Kuna. When he answered the door, I told him that I was David Korn and that I had been at the orphanage for three years. He asked when I arrived at the orphanage and I told him October 1942. At that point, he brought out a book and looked through it until he found that month and year. "Oh!" he exclaimed, "you have a brother, Jacob Korn; your mother is Miriam Korn and your father is Abraham Korn, and you came from Stará Ľubovňa."

He remembered me! We had a long discussion. I asked him about his brother, who had been a hero of the Slovak resistance and had helped to liberate the country. Pastor Kuna told me that his brother, Pavol, had passed away nearly ten years earlier and that, under the Communist regime, his brother had been deprived of his military rank, as had so many other generals and army officers. Can you imagine the communist logic? I was shocked. His brother had helped to liberate Slovakia during the war and had been a general in the

Czechoslovak army after the war! Pastor Kuna even had a bust of his brother in his room. It was all so sad.

From our discussion, I learned most of what transpired in the orphanage when I had been there. He said that after the war, in 1950, the Soviets closed the orphanage because it was run by a religious organization. In communist ideology, there is no room for religion. Pastor Kuna was still able to continue working in the parish in Liptovský Mikuláš and was then moved to a parish in Partizánske until his retirement in 1972. His financial situation was very bad, so I left him some money. One further point about Pastor Kuna — when I spoke to him, I had a question: Why had he taken the risk of hiding Jewish children, especially knowing the risk to his family, his wife and son? He quoted St. Paul in the New Testament, Corinthians One, verse twelve, that God told the Christians that both Christians and Jews are of the same body and spirit, and that they should be treated equally. This passage, and others about love for all peoples, guided him.

A year later, when I was in Jerusalem, I managed to arrange a pension for Pastor Kuna through Yad Vashem. People were donating money for the express purpose of helping those who had helped save Jews during World War II. From this fund at Yad Vashem, Pastor Kuna would get a monthly pension until he died.

I continued to correspond with Pastor Kuna, and in his many letters he was very precise when writing out the history of his orphanage. He eventually donated all the documents from the orphanage to the local church.

We communicated until he died in 1996. After his death, my brother continued to correspond with his son, Milan. Every Easter, we send Milan some money. He is also an engineer, and we have a very good relationship. In 2004, on the hundredth anniversary of Pastor Kuna's birth, there was a ceremony at the church in Liptovský Mikuláš; many dignitaries came, and one recited all the names of the Jewish children Kuna had saved. There is a bronze plaque in the church in his honour.

Pastor Vladimir Kuna, the director of the orphanage, was recognized for his heroism by both the Lutheran authorities and, as I eventually found out, by Yad Vashem in 1972, when the title of Righteous Among the Nations had been bestowed upon him and Yad Vashem planted a tree in his honour and memory.

However, I would also like to express my appreciation for the devotion that Sister Maria showed all the children in the orphanage. Her duties and work were non-stop, seven days a week, twenty-four hours a day, and three hundred and sixty-five days a year. She richly deserves honourable mention for her dedication to the orphaned children.

There were seventy children in the orphanage, twenty-six of whom were Jewish. It was superhuman how Pastor Kuna and his staff risked their lives to save ours. If they had been found out, they would have been executed. Nobility should not be hereditary — an individual, based on their deeds, should merit it. Nobility deserves to be bestowed upon Pastor Kuna, Sister Maria and the staff of the orphanage for saving twenty-six innocent Jewish lives.

There is something a professor of French literature once told me that I think perfectly sums up my experience during the war. After I recounted my story of survival to him, he said, "You had an angel on your shoulder!"

When Pastor Kuna reported to the higher authorities of the Lutheran church that he would be accepting Jewish children, they told him that he would have their support, but that ultimately the responsibility would be his. It was ordinary Slovak people who helped Jews, and many Jews were also sheltered by private citizens, according to the numbers given by Yad Vashem. I would like to give all of these people credit and recognize them for their courageous deeds.

I believe that one should judge both people and religions on how they behave during a crisis. The Catholic Slovak church and establishment, hostile to the Jewish plight, failed this test. The Lutheran church passed with flying colours. My survival during the war is a testament to humanity winning over evil.

In my opinion, the Slovak government, too, failed for a very long time — they did not take responsibility for their role in deporting their Jewish citizens. Up until the end of Communist rule in 1989, the narrative was that Slovakia was yet another victim of Nazi Germany. It was not until the mid-1990s that Slovakia's Museum of Jewish Culture opened in Bratislava, and it took until 2016 for a Holocaust museum to open in the town of Sereď. Various governmental representatives have apologized for Slovakia's role in the Holocaust since 1990; yet, as late as 2010, I received a book about culture and memory in the Lower Tatra Mountains, and in it the authors state that the Jews were deported by the Germans! So, there is still a lot of misinformation, and I don't think that all of Slovak society has really come to terms with the fact that the Slovak wartime government was responsible for deporting its Jewish citizens. From what I have read, there is still a lot of antisemitism in Slovakia.

Epilogue

In 1997, I was in Israel with my brother, visiting family — both my aunt Libusa and my uncle Martin happened to pass away later that year, so I was lucky to see them one last time — and I went to Yad Vashem in Jerusalem. I found a file consisting of the testimony given by two women about Pastor Vladimir Kuna: they were Marta Nimrod from Kibbutz Ein HaHoresh and Marta Rakovsky from Kibbutz Ein HaShofet. I added my testimony to the same file. I intended to visit both women, but regrettably, I was only able to visit one, Marta Nimrod, in Kibbutz Ein HaHoresh.

Actually, both my brother and I visited Marta, who we had been with in the orphanage. Marta was manufacturing Chanukah candelabras and I bought one from her to add to my collection as a remembrance. Marta was about four years older than me, and we discussed our experiences from that time long ago. Surprisingly, she told us that Sister Maria Wagner was Jewish! In addition, she told us that several of the women who had worked in the kitchen or as cleaners were actually the Jewish mothers of children in the orphanage. I recalled that Pastor Kuna had mentioned this to me; in one of his letters, he wrote the name of one woman, Mrs. Rosenzweig.

I was skeptical about Marta's claim about Maria until one day in 2005, when I was staying in a condo in Miami that was frequented by Hungarian and Slovak Jews, I asked an elderly widow whose husband had been a Slovak doctor if Wagner (Wagnerova in Slovak) was a Jewish name. She said that she knew of a Jewish doctor by the name of Wagner in a town near Bratislava, so it was indeed possible. But I do not know for certain whether Maria was Jewish, and I probably never will.

In 2007, the International Tracing Services (now called the Arolsen Archives) opened up files from World War II that had not been open to the public for about sixty years. My brother contacted the agency to see if they could trace any more details on what happened to our parents. In August 2009, we learned that our parents had been apprehended about a week after they put us in the orphanage, and they were deported from Žilina, Slovakia, to Auschwitz on October 20 or 21, 1942. Apparently, according to this source, my father died around four months later in Auschwitz on February 18, 1943. As for my mother, they still don't know what happened to her.

Photographs

David's mother, Miriam Steiner (later Korn), in her hometown of Český Těšín, Czechoslovakia (now Czech Republic), circa 1932.

1

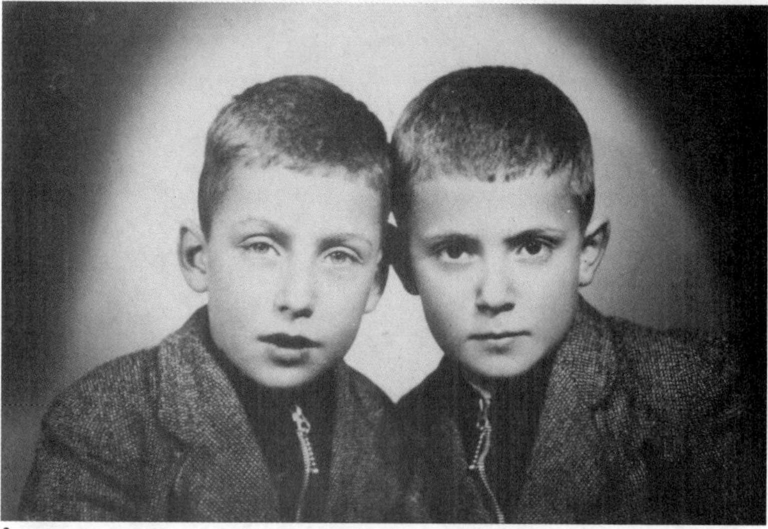
2

1 The wedding photo of David's parents, Abraham and Miriam Korn. Spišská Stará Ves, Czechoslovakia (now Slovakia), 1934. David received this photo — the only one he has of his father — from a relative in July 2020.

2 The only wartime photo of David (left) and his brother, Jacob. Liptovský Svätý Mikuláš, Slovakia, circa 1943.

David (right) with Jacob and their uncle Martin by the Eiffel Tower in Paris, France, 1948.

1

2

1 David (left) with a teacher (centre) and his friend Michael Faskas in front of Kfar Batya, the children's village and school where he lived soon after arriving in Israel. Ra'anana, Israel, circa 1953.

2 David on Kibbutz Sa'ad. Israel, 1957.

1

2

1 David's high school graduation photo, class of 1955. David's photo is in the far-left column, on the bottom.

2 Graduation photo from the Technion — Israel Institute of Technology, class of 1964. David's photo is in the right-hand column of six photos, at the bottom left.

1

2

3

1 David and Yona's wedding photo. Haifa, Israel, August 3, 1966.

2 David with his children, Miriam and Gil. Halifax, early 1970s.

3 David and Yona in their sukkah outside their home. Halifax, Nova Scotia, circa 1980s.

1

2

3

1 David working on the restoration of the Halifax Citadel National Historic Site. Halifax, Nova Scotia, circa 1978.

2 David restoring the Centre Block of the Parliament Buildings. Ottawa, circa 1994–1997.

3 David (right) at the top of the Parliament Buildings with a co-worker. Ottawa, circa 1994–1997.

1

2

1 David's family in Israel. From left to right: Aunt Libusa, Uncle Feri, Aunt Lia, Uncle Martin and David's cousins Yigal, Naomi's son, Ohad Liran, and Naomi. Circa 1980s.

2 Uncle Feri and Aunt Libusa Frish. Israel, early 1990s.

1 David's daughter, Miriam, with her son, Ilan. Halifax, 2010.

2 David's grandson, Ilan Yehuda Korn. Halifax, 2019.

3 David's son, Gil, holding his daughter, Aviva. Halifax, 2012.

4 David's granddaughter, Aviva Azaliah Korn. Halifax, 2019.

1

תעודת כבוד

Certificate of Honour

THIS IS TO CERTIFY THAT IN ITS SESSION OF JANUARY 30, 1972 THE COMMISSION FOR THE DESIGNATION OF THE RIGHTEOUS, ESTABLISHED BY YAD VASHEM, THE HOLOCAUST HEROES & MARTYRS REMEMBRANCE AUTHORITY, ON THE BASIS OF EVIDENCE PRESENTED BEFORE IT, HAS DECIDED TO HONOUR

Pastor Vladimir Kuna

WHO, DURING THE HOLOCAUST PERIOD IN EUROPE RISKED HIS LIFE TO SAVE PERSECUTED JEWS.
THE COMMISSION, THEREFORE, HAS ACCORDED HIM THE MEDAL OF THE RIGHTEOUS AMONG THE NATIONS.
HIS NAME SHALL BE FOREVER ENGRAVED ON THE HONOUR WALL IN THE GARDEN OF THE RIGHTEOUS, AT YAD VASHEM, JERUSALEM.

Jerusalem, Israel
JUNE 21, 1992

WHOEVER SAVES ONE LIFE IS AS THOUGH HE HAD SAVED THE ENTIRE WORLD

2

3

1 Pastor Vladimir Kuna in a photo taken by David when they met after the war. Liptovský Mikuláš, Slovakia, 1991.

2 A copy of the Yad Vashem certificate of honour naming Pastor Vladimir Kuna as Righteous Among the Nations in 1972.

3 The orphanage where David was hidden during the war. Liptovský Mikuláš, Slovakia, 1991.

1

2

MESTO LIPTOVSKÝ MIKULÁŠ

udeľuje

ČESTNÉ OBČIANSTVO
in memoriam

Vladimírovi Kunovi

(evanjelický a. v. farár, učiteľ, správca sirotinca)

za vysoko humánny čin záchrany 26 detí
židovského pôvodu

V Liptovskom Mikuláši
16. novembra 2010

Ing. Ján Blcháč, PhD.
primátor mesta

3

1 David (right) with his brother, Jacob. Halifax, 2010.

2 David (right) with his cousin Yigal on a visit back to where David grew up in Spišská Stará Ves, with the Červený kláštor monastery in the background. Slovakia, 2010.

3 A certificate issued by the town of Liptovský Mikuláš honouring Vladimir Kuna for saving the lives of twenty-six Jewish children during the war.

Liptovský Mikuláš,18.marec 1992.

Vážení a milí Kornovci!

Balík,ktorý ste nám poslali sme obdržali.S obsahom balíka sme sa podelili,rodina Kunovie s rodinou Mentelovie s rozpomienkami na minulosť,na všetko,čo sme prežili, keď ešte účinkoval Evanjelický sirotinec v Lipt.Sv.Mikuláši, ktorý sa po toľkých rokoch reportážami dostal do popredia a dostane sa ešte na Slávnostnom zasadnutí,ktoré má byť v Banskej Bystrici od 23 marca do 27.marca t.r.

Na požiadanie niektoré spisy-listy týkajúce sa býv.sirotinca poslal som p.Dr.Dezsiderovi Tóthovi do Banskej BystriceKapitulská 23-97401-Múzeum SNP. Spisy poslal som len prečítanie,lebo chcem ich mať v"rodinnom archíve" pre svoje dietky,vnukov a pravnuka.Medzi spisami sú aj hebrejské noviny s poslednou fotografiu dietok sirotinca z r.1950.Hebrejské noviny s prekladom nemám,neviem,čo je v nich napísané.

Mnohé dietky odchované-zachránené v mikulášskom sirotinci spomínajú si na všetko,čo prežili v sirotinci. O tom som sa presvedčil pri návsteve Editky Breinerovej,rod. Kxxxxxxx Ferencziovej z Humenného,ktorá ma so svojím synom, častým navštevovateľom Izraela navštívila.Do sirotinca som ju prijal 25.4.1943 a sirotinec opustila r.1945.Jej starých rodičov v Podturni som veľmi dobre poznal,keď som bol farárom v Lipt.Sv.Jáne/1931-1938/.Podtureň bola fíliou cirk.zboru svätojánskeho.Na evakuáciu do Ružomberka sa veľmi dobre pamätá.Jej návšteva ma potešila.

Váš list zo dňa 2.marca t.r.som obdržal,vďaka Vám,že si na mňa spomínate a sprítomnjete mi minulosť,ktorú som z milosti Božej prežil,v ktorej si spomínam na dietky sirotinca,medzi ktorými ste aj Vy-milí bratia Kornovci.

Vďaka Pánu Bohu,že nám dobré deti,vnukov,pravnuka,ktorí ma navštevujú a sviatky pre nás znamenali milé rodinné posedenie so spomienkami na tých našich drahých,ktorí nás predišli do večnosti. Spomienky viažu aj Vás milí bratia Kornovci,spomínate si na diakonisy,ktoré boli vychovávateľkami v sirotinci.Výchovu dietok viedla s pomocou sestry diakonisy Márie Vágnerovej pi vd.Emília Šoltésová až do apríla r.1944 od 1.1.1939.Na jej vedúce miesto nastúpila 2.5.1944 sestra diakonisa Juliška Rigáňová so sestrou diakonisou Vierkou Faškovou. Krajčírske práce od r.1943 až do konca apríla 1945 svedomite konala pani Irena Rosenzweigová,ktorá sa so svojím synom Lackom zachránila i keď sirotinec bol obsadený nemeckým vojskom.

Keď prestalo xxxxx účinkovanie sirotinca /1917-1950/ niektoré býv.diakonisy stali sa ošetrovateľkami v Št.nemocnici.Diakonia na Slovensku bude obnovená. Vďaka za hebrejské noviny.Bol by som rád,keby som sa v ich preklade oboznámil/v preklade/ s obsahom. Zdravotný stav sa mi zhoršuje, slabosť nôh pokračuje,ale sa to dá s pomocou Božou vydržať.

Srdečne si Vás pozdravuje

Vlad. Kuna s rodinou

One of the many letters sent to David and his brother from Pastor Kuna. Translation of edited text on the following page.

Liptovský Mikuláš, March 18, 1992

Dear and Esteemed Brothers Korn,

We safely received your parcel. We shared its contents with the Kuna and the Mentel families, together with the memories of the past and everything we had experienced during the existence of the Lutheran Orphanage in Lipt. Sv. Mikuláš, which after all those years was resurrected by articles in the press and will continue doing so — at a ceremonial session to be held in Banská Bystrica on March 23 to March 27 of this year.

At the request of Dr. Dezider Tóth I sent some of the files — letters related to the former orphanage — to the Museum SNP in Banská Bystrica, Kapitulská 23-9740. I loaned the files for reading only as I want to keep them in our "family archive" for my children, grandchildren and my grandson. The files include a Hebrew newspaper with the last photograph of the orphanage residents, from 1950. I don't have the newspaper translation and do not know what is written in it.

Many of the children raised [who were] saved in the Mikuláš Orphanage remember everything they had experienced in the orphanage, as I could observe during the visit of Editka Breinerová [...] She recollects the evacuation to Ružomberok very clearly. Her visit pleased me very much.

I have received your letter, dated March 2 this year — thank you for thinking of me and keeping fresh the memory of the past which I have, with the Grace of God, survived and which includes the little residents of the orphanage, including you, dear brothers Korn.

I thank the Lord that I have good children, grandchildren and a grandson who visit me, and holidays always mean nice family reunions and remembrance of our dear ones who preceded us to the Eternity. You, too, dear brothers Korn, carry memories; do you remember the deaconesses who were the orphanage caregivers? Mrs. Emília Šoltésová, the chief caregiver, with the assistance of sister deaconess Mária Vágnerová were in charge of education from 1939/01/01 to April 1944. She was succeeded by sister deaconess Juliška Rigáňová on 1944/05/02 and sister deaconess Vierka Fašková. From 1943 until April 1945 all sewing was diligently done by Mrs. Irena Rosenzweigová who, with her son Lacko, were saved, even [at the time] when the orphanage was occupied by German troops.

When the orphanage ceased to operate /1917-1950/, some of the former deaconesses became nurses in the State Hospital. The Samaritan work will be revived in Slovakia. Thank you for the Hebrew newspaper. I would love to know its contents through translation. My health is deteriorating, weakness of the legs persists but that, with God's help, can be endured.

With sincere greetings,
Vlad. Kuna with family

Liptovský Mikuláš,15.október 1993.

Vážení a milí bratia Jakub a David s rodinou,

vďaka Vám za poslané peniaze,ktoré som obdržal i za želanie všetkého najlepšieho na nový rok,ktorý očakávame. Srdečne si Vás pozdravujem so želaním všetkého dobrého vo Vašom živote s i rozpomienkami na pobyt v bývalom Evanjelickom sirotinci v Lipt.Sv.Mikuláši,keď som bol správcom v sirotinci, ku ktorému sa viažu moje pekné rozpomienky najmä v tom,že zachránené boli mnohé dietky medzi nimi aj vy,aby mohli žiť a rozpomínať sa na tomčo prežili a ako.boli zachránené.

Budova bývalého sirotinca bola pekne opravená a v-nej je škola evanjelická a rímsko-katolícka.Budova vilky,v ktorej som býval so svojou rodinou čaká na opravu,sme zvedaví,kto v nej bude bývať? Budova diakonie nie je opravená,už nie je taká pekná ako ste ju vy videli,poznali.

Vo svojej starobe prežívam rozpomienkami väe všetko,čo som prežil vo svojom kňazskom povolaní z milosi Božej a čo prežívam teraz v starobe pri veľmi zhoršenom zdravotnom stave,pxke som nútený byť doma a čítať si svoje životné záznamy od mladosti až do staroby,ktoré mi pripomínajú,že hodno bolo žiť,hodno bolo aj trpieť a z milosti Božej aj pokojnejšie časy očakávať s rozpomienkami,čo sme to len v našom živote prežívali

Srdečne si Vás pozdravuje
Váš

Vladimír Kuna s rodinou

One of the many letters sent to David and his brother from Pastor Kuna. Translation of edited text on the following page.

Liptovský Mikuláš, October 15, 1993

Esteemed and dear brothers Jakub and David with families,

Thank you for the money you last sent to me and for the wishes of all the best in the New Year that is ahead of us. I am sending my cordial greetings with best wishes in your life and with memories of [your] stay in the former Lutheran Orphanage in Lipt. Sv. Mikuláš, where I was the custodian and which is associated with my nice memories, especially because many a child — you included — was saved in order to stay alive and remember what they experienced and how they were saved.

The building of the former orphanage was nicely restored and now it houses Lutheran and Roman Catholic schools. The building of the little villa where I lived with my family has not been repaired, and it is far from being as beautiful as you had seen it and remember it.

I spend my old age going through my memories of all I had, with God's grace, gone through during my pastoral work and what I am going through now, as an old man with deteriorating health; I am forced to stay at home and re-read the records of my life, from my early years until my old age, and which remind me that my life was worth living, the suffering was worth it and that with the Grace of God, I was able to look forward to more peaceful times, remembering what we had experienced in our lives.

With heartfelt greetings,
from
Vladimir Kuna and family

Liptovský Mikuláš, Sep. 9, 1991

Dear Brothers Korn,

[...] What I experienced in Ružomberok is hard to forget. In March 1945 the German commander, Oberstleutnant Otto, ordered the evacuation of the population of Liptovský Mikuláš as well as our orphanage. Therefore on March 23, 1945, I, with my family and all God's children, over 40 of them, evacuated to Ružomberok.

We were given a bus and some trucks at our disposal. In Ružomberok, the orphans were housed in the Lutheran Primary School. On the morning of April 5, 1945, we witnessed retreat of German troops through Ružomberok, escaping the 4th Czechoslovak Independent Brigade whose organizer was my brother Pavol, the Uprising commander and a lieutenant. The 4th CZ Independent Brigade liberated Lipt. Sv. Mikuláš on April 4, 1945, and Ružomberok on the next day, April 5, and the entire brigade were decorated with the Order of Bohdan Khmelnytsky of the Second Class. Pavol was promoted to the rank of Brigadier Major General. Meeting my brother after a considerable time was a joyful occasion. Our soldiers used their trucks to help us return the little orphans to the orphanage on April 21, 1945.

During 9 weeks of artillery attacks on Liptovský Mikuláš, the building of the orphanage received 455 minor and 7 full hits. ... as many as 45,000 grenades and mines were deployed in Liptovský Mikuláš and surroundings. Seventeen ecclesiastical buildings were damaged and restored in 1945....

During our evacuation, in my mind I was going through everything I had experienced up until then. The nice memories since 1937, teaching religion and overseeing the local schools. The sad memories, when I was arrested and imprisoned in Ružomberok by the German Gestapo from Nov. 17, 1944 to Dec. 31, 1944, and then in Bratislava until Jan. 7, 1945. I still bear the consequences of the Gestapo prisons.

I am glad that the Minister of Defence, Luboš Dobrovský, recalled the 1948–1950 decrees whereby 14 generals of the Czechoslovak Army were stripped of their ranks, my brother Pavol (1895-1982) included. His military rank of Brigadier Major General was restored. I, too, was rehabilitated at my high age of 86!

Sincere regards with the wishes of all the best in your life and in the lives of your family.

Yours,
Vladimir Kuna

Translated and edited extract of a letter from Pastor Kuna about the evacuation of the orphanage in 1945.

David Korn, 2019.

The Survival Story of a Six-Year-Old Boy

Fishel Philip Goldig

POLAND, 1939–1945

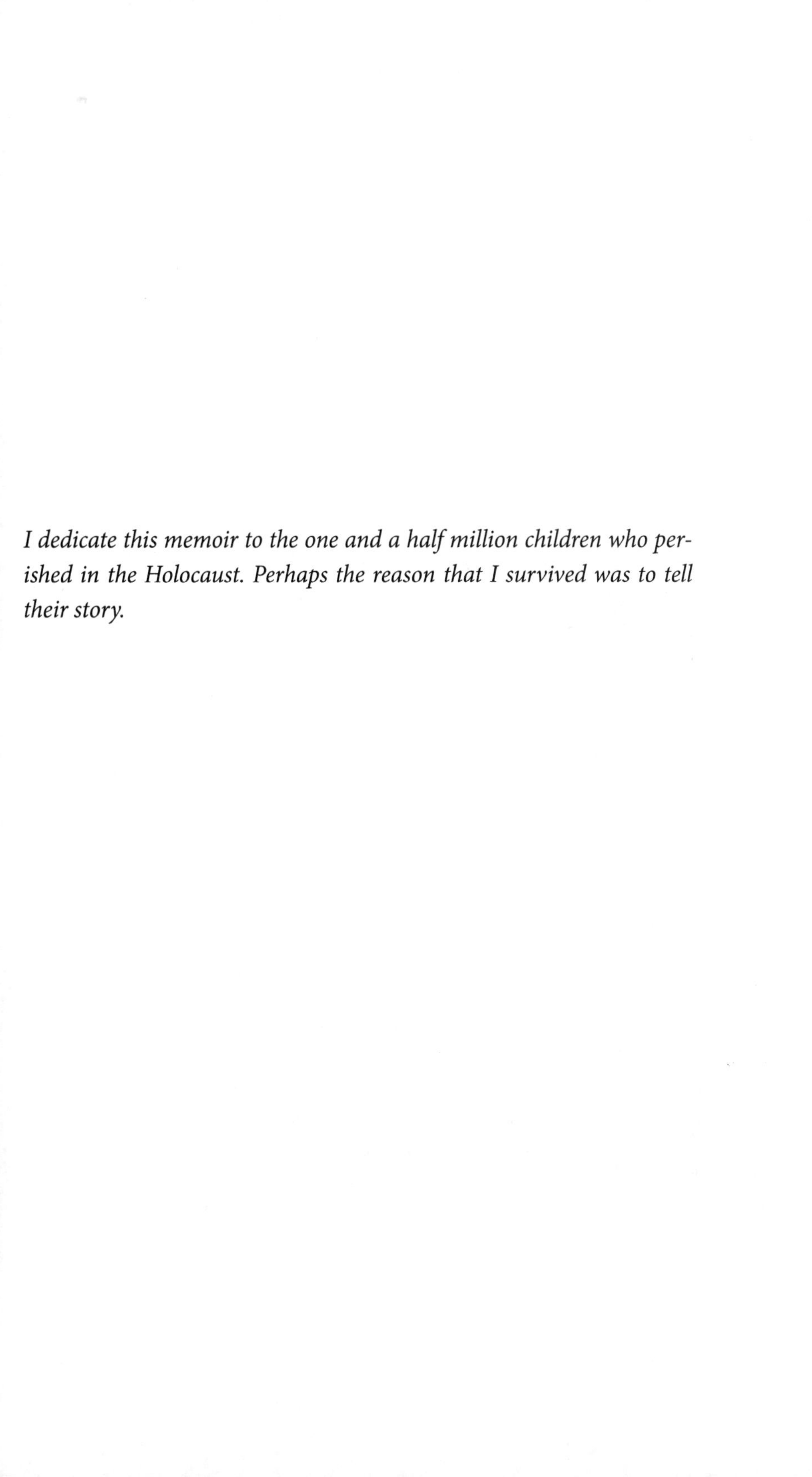

I dedicate this memoir to the one and a half million children who perished in the Holocaust. Perhaps the reason that I survived was to tell their story.

Preface

It has occurred to me that the time has come to take pen to paper and record my life story for my family and friends, as well as for anyone else who might be interested, and in particular, to tell of my experiences during the Holocaust and of my survival. My experiences of the war years, 1939 to 1944, are based on my memory as a six-year-old boy when the war started, and a ten-and-a-half-year-old when it ended, as well as on the memories of my parents and other family members, who told me their stories from that awful time.

As we all know, there comes a time for all of us to depart from this world, with all the good and the bad that it has to offer. The greatest honour you can bestow upon me would be to read my story and to pass it on to your children, grandchildren, and to their descendants to come, so that not only the Jewish people, but all people, will never forget the historic and tragic event called the Holocaust.

I am now in my eighty-seventh year. With the exception of my survival as a child during the Holocaust, I have had a mostly happy life. But there is more to be done. I want to tell my life story to many more people. I want to see my family happy and healthy and growing in strength and in spirit. I want to help young people to become better singers and actors. I want to continue to sing and see a smile on peoples' faces. I want to visit more places and see the beauty of this earth.

I don't know if I will achieve all of this or how long I will be around to even try. It does not matter. As long as we are here, we must try to accomplish as much as possible. We must, also, reach out to our children and grandchildren to continue where we left off — to make a better world.

In 2015, I was diagnosed with Hodgkin's lymphoma and underwent a series of chemotherapy treatments. Going through this cancer episode gave me a completely new perspective on life. I realized that I had been missing out on the importance of telling my survival story — I should have started to tell it years ago. But we are where we are. Now, it is my obligation to tell my story to anyone who will listen. I am concerned about our legacy. Who will tell our stories when we, the survivors, are no more? This is my project now, and I hope it will be the project of all survivors. Our sages tell us, "It is not upon you to finish the work, but you are not free to ignore it."

In April 2015, I took part with my wife, Lorna, in an event of great importance, the March of the Living. This was a trip of a lifetime, and it changed my perception of the Holocaust. I had rarely spoken outside of the family about what I had gone through during the war, but this trip gave me the chance to speak about it more publicly. I spoke about my survival story to around 180 young people who were sixteen or seventeen years old, and to the chaperones who accompanied us on the trip. It was a wonderful, memorable trip, especially when, at Auschwitz on Yom HaShoah, Holocaust Remembrance Day, we encountered thousands of youngsters from all over the world, and it was the first time I was asked to tell my story in Spanish to a group of young people from Mexico.

When we returned from our March of the Living trip, I joined the Montreal Holocaust Museum and started to give my testimony to students from schools, CGEPS (colleges) and universities. I feel very gratified when I have the opportunity to speak to these youngsters, both Jews and non-Jews, either in French or in English, to tell my story of survival, answer their questions and see the interest they have in knowing more about the Holocaust.

At the end of my testimony to these young people, I tell them that we, the survivors, have an obligation and a mission to tell our survival stories to the future generations, but that they, too, have an obligation. Their obligation is to make sure that what happened to us will never happen again and that when they arrive at university, and beyond, they must fight against antisemitism, Holocaust denial, and all kinds of prejudice and hatred that exists in the world today.

Early Life

I was born in Poland in 1933, in the town of Mielnica, which is now called Melnytsia-Podilska and is part of Ukraine. My father was Baruch Goldig and my mother was Rachel Kimmel. My father came from a religious Chasidic family from the town of Yagelnitza, as it was called in Yiddish (now Yahil'nytsya, Ukraine). My grandfather died before I was born and I was named after him. Although my grandmother and two of my father's brothers, Willie and Hershel, would visit us when I was young, I have memories only of my uncle Hershel, who used to visit quite often and whom I loved very much.

My father was quite a sociable person — full of energy and always telling jokes and participating in discussions. Because of his Chasidic upbringing, my father was well versed in Talmud, and the shul, the synagogue, was still of great importance in his life. It is there, in the community among his friends and acquaintances, where he shone.

My father used to tell me a story about his father, who was a Chasid of the Chortkover Rebbe, part of the Ruzhiner Chasidic family. As with all Chasidim, my father and his brothers had beards and *peyos*, sidelocks. When he was eighteen, my father discovered Zionism and became a committed Zionist for the rest of his life. He joined a religious Zionist party and cut off his beard and *peyos*. My grandfather, needless to say, was upset with his son's new way of life and took my father to face the rebbe. My grandfather said to the rebbe, "Look what has happened to my son." The rebbe looked him over and said, "I'm not worried about your son, but I am more worried about *his* son!"

My father was strict about my education, especially my Jewish education. As far back as I can remember, I always went to cheder, Jewish school, after my regular school. And I cannot remember a Shabbat when I didn't go with my father to shul.

My mother came from a large family of six children. Her father, my grandfather Kimmel, owned a large produce company that exported produce to Western Europe. His sons and sons-in-law, including my father, all worked in this business with him. Pesach Kimmel was a stern, dictatorial man. Everyone except my aunt Mina — who happened to be the only one of her siblings to receive more than a few years of formal education — was afraid of him. My grandmother, Tauba, was a small, sickly woman who loved her grandchildren and also loved to cook. I remember her as kind and loving. When we came into her home, she would go around to all the children and blow our noses into her apron! I remember best my uncle Levi, the youngest of my mother's six siblings. He used to visit us often, and I adored him.

After my parents got married and I was born, my mother's main concern was to care for our family. She worked hard all her life to make sure that we had a good life. She had learned early on, perhaps because she had gone through the struggles of World War I, that you must preserve every penny and not spend foolishly. She stubbornly guarded every penny that was spent! In contrast to my father, my mother was not a very happy person, possibly because of her younger years at home, and she was never interested in the social activities of my father. But she was caring and loving in her own way.

I was born with a disease called rickets, which affects the bone structure in children's legs and feet. At that time, the only medical specialist in this field lived in Lwów, which was more than two hundred kilometres away. My parents took me often, at great cost, to see this specialist. One day, my grandfather Kimmel asked my father how expensive it was to make these trips to Lwów to see this doctor. My father answered that it was indeed very expensive, but well worthwhile. My grandfather replied that money is difficult to get but you can always have another child! My father was extremely upset by these remarks. He quit his job at Grandfather's business and opened up his own. He didn't speak to his father-in-law until many years later, when events forced us together in the ghetto.

My parents always quarrelled. However, even though their relationship was not great, they loved each other in their own way, and in a crisis — of which there were many — they cared for each other without reservation.

One thing was certain: both of them loved me very, very much. So, from the day I was born until 1939, I had a loving family and a normal life.

The Survival Story

Life Under the Soviets

In 1939, I was six years old. As I was coming home from school one day I was attacked by some other boys and beaten up. The attackers ran away and left me, just a little boy, on the ground in pain. Among the terrible names that they had called me was "dirty Jew." When I finally made my way home, crying, I told my mother what had happened and asked her, "Why? I haven't done anything wrong." "My son, you better get used to it," she answered. "We, the Jewish people, have been persecuted for many centuries."

That was my introduction to what is called antisemitism. It is comprised of ignorance, prejudice and hate, and it is where my story of survival starts.

Before World War II, our town, Mielnica, was in the Tarnopol region of Poland. The majority of the population was Ukrainian. Shortly before the war started, Germany and the Soviet Union made a pact known as the Molotov-Ribbentrop. Both countries agreed to invade Poland — Germany from the west and the Soviet Union from the east.

In mid-September 1939, the Soviets came into our town. Soon they started to arrest most of the wealthy people. They sent some to toil in Siberia, in the north of Russia, or to labour camps in Kazakhstan, and others were expelled from our town and forced to move to another town in the region. My uncle Mendel was arrested and sent to Siberia, and we never heard from him again. After the war, people who had been with him told us that he had died after falling off the roof of a crowded railcar.

One Sunday afternoon, while my parents and I were eating lunch, the secret police known as the NKVD and two police officers carrying rifles entered our home. I still remember this clearly, even that we were eating chopped liver for lunch. One of the police officers pulled out a document and read it to my father. It said that we had to move to a different city. My father said, "Why? What have I done?" The men said that we were considered to be capitalists, part of the rich bourgeoisie class! We had three days to leave our house and the town. I didn't understand what was happening, but I was scared.

We were not wealthy. My father had a small business and earned just enough to feed his family. He protested, but we had no choice; we had to start packing. Before we left, my father, angry and upset, decided to write to Stalin, the ruler of the Soviet Union, complaining that a mistake had been made in our case and that we should be granted permission to return to our town of birth. At that time, to complain to the authorities, and in particular to write to Stalin, was very dangerous, and it could have meant being sent to prison or to Siberia.

We left our town and settled in Jezierzany (now Ozeryany, Ukraine), which was my mother's birth town, approximately forty kilometres away. We rented a house, and my father found a job and arranged for me to go to a cheder.

Late one evening, about one and a half years later, two officers from the secret police came to our door, asking my father to accompany them to the police station. My mother and I were crying when he left, sure that we would never see him again. At the police station, the officers asked him if he had written a letter to Stalin. My father had no choice but to admit that he had — his signature was on the letter. He was then told that our case had been reviewed and that an error had been made. We had permission to return to our town!

And so, in the spring of 1941, we returned to Mielnica, to our house. But Soviet officers were living there, so we had to find somewhere else to live. My father found another job, and for a while, everything was okay.

Life Under the Nazis

Months after we moved back to Mielnica, Nazi Germany broke the pact with the Soviets and soon conquered the entire region. Before the Germans arrived, there were approximately three days when no one was in control of the town. News spread in the Jewish community that a large mob of Ukrainians was gathering with pitchforks and axes and had started walking toward the centre of town, where most of the Jews lived, in order to kill the Jews and confiscate their belongings. Fear and confusion engulfed us. What happened next, which my father told me, was even more astonishing. A Ukrainian priest engaged the mob and admonished them for attempting to do this awful thing. He told them that they were about to commit a terrible sin and that they would be punished by God. After pleading with them for some time, the crowd dispersed.

When the Nazis arrived in the summer of 1941, they slowly imposed many restrictions on the Jewish community. First, Jews had to wear a white armband with a blue Magen David, the Star of David, on it. If anyone refused, the Nazis could deport them or shoot them on the spot. It was clear to us that we had to do whatever they wanted or we wouldn't survive. Then, there was a night curfew, no travel without a special permit and no congregating on the streets. Soon Jews were not allowed to travel outside the town, and the authorities took our passports and birth certificates. The Nazis would announce these restrictions through a big loudspeaker that was on top of a small truck that would drive around town. "Achtung! Achtung!" (Attention! Attention!), a voice would call out, and then it would tell us what they wanted us to do.

Eventually, that truck came around announcing "Achtung!

Achtung!" again, and the Nazis proclaimed that all Jews in our town and in the surrounding towns and villages had to abandon their homes. We were allowed to take only what we could carry and had to travel to a ghetto in a larger town called Borszczów (now Borshchiv), approximately thirty kilometres away. Again we had three days to pack and were forced to move.

Life and Death in the Ghetto

The Nazis had created the ghetto in Borszczów in a small part of the Jewish sector of town. The ghetto covered about eight to ten square blocks and was at first "open," but I remember it later being encircled by barbed wire. Life in the ghetto was inhumane. With the influx of so many people, living conditions were horrible. Entire families lived in one or two rooms. In the building we lived in, my parents and I had one room, but there were other families with many children that also had only one room. On our floor, at the end of a corridor, there was a bathroom with a shower, and that was the only bathroom available on that floor.

We lived crammed together. My parents had a bed and I was sleeping on the floor, on a blanket. That was just the beginning. We were given some food rations, but it was not enough. Some people had money or jewellery and could exchange it with non-Jewish neighbours for food. But many people were dying, some of them from hunger, particularly little kids. I was always hungry. There were epidemics of typhus and dysentery; there was never enough drinkable water. Many able-bodied men were taken to work as forced labourers. Those who resisted were rounded up and sent mainly to the Belzec death camp.

In spite of the terrible conditions, my father insisted that I study. He found a teacher, and we went to cheder in a little room, five or six of us. When my father said I had to go, I had to go. It was non-negotiable. I was afraid. If the Nazis found us studying, they would shoot us because it wasn't allowed. Yet, I enjoyed studying because I felt that maybe I was doing something good, something worthwhile. But I spent most of the day at home. Sometimes I played outside with some of my friends. Whenever we saw police officers go by on motorcycles, everyone grew quiet. There was fear, but you learned to live with fear. However, the worst was still to come.

By 1943, the Germans would choose a day, usually a Jewish holiday, known as *Aktionstag* (action day). On these days, they would come early in the morning and surround the ghetto with German SS troops and Ukrainian Auxiliary Police, Nazi collaborators. Every Jew caught during that day was brought to the cemetery, where other Jews had been forced to dig huge graves. There, everyone was shot and buried in those graves. Anyone who refused to go to the cemetery or who tried to escape was shot on the spot. The shooting would go on all day.

To have any chance of surviving, people had to find hiding places. Some people built false walls or ceilings about thirty inches distant from existing walls and ceilings, and they would hide in that space. Everybody had to hide. If you didn't, you were dead — as simple as that. In our apartment building, there was an engineer who built one of these special hiding places for the people who lived there. There was an outhouse in the back of the building with a small wooden platform at the entrance. The platform was removed, and some of the men dug a bunker underneath it. A small opening was made for people to enter. Then they dug deeper, longer and wider to accommodate all who lived there. Whenever we heard shooting, we knew it was going to be a killing day, *Aktionstag*, and anyone who could would run into the bunker and stay until nightfall, when the shooting would finally stop.

I remember once, after an *Aktionstag* on the Passover holiday, we came out of a bunker we were hiding in and I saw some of my friends, who had been shot, lying in the street. Their bodies were picked up from the street and thrown onto a horse-drawn buggy and taken to the cemetery.

During another *Aktionstag*, which started on the holiday of Shavuot in the summer of 1943 and lasted for many days, I lost my Kimmel grandparents and my aunt Zlate and her children, Motel and Eva. We were told that my grandfather Kimmel had refused to go to the cemetery and was killed by the police with the butt end of a rifle. One of my aunts witnessed this. She escaped on the way to the cemetery and managed to get back into the ghetto and find a place to hide. Eventually she was found, and she, too, was killed.

Soon, we heard rumours that the Germans had decided to liquidate the ghetto. They were going to kill everyone in the ghetto over a period of days, until all the Jews were dead, but no one knew exactly when.

It is worth mentioning that well before the liquidation of the ghetto, a small group of young men had formed a resistance group. By 1942, they had managed to acquire some arms, and by the summer of 1943 some of these fighters had escaped to the forest, where they banded together and where, for a few months, they organized attacks on Ukrainian Auxiliary Police and Ukrainian nationalists, as well as some Germans. Ultimately, a large force of Germans attacked the resistance group and most of the Jewish fighters were killed.

~

Eventually, it came — the liquidation of our ghetto. I was nine years old. We heard the shooting and people began running in every which way to save their lives. We heard that in one sector of the ghetto, some people were able to cut the barbed-wire fence and escape through to the non-Jewish area of town, running into the fields and into the forest beyond. So my parents and I, my cousin Julek, who was one year younger than me, and his parents, Rivka and Issie, decided to try to escape through this opening. There were hundreds of people pushing through this small breach in the barbed wire, and we got separated from my father and uncle who were running ahead of us. My mother and I and my aunt and cousin were still some distance away from them. However, when we got to the fence, the Germans had already arrived with two trucks with mounted machine guns on top, one on each side of the street. As people tried to run across, they were shot down. The street was full of dead bodies. My father and uncle had managed to get through the opening ahead of us, but we didn't know what happened to them. We didn't know if my father had been killed.

We decided to return to the ghetto because to try to cross the street was certain death. We started to look for a place to hide. At the back of a building, we found an old abandoned shed without doors. It was divided into two sections by a wall made of wooden planks approximately four to six inches apart. My aunt and cousin went into one of these sections and my mother and I went into the other section of the shed. My aunt found two large wash basins, and she and my cousin covered themselves with them. My mother and I found two large straw mattresses, and my mother covered me with one of them and herself with the other.

I was lying diagonally under the mattress that was closest to the entrance. Some time passed, and then we heard the voices of two Ukrainian police approaching the shed. They first entered on the side where my aunt and cousin were hidden, lifted the wash basins and shot them on the spot. Then, one entered our side of the shed, lifted the corner of the mattress — the side opposite where I was lying — and said to the other, "There is nobody here," and they left.

That was the closest I came to dying.

We waited several hours until nightfall without moving, listening to the moans of my aunt Rivka and my cousin Julek, who were dying on the other side of the shed — until there was silence.

Escape

Finally, it was dark. We left the shed and ran through to the non-Jewish sector of the town and into the fields. We were trying to reach the forest, but we did not know the way and got lost. We wandered around in the fields for about a week or so, hiding among the tall rows of corn and wheat. We ate the raw corn and wheat for food and we slept on the bare ground. And every day we looked for a way out. Most likely we were just going in circles.

One day a gang of about ten to fifteen Ukrainian teenagers discovered us and started to throw stones at us. I was bleeding and my mother was pleading with them to stop, saying, "We didn't do anything to you, why are you doing this?" but to no avail. Suddenly, we saw a man on horseback coming toward us. It was the farmer who owned that piece of land. He had seen that there was something going on and yelled at the youngsters to get off his property, and he chased them away. Then he took us to his house about half a kilometre away, washed and bandaged our wounds, gave us some food and water, and walked with us to show us how to get to the forest, which turned out to be close by. To us, this man was not a farmer but an angel from heaven!

Many people were hiding in that forest, groups of fifteen to twenty people scattered throughout. When we encountered members of other groups, my mother would ask, "Is there someone in your group by the name of Baruch Goldig?" One day, one of these people said that there was, and that is how we reunited with my father. We were a family again. My uncle, who had run from the ghetto with my father, had been shot and killed just outside the ghetto.

I think we spent about three months in the forest. Life there was very difficult. There was a lot of rain, but we couldn't make anything that looked like a shelter because we didn't want to be discovered. The Germans knew there were Jews in the forest, and from time to time, there were German patrols looking for Jews who had escaped from the ghetto. So we constructed shelters from leaves and branches, and we were on the move every few days. There was also very little to eat. Some of the men in our group would go out at night into the fields and steal corn and potatoes. We would put them on a stick and cook them over a fire, making sure that the fire didn't get too big so it wouldn't attract attention. But this, too, was dangerous.

It was getting cold, and we were desperate to get out of the forest and find another hiding place. Occasionally, some farmers would come and exchange food for money, jewellery or anything of worth. These farmers were taking a chance — if the Germans caught them, they would kill them. My father became friendly with one of these farmers, Alexi. He asked Alexi to do him a favour, to go to our town, which was not far away, and see if he could find my uncle Leon and aunt Mina and ask them if they had a place where we could hide.

When we had been ordered to leave my hometown of Mielnica and go to the Borszczów ghetto, the only Jews who were allowed to remain were my aunt Mina and my uncle Leon, who were doctors, as well as their daughter, my three-year-old cousin, Eva, and one other Jewish doctor. The Germans kept them in town for the surrounding population's medical needs.

At the time the Germans were going to liquidate the ghetto, they were also going to get rid of all the Jews in the area, including doctors, nurses and other professionals. My aunt and uncle found out what was about to happen and started to look for a place to hide. One of my uncle's patients was a young boy who had some terrible disease and whose father was a well-known and honourable man, Mr. Kukurudza. My uncle asked him if they could hide on his farm. Mr. Kukurudza, who was a good soul, said that it would be impossible to hide on his farm because the Germans frequently came to his house. But he said that he would find some other farmer in the area to hide the family. After some time, he found a poor potato farmer named Nikolai Kravchuk who was willing to hide my uncle and his family.

Alexi went into the town to relay the message about hiding us to my aunt and uncle. He came back with the news that he had found them and they had asked him to bring us to the village, and to the farm, approximately ten kilometres from Mielnica. And so, we arranged for Alexi to come one night and to bring us over to that village. It took us two days to get there because we could only travel at night. During the days, he would leave us in the field, and he would come back at night.

With the help of Mikhail Kukurudza, we had found a hiding place in a small village called Babince (now Urozhaine), at a farm owned by Nikolai and Yulia Kravchuk, who lived with their three children, nine-year-old Yaroslava, six-year-old Irina and a younger brother, whose name I never knew. My aunt and uncle and cousin joined us soon after we arrived.

The Cave

At first, we stayed in the attic of the farmer's house. But this was very dangerous because the children, who at first did not know we were there, would occasionally go up to the attic to bring down some toys or play. Some of the neighbours' kids often came to play, especially in winter, and if even one person had said anything about us being there, we'd all be dead. We had to find another place to hide.

The farmer's yard extended back to a small hill, and, years before we arrived there, he had dug into that hill and constructed a cellar, which was like a cave, with walls and a ceiling made of stones. He stored his supply of potatoes there over the winter.

We thought that we could hide in this cave, but people were coming and going, buying the farmer's potatoes, and the kids played near there as well, and we were afraid that the children would hear us. And so, in the middle of the night, my father, uncle and the farmer removed a few large stones at the base of the wall of the potato cave and dug further into the side of the hill to make another bunker for us to hide in. The opening of the cave was small and narrow, just wide enough for us to crawl through. We then made it wider, longer and higher to accommodate my parents, me, my aunt and uncle, and my three-year-old cousin Eva. When we were inside the cave, we would replace the stones, so that it could not be detected by anyone who might come inside the potato cellar.

The cave was not very high. When I stood up, I had to bend my head. It was warm and dark, and we had kerosene lanterns and some candles for light. There was a wire mesh over the window that was in the door to the cave, and so we also had some air. Kravchuk gave us a small table, blankets to put on the ground and to cover ourselves with, as well as some old clothing that had belonged to his children.

Once a day, early in the morning, Kravchuk would bring us some food and remove the waste. He would also bring us a big pitcher of water to wash with and for drinking. Once in a while he would spend some time talking to us. He was a nice, gentle man, though he and his wife were afraid of hiding us — they were often afraid to even come into our hole because they were worried neighbours would see them. There was always the fear of betrayal.

About once every two weeks, Kravchuk would go into Mielnica and bring us back a Ukrainian newspaper, and reading that, we would get a sense of where the front was. We would read that paper from one end to the other. My aunt and uncle had brought some books with them, mainly in Polish, and I remember seeing a couple of medical books as well. I didn't understand a word of them.

My parents, aunt and uncle would spend a lot of time talking, all kinds of things that adults talk about, and I would listen and sometimes play with my little cousin. My father had brought a small, thick *siddur*, a prayer book, with him. He used to always have it with him. He would ask me to read and translate from the *siddur*. At the back of the *siddur* was a Chumash, and he would tell me to learn the *parshah* (portion) of the week and then quiz me about it. He did this throughout my life. Whenever I studied Gemara, he would ask, "Which Gemara are you studying?"

We spent a lot of time just sitting quietly because we didn't want our voices to be heard outside. We had to be very careful.

The big question was what to do with a three-year-old? We had to keep my cousin quiet, so we started to teach her to read. For months, she was sounding out letters and words, "Ma...po...beh...bah...," making noises, putting together letters to make words. By the time of liberation, Eva could read three languages: Polish, Ukrainian and Hebrew, and maybe some Russian, too. She had become my little sister, and we grew up together. Later in life, Eva became a world-renowned geneticist; she has travelled all over the world giving papers and lecturing. Eva (née Deutsch, now Andermann) and I are still very close.

In the first few months that we were hidden, we were able to come out to the yard for fresh air for an hour or so, but only in the middle of the night every ten days or so. By the start of the new year, it became too dangerous for us to leave the cave. Another Jewish family hiding nearby had been found and shot, along with the farmer who was hiding them and his wife and children. If anyone had found us, the Germans would not only have shot us, but also the farmer and his whole family.

Nikolai Kravchuk was a simple and good man, and he despised what was being done to the Jews. Additionally, my aunt had some coins that she had gotten from her grandmother, and she gave them to the farmer from time to time. Kravchuk had to be careful with where he used them, though, because where would he get such an old coin? There was nothing to stop him from killing us or calling the police and taking whatever possessions we had. But he didn't do that because he was a decent human being. The same is true of Mr. Kukurudza, who would occasionally come to the farm to see how we were doing.

During the time we were in the cave, I was often bored and wanted to leave. But I knew what I had to do. I had to survive. That was my lesson during that entire time. When many survivors are asked how it was possible to survive such a thing, they answer: the instinct to live just one more day, or just another week. That's what pushes you. You're hungry, you're tired, you're dirty. But the instinct in you is to fight to live for just one more day.

So, we stayed there, underground, until the spring of 1944.

Liberation

The spring in 1944 was very wet, with lots of rain and melting snow, causing us some serious problems in the cave. Large pieces of earth began to fall from the ceiling. One piece fell inches from Eva, which could have caused her major injuries. Kravchuk brought us some wood to shore up the ceiling. But we always were afraid that at any time the whole cave would collapse and bury us alive. We knew that the Soviets were coming, but we didn't know when.

Finally, one day in April 1944, Kravchuk removed the stones to our entrance and announced that the Germans had gone and that the Soviet army had arrived. We were finally able to crawl out of our hiding place and see the sun for the first time after many, many months of darkness.

After a couple of days, my parents decided to return to our hometown, Mielnica. Eva and her parents decided to stay with the farmer longer, as the situation was still very confusing and unsettling. We arrived in Mielnica and went directly to our house, which was abandoned. A few days after we returned home, something strange happened to us. Suddenly, we could not walk. For my parents, it was painful just to take a few steps. I was more fortunate. I could walk a little, but I could not run. I had to be the one to go out and get food. It seems that being in the bunker for so long and not using our leg muscles had made the muscles atrophy from lack of exercise and regular, normal movement. Slowly, with time, our leg muscles began to function properly.

We managed to get some food, furniture, and pots and pans, and we started to live somewhat normally. But about ten days after we arrived something happened that disrupted our lives once more.

Without any warning, the Soviets left the town and the German army, consisting of thousands of soldiers with heavy artillery and tanks, returned. It seems that the Soviets had encircled the retreating German forces, who retreated into our town and the surrounding area. The Germans were trying to escape by building bridges across the Dniester River, leading to Romania. Every night, they would build a bridge, and every day, the Russian planes would bomb and destroy them.

In the meantime, we left our home once again and found an abandoned house nearby with an empty cellar to hide in. The cellar had one of its walls bombed out and there was snow coming in. We lived mainly on half a loaf of bread, which we had brought with us when we had left our house, and some snow, for several days. We could hear the tanks and trucks moving around town. Also, some German soldiers, seeking shelter from the cold, were occupying the floor above us!

Finally, the Germans left. The town had grown quiet. We were in this cellar wondering if they would come back. Should we stay there a little longer or try to return to our home? Hunger convinced us to return. For a day or two, there were no Russians or Germans in town. And then, a small group of Russian soldiers appeared and proclaimed that the Germans had been chased out of town and our region. So, we started to re-adjust to our lives under Soviet rules.

Soon, the Soviets were recruiting people for the war effort. My father, who was still in the age group for recruitment, was afraid that he would be drafted into the Soviet army. With the help of some high-ranking Russian-Jewish officers, he was able to change his age on his identity documents to seven years older, so that he would not be drafted. Our original birth certificates had all been destroyed by the Germans. However, my father had to serve in the local militia, which was fighting the Banderivtsi, Ukrainian partisans who hated the Russians. They would attack the Soviet police and soldiers as they travelled from town to town. One day, when my father was travelling with a group of militia men to one of the villages, they were attacked and my father was almost killed. As he was running, several bullets went through the side of his open coat, just missing his body.

Displaced

We lived in Mielnica from 1944 to 1945. When the war ended in 1945, I went to school, and my studies in Grade 4 were in both Russian and Ukrainian. Then the Soviets proclaimed that this part of Poland would be returned to "Greater Ukraine" and that all citizens with Polish passports had the right to live in Poland proper.

We moved to Katowice, where I attended school for Grade 5, and my studies were now in Polish. After regular school, I attended a cheder that was partially organized by my father, where I studied religious themes.

My father was actively involved in the black market, buying and selling all kinds of products. A Soviet soldier was told that my father dealt in the black market, and he showed up one day with a truckload of prayer shawls, *taleisim*, for sale. He admitted to my father that he had gotten them from one of the concentration camps. My father bought the truckload with the help of some other men from his synagogue and donated everything to the synagogue, except for one *tallis*, which he kept for himself and had until his death.

Our goal was to leave the Soviet-occupied countries and immigrate to Canada, where my mother's brother William (Veve) Kimmel had lived since 1931. In 1946, my father found some smugglers who could get us across the border between Czechoslovakia and the American Occupied Zone of Germany. It was expensive and dangerous. First we had to travel to Prague and wait there for the proper time to cross the border. We stayed there for about two weeks. Then the smugglers came with a covered truck and took us to the border, where we were met by other smugglers who walked us across to the American Zone. Then another covered truck took us to a displaced persons (DP) camp in Bavaria called Pocking, or Pocking-Waldstat. During the war, this place had been a subcamp of the Flossenbürg concentration camp, where forced labourers worked on an airfield and built defences.

The camp was quite large. At one point at least seven thousand people from all over Europe were staying there. We lived in former army barracks, and my family and I stayed in one large room. We received food and clothing from the United Nations Relief and Rehabilitation Administration (UNRRA) and from the American occupying army in Germany.

Everyone in the camp had a goal to go somewhere they could live a normal life. People went to the United States, Canada, Australia and Argentina, and many went to Palestine, which became Israel in 1948, by way of Aliyah Bet — which meant that they had to be smuggled illegally into Palestine. Some of the boats and ships that were caught had to return to their country of embarkation or the passengers were sent to Cyprus, where they were kept in internment camps surrounded by barbed wire. Three of my friends were among the 4,500 Holocaust survivors on board the famous ship the *Exodus*, which in 1947 was stopped from entering Palestine by the British authorities. This situation caused a world outcry and not long after that incident, the State of Israel was established.

For me, there were some very positive things happening in the DP camp. I played on a soccer team and there was an outstanding school, with teachers who had survived the Holocaust as well as teachers from Palestine. The language in school was mainly Hebrew and some Yiddish. The problem was that there were many students from all over Europe who spoke different languages. So it was important to establish a common language, and this ended up being Hebrew. After two years in that school, I became proficient in Hebrew, and I speak it to this very day.

Many envoys, *shlichim*, from different organizations came to establish political and social Zionist groups in our camp. I joined Bnei Akiva, a religious Zionist club. We had meetings where we sang Hebrew songs. It was around this time that my voice started to change and singing became a serious part of my life. At the age of thirteen, I was singing in choirs and sang solos in the DP camp. We also learned about Zionism and Jewish history, and we read biographies about Jews who had immigrated to pre-state Israel.

Most of the people in the DP camps wanted to go to Eretz Yisrael, the Land of Israel. Some of the *shlichim* who came to the DP camps in 1946, 1947 and the beginning of 1948 were members of the Zionist military organizations, the Haganah and the Irgun. They came to teach young people in the DP camps the military arts. Of course, this was illegal, as the British were still occupying Palestine under the UN mandate. But these envoys began preparing young people to become soldiers as soon as they could reach Palestine. They recruited youngsters from the age of sixteen and taught them how to use a gun, a knife and a stick called a *makeil* in Hebrew. Although I was only fourteen, I was big for my age, and I was recruited along with a group of older boys to learn how to be a soldier — how to march and use a gun.

My parents were in constant contact with Uncle Veve in Canada, who ended up sponsoring us to immigrate. When my parents told me that we were going to Canada, I refused. I wanted to go to Palestine. We argued and my mother and I cried. I begged them to let me go. I remember my parents saying to me that since we survived the Holocaust together, we must stay together.

We had to travel to the Canadian Consulate in Amberg, Germany, to receive our visas for Canada. The people there were rude, and we felt that they were prejudiced toward Jews and made the process of getting the right documentation and medical exams very difficult.

Our trip to Canada was postponed for six months because of a stye on my father's eyelid — something that disappeared within a few days.

Finally, in July 1948, we travelled by train to Genoa, Italy, and boarded the Greek ship *Nea Hellas*, headed for Canada. On board, my mother suffered terribly from seasickness and thought that she would die. One day, she called me to her sickbed and told me not to forget her and to tell my uncle Veve that she loved him and that she had been looking forward to seeing him after so many years, but that it was not to be. She started to cry and asked if she would be buried at sea. Of course, she began to feel better as soon as the ship docked in Halifax, Nova Scotia. Immediately after arriving, we boarded a train for Montreal.

A New Beginning

I must declare that, actually, my "real" life began when we reached Canada in 1948. Everything before that was bad dreams and awful memories. Although, for the first few years in Canada, life was quite difficult.

When we arrived in Montreal, we were greeted by Uncle Veve at the train station. He drove us to Perth, Ontario, where he lived with my aunt Lily and my cousins, Earl and Miriam. After about a week or so, my father asked my uncle to drive us back to Montreal so that my parents could find work and rent a place to live. I stayed in Perth for several weeks while my parents were gone. Aunt Lily did not like my name, Fishel — it didn't sound very Canadian! — so she "christened" me Philip, the name I'm referred to 50 per cent of the time to this day.

We were survivors of the Holocaust and immigrants in a new country, and we could not speak English or French. My parents rented the third floor of a triplex in Montreal. It was difficult in those days to find a flat without paying five hundred dollars in key money. We had arrived with only fifteen US dollars. So my father had to borrow money from the Hebrew Free Loan Association, which Uncle Veve guaranteed, to pay this key money.

My father got a job in a rubber factory at a weekly salary of fifteen dollars. My mother worked as a dress finisher in a factory at fifteen to seventeen dollars a week. As for me, I wanted to get a job to help out at home, but my father would not hear of it. I had to go to school. My mother also had her own little business that she ran in the evenings and on weekends. My uncle Veve was an egg distributor and sold eggs to wholesalers and stores. Every week he would deliver one or two cases of eggs to our house, which my mother bought from him. She would then sell to our neighbours. I was designated as her helper in this venture, climbing the multiple stairs to deliver the eggs.

In the summer of 1948, after settling into our new premises, in what today is referred to as the "Le Plateau" area, I remember passing by Fletcher's Field, a park between Park Avenue and Esplanade Avenue, where some youngsters were playing soccer. Since I had played organized soccer in the DP camp in Germany, I ended up joining a junior team of immigrant kids just like me.

At the end of August 1948, my father said that we had to go to the Talmud Torah to register me for school. Half the curriculum there was Jewish studies and the rest was secular studies. We arrived at the school and met a Mr. Beutel, who interviewed me, saying that my knowledge of Jewish subjects was very good but not speaking English was a problem. He added that we would have to pay school fees. My father explained that we were newly arrived immigrants and had just started working, and that as soon as he started to earn a better salary he would pay, on a monthly basis, until the fees were all paid up. Mr. Beutel said that this was not acceptable and referred us to a yeshiva just down the street.

At the Yeshiva Merkaz Hatorah, we met the principal, Rabbi Leib Baron, who interviewed me. He was satisfied with my studies to this point and told me to come back to school in September. When my father asked him about the school fees, he said something I will never forget: He told my father that he could pay as much as he was able to, whenever he could. I attended that school for four years and graduated high school there. Due to a wonderful and inspiring teacher, Mr. Paul, I acquired a lasting love of poetry and literature.

When school started in September of that first year, I had no problem with the Hebrew studies, but since I did not speak English, I was not at the same level as the others in the class when it came to secular subjects, except for in mathematics.

After three months, when I could converse a little in English, Mr. Paul, who had taken an interest in my progress, decided to include me in a class project, writing an essay on a variety of subjects. For me, he chose three simple topics, one of which was "hats." And so I went home and wrote an essay, which started with the words and spelling as follows: "In the velt [Yiddish for world] is many heds." Somehow, one of my classmates got a hold of the essay and read it out loud to the class. To my chagrin and embarrassment, there was great laughter in the classroom!

Within six months I became more proficient in the language and had arrived at the same level as everyone else. My fellow students, however, never forgot my essay. For the next four years, whenever we had a conflict or disagreement of any sort, they would bring up the first sentence of that essay and sing it to me to the tune of "Old MacDonald Had a Farm."

After graduating in 1952, my parents wanted me to continue my education and to have a profession of some sort. Stupidly, I refused and worked mostly in menial jobs. However, I read a lot of wonderful writers in those years, both of poetry and prose — Keats, Shelley and Browning, plus most of Shakespeare's plays, Dickens, Tolstoy, Pushkin, Voltaire and Sartre. In Yiddish, I read most of the works of Sholem Aleichem, Peretz, J.J. Segal, and Sholem Asch. I also had, and still have, an interest in reading books about philosophy, political science and history.

Although we were thankful for being allowed to come to Canada and to start a new life in a democratic and free country, there was a dark side. The government of Canada had not at all been welcoming to Jews, and many officials were slightly antisemitic. Yet, since we were used to so much worse, overt antisemitism, this was of little concern.

Our relationship with the Jewish community was of much greater concern. It seemed that people had no interest in hearing the survival stories of the thousands of Jewish immigrants who had arrived in Canada after the war. Jewish people in Montreal did not want to have any relationship with survivors, and it was very difficult for us to integrate into the local Jewish community. We were subjected to being called "greeners," "mockies" and other insulting names. I can recall many times being called these names. This was very hurtful, especially after having gone through the horrible experience of Nazi oppression.

Even in the Jewish school, the yeshiva I attended, where there were only Jewish students, in the four years I studied there, no one ever asked me how I had survived the Holocaust.

It is important to note that this attitude existed in Israel, too. Even Prime Minister David Ben-Gurion stated, "Among the survivors of the German camps were people who would not have been alive were they not what they were — hard, mean and selfish — and what they have been through erased every remaining good quality from them." Later on, Ben-Gurion apologized for these remarks, according to Yad Vashem's chief historian, Dina Porat. Nothing was simple in how we were treated. At another time after the war, on visiting a DP camp, Ben-Gurion said of survivors, "The majority are precious Jews, precious Zionists with deep Zionist instincts, ready to undergo again all these troubles — if this is what Zionism needs — with fervour for unity and fervour for the survival of the Jewish people."

Nevertheless, regardless of the variety of attitudes and beliefs people held about us, we overcame it all. We survived and prospered and integrated into society wherever we lived.

Circles of Life

In the early 1950s, my cousin Miriam Kimmel introduced me to Beatrice Gurevitch, and in 1955 we were married. We rented a modest three-and-a-half-room apartment on Barclay Street in the Côte-des-Neiges district of Montreal. Beatrice became pregnant in 1957, and we were gifted with our first wonderful son, Billy. In 1959, our beautiful daughter, Carrie, was born. In 1963, when we were expecting our next child, we bought a small bungalow in Chomedey, Laval, north of Montreal. In 1964, another blessing came along with the birth of our son Loren.

In the early 1960s, I started to take singing lessons from Professor Bernard Diamant, who was one of the greatest voice teachers in Montreal. Unfortunately, I only studied with him for less than a year. At the same time, I studied music and theory with a teacher from the music school Vincent-d'Indy. But I had to stop my studies because music lessons were expensive and I was earning very little money and, at the time, had young children to support.

I had such a passion for performing ever since I was a teenager in the DP camp, but when we first arrived in Montreal, I sang only at parties and at the yeshiva, where I could conduct services on Shabbat and the holidays. My parents loved to hear me sing but were not enthusiastic about me taking lessons in voice and music to establish a career in singing. I had wanted to have a career as an opera singer, but since there were few opera companies at that time in Canada, I would have had to travel to the United States or Europe. The reality was that I simply could not afford to do this. So I decided to do some professional concerts from time to time and to sing in the synagogue choirs in the Montreal area in order to make a few extra dollars, a pastime that lasted for about forty-five years. Part of that time, until 2014, I was also a cantor for the High Holidays. Occasionally, I was fortunate enough to be accompanied by a choir. One of the greatest joys I had as a cantor was the year my son Billy and his wife, Terri, who both have marvellous voices, joined me in singing the High Holiday services.

In 1971, my dearest friend Sidney Zoltak, who was a member of the Dora Wasserman Yiddish Theatre, asked me to join this wonderful group, which put on Yiddish productions of musicals and dramas. I started a non-professional theatrical career that lasted some forty years and, to a lesser extent, is still continuing. We performed plays by some of the greatest classical Yiddish writers, such as Sholem Aleichem, Peretz and Singer. The role that probably gave me the most gratification was that of Tevya in the production *Fiddler on the Roof.* I played the part in Yiddish with Dora's group and in English with the Lyric Theatre.

Dora Wasserman was a great influence on my artistic life and my life in general. Dora was so much more than the founder and director of the Yiddish Theatre in Montreal — she was a teacher, a mentor, an advisor and a trusted friend. She instilled in me a love for the theatre and taught me the skills of the actor. She made me a better singer and, I believe, a better person. I will never forget this extraordinary person who came into my life.

~

In 1962, I was fed up with my job at a supermarket and desperately wanted to go into business. With the help of my lifelong friend, Reuben Richman, and another partner, I started a new company called Bell

Metals. We were in the scrap metal business. The partnership didn't last long, but I continued in the scrap business, and later in the buying and selling of new and used steel, for twenty years. In 1982, I decided to leave the steel business to get into the auctioneering business, and I worked with a local auctioneer for ten years. In 1992, I made the decision to open a new company, Nova Auctioneers, with my partner, the late Yosie Deitcher, an old school friend. The company is still in existence.

My father, who had been in business as a food distributor, was forced to leave the work when he started to develop heart problems, and he joined me in my business ventures. Sadly, in 1968, my father had a heart attack while he was in our office. I was visiting a customer nearby when my father called and asked me to come back to the office immediately because he wasn't feeling well. I rushed to the office, put him in the car and sped to the Jewish General Hospital. He passed away several hours later.

My father was very special to me. He loved me, of course, and I loved him, too, but there was more. Since I never had any siblings, he was my mentor, advisor, confidant and my best friend. He was involved in all aspects of my life, from discussing business issues to the education of my children. Yet, I never realized just how much I would miss him.

About two or three years before my father died, we wanted to have another child, but it was not happening. Interestingly, a few months after my father's death, Beatrice became pregnant with our fourth child. In 1969, she gave birth to a beautiful boy, whom we named Baruch, after my father, and in English we called him Brian.

After my father's death, my mother lived alone on Bourette Street for several years. During those years, she would vacation in Miami Beach during the winter. On one vacation, she met a gentleman named Isaac Finkelstein, from New York, who was staying at the same hotel. When I met Isaac, I found him to be nice, religious and knowledgeable, and a little like my father. My mother and Isaac married in 1973 and lived together in Florida for the next five years. Unfortunately, Isaac had heart problems and died in 1979.

My mother lived in the condo they had bought in Miami Beach for more than twenty years and I came to visit her at least once or twice a year. Every time I went there, she insisted that I perform a concert for her friends and neighbours. Two weeks prior to my arrival, posters and notices would be placed in the elevators and in the lobby, announcing the time and date of the concert! The concerts took place in a room in my mother's building that was designed to hold thirty people but there would be at least seventy people by the time my performance began, with lots of people standing in the back. Each time I performed there, my mother would walk around the room, nodding her head, left and right, and accepting congratulations from the audience. Sometimes I had to ask her to sit down so that I could start the concert!

Eventually, in the 1990s, as her health started to decline, my mother moved back to Montreal to be closer to our family. My mother became quite ill and was diagnosed with stomach cancer. She spent several weeks at St. Mary's Hospital. Her health declined each day until the day before Yom Kippur in 1995, when we received a call from the hospital that she was not doing well and that it was just a matter of days.

On the day of Yom Kippur, during the afternoon break from synagogue services, we received another call from the hospital, saying that death was imminent and could happen within hours or minutes. Since I was the cantor conducting the services and had to return to the synagogue to sing the Ne'ilah service, the last prayer of the day, a decision had to be made on whether to return to the synagogue or go to the hospital. My son Loren suggested a solution: He would go to the hospital, the rest of the family would return to the synagogue, and immediately after the services we would all go to the hospital. So, we went back to the synagogue and just when I was in the midst of the Ne'ilah prayer, I saw Loren coming into the synagogue. I knew it was over. Finishing the prayers was extremely difficult and emotional. On Yom Kippur day, in 1995, my mother passed away at the age of ninety.

~

In 1989, Beatrice and I decided to separate. After living on my own for a few years, two of my good friends arranged a blind date for me to meet a woman named Lorna Gerson. On April 11, 1992, I met Lorna at her flat. We sat and talked for hours, and I found her interesting and intelligent. Lorna is smart, funny, beautiful and has a *guteh neshomeh*, a good soul, and I don't know what I would have done without her. She is the love of my life and my best friend. She has fulfilled my heart, and I feel very lucky.

On September 12, 1993, we got married in an apartment that I was renting on Melrose Avenue in Montreal. Our wedding was a fantastic and unusual event. We had over seventy guests who ate, sang and danced in a very small space to the music of the one-man band Yaacov Sassi until late at night. Without question, one of the best moves of my life was to marry Lorna. Her only fault is that she can still stand my crazy shtick! When I went through my health crisis in 2015, I don't know if I would have survived if not for Lorna's love, help, determination and insistence that things would get better. I am sure that I will never be able to thank her enough for what she did for me during this crisis.

I am lucky to be surrounded by so much family, so much joy — my son Brian; my son Billy and his wife, Terri Budovitch, and their children, Zack, Phoebe and Katie; my daughter, Carrie, and her children, Michael (Mikey) and Rachel; and my son Loren and his wife, Francesca Astengo, and their children, Luca and Chiara.

Our Ukrainian Families

After the liberation, as we were wandering from country to country, we continued to have contact with the Ukrainian families who had saved us. We sent them letters and parcels until the mid-1950s. Then the letters started to come back to us, and we lost contact with them. We had no idea what happened to them.

Then, in 2006, a wonderful and memorable event occurred. My cousin Eva, her husband, Fred, and their children, Lisa and Mark, along with their spouses, visited the village of Babince, where we had been hidden, and found a sister of Yulia Kravchuk, the wife of the farmer, Nikolai. Yulia's sister was ninety-nine years old and blind. She told them that the family had moved away many years ago. Kravchuk had had a poor harvest season and found a job in the coal mines of Ukraine. His sister-in-law gave my cousins the addresses and phone numbers where the remaining family — the farmer's two daughters and their families — now lived. And so, after many years, communication was re-established with our Ukrainian families.

Upon returning to Canada, Lisa and her husband, Michael, took the initiative to have the Kravchuk and Kukurudza families designated as Righteous Among the Nations. This honour is bestowed by Yad Vashem, the World Holocaust Remembrance Center, upon non-Jews who saved Jewish lives during those terrible years. It took approximately eighteen months before the museum finally accepted our application for these families to be recognized and honoured.

In 2009, the Israeli Embassy in Kiev invited our families and the children and grandchildren of the Kravchuk and Kukurudza families to come to the ceremonies at the embassy to receive the medals and certificates on behalf of their parents and grandparents who had all since died. I travelled with my wife, Lorna, and my cousin Eva and her husband, Fred.

We were asked to arrive at the embassy on the morning of October 1, 2009. There, we were escorted to a large room where other Ukrainian families were also being honoured. The last time Eva and I had seen the two daughters of Mr. and Mrs. Kravchuk was sixty-five years earlier, when Yaroslava and I were close to eleven years old, Irina was nine and Eva was almost five. When we entered the room, we looked around, and then I pointed to the group sitting on the opposite side of the room and said to Lorna that I thought this was "our family." As we approached them, Irina and Yaroslava stood up and started to walk toward us, recognizing us as well.

After sixty-five years, the impact of this emotional event was something we will remember for the rest of our lives.

We kissed, we hugged, we cried and we laughed. We were all so overcome by emotion. We were introduced to Yaroslava and Irina's children and grandchildren, and Maria and Vladimir, the grandchildren of Mr. and Mrs. Kukurudza.

Every year, the Israeli Embassy in Kiev combines this ceremony for the righteous with an annual memorial day for the close to thirty-four thousand Jews killed by the Nazis in Babi Yar, just outside of Kiev, in 1941. The ceremony took place in a synagogue and was attended by various dignitaries such as Kateryna Yushchenko, the wife of the then president of Ukraine, who spoke eloquently; the ambassador of Israel to Ukraine; the mayor; church officials; and leaders of the Jewish community of Kiev. After the official speeches were over, all the Ukrainian families received their medals and certificates — Yaroslava and Irina on behalf of their parents, and Maria and Vladimir on behalf of their grandfather Mikhail Kukurudza. My cousin Eva spoke, and

I sang *El Maleh Rachamim*. It was a beautiful ceremony and it was recorded and shown on the six o'clock news later that day.

When it ended, we invited the two families to stay with us at our hotel. The embassy had sent return train tickets to all the Ukrainian families who were being honoured that day, so they were supposed to return to their towns that evening, but we didn't want that to happen. That evening, we all went to a Ukrainian restaurant, where we consumed a lot of food and about a barrel of vodka. We sang and drank until very late that night. I went up to the trio that was playing music and sang pretty much every song I knew. The restaurant had to throw us out at one in the morning!

The next day we hired a mini-bus and a guide who spoke Ukrainian and English, and all fifteen of us spent the day visiting the sights of Kiev, which they had never seen before. As we brought them to the train station later in the day, it was again very emotional and difficult to say our goodbyes. I've stayed in touch with the families, keeping up a regular correspondence, but I never went back to Babince or Mielnica. I still have bad dreams about my time there.

Epilogue

In October 2011, Lorna and I visited Yad Vashem in Israel and saw the names of these courageous and brave people displayed on the Wall of the Righteous, for eternity. These were people who risked their lives and the lives of their children in order to save another human being.

When I think of the human tragedy of the Holocaust, the lost six million Jews, and among them one and a half million children, I think about how Eva and I could have been among those children if it had not been for our wonderful Ukrainian families.

Photographs

Wedding photo of Fishel's parents, Rachel and Baruch Goldig. Mielnica, Poland, circa 1930.

1

2

3

1 Fishel at three years old. Mielnica, 1936.

2 Fishel's maternal grandmother, Tauba Kimmel, before the war. Date unknown.

3 Fishel, age five, with his uncle Hershel Goldig. Mielnica, circa 1938.

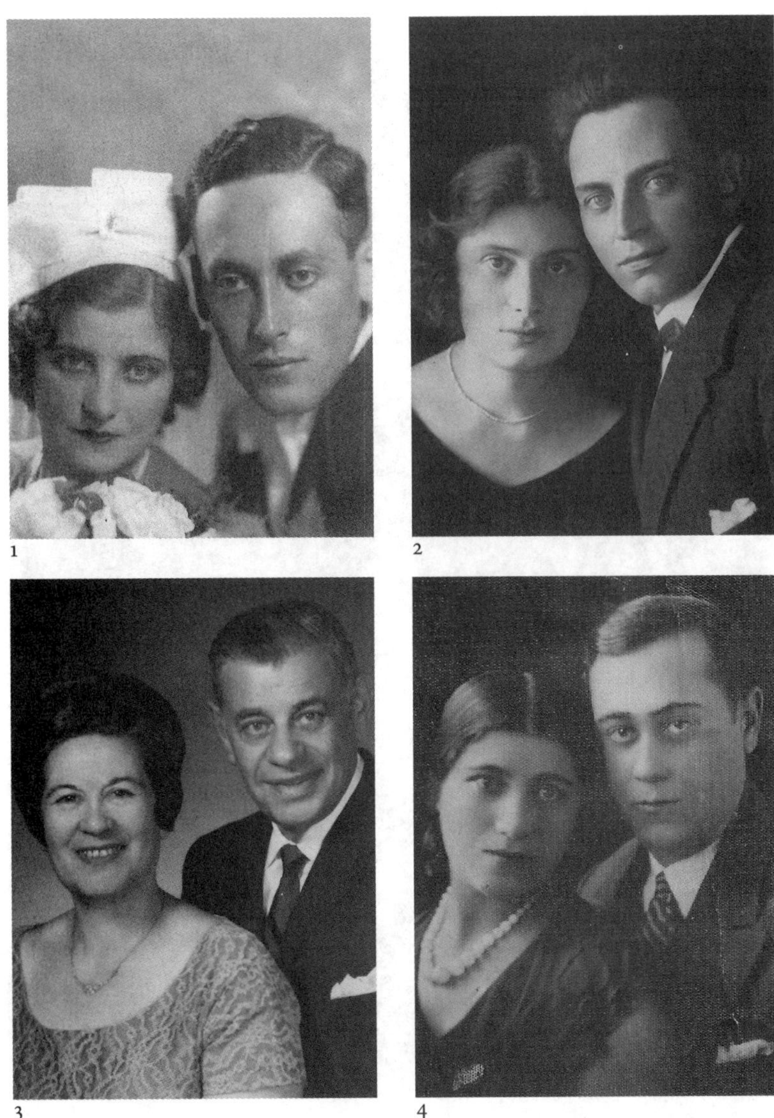

1 Wedding photo of Aunt Mina and Uncle Leon Deutsch. Lwów, Poland, 1938.

2 Aunt Zlate and Uncle Mendel Schaffer, who were killed in the Holocaust. Mielnica, Poland, date unknown.

3 Aunt Lily and Uncle Veve Kimmel, who sponsored Fishel and his family to come to Canada. Montreal, date unknown.

4 Aunt Rivka and Uncle Issie, who were killed in the Holocaust. Mielnica, date unknown.

Fishel, age six, with his parents in the last photo taken before the war. Mielnica, 1939.

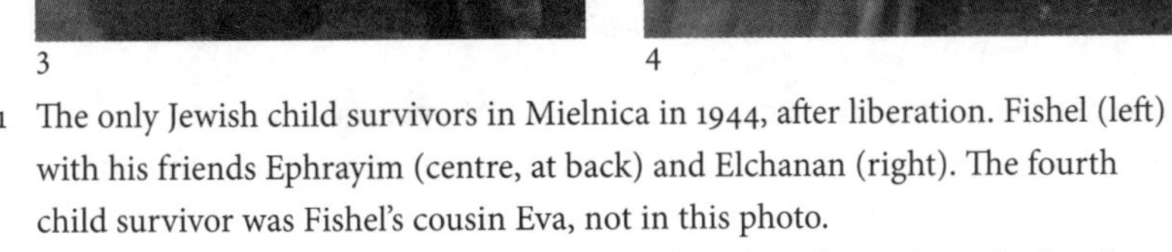

1 The only Jewish child survivors in Mielnica in 1944, after liberation. Fishel (left) with his friends Ephrayim (centre, at back) and Elchanan (right). The fourth child survivor was Fishel's cousin Eva, not in this photo.

2 Fishel (back row, second from the left) with friends at the Pocking displaced persons (DP) camp. Germany, circa 1946.

3 Fishel with his father, Baruch, on the occasion of his bar mitzvah. Pocking, Germany, 1946.

4 Fishel's parents living in barracks in the DP camp, circa 1946.

1

2

1 Fishel and his parents on their arrival in Canada. Montreal, 1948.

2 A yearbook photo of Fishel (seated, third from the right), with rabbis, teachers and classmates learning Torah at Yeshiva Merkaz Hatorah. Montreal, circa 1950.

Fishel in his cantorial attire. Montreal, 1982.

1

2

1 Fishel (left) performing in the play *Andorra* with his son Billy (right). Montreal, 1982. Photo courtesy of Ron Diamond.

2 Fishel in the role of Tevye in *Fiddler on the Roof*. Montreal, 1991. Photo courtesy of Burney Lieberman.

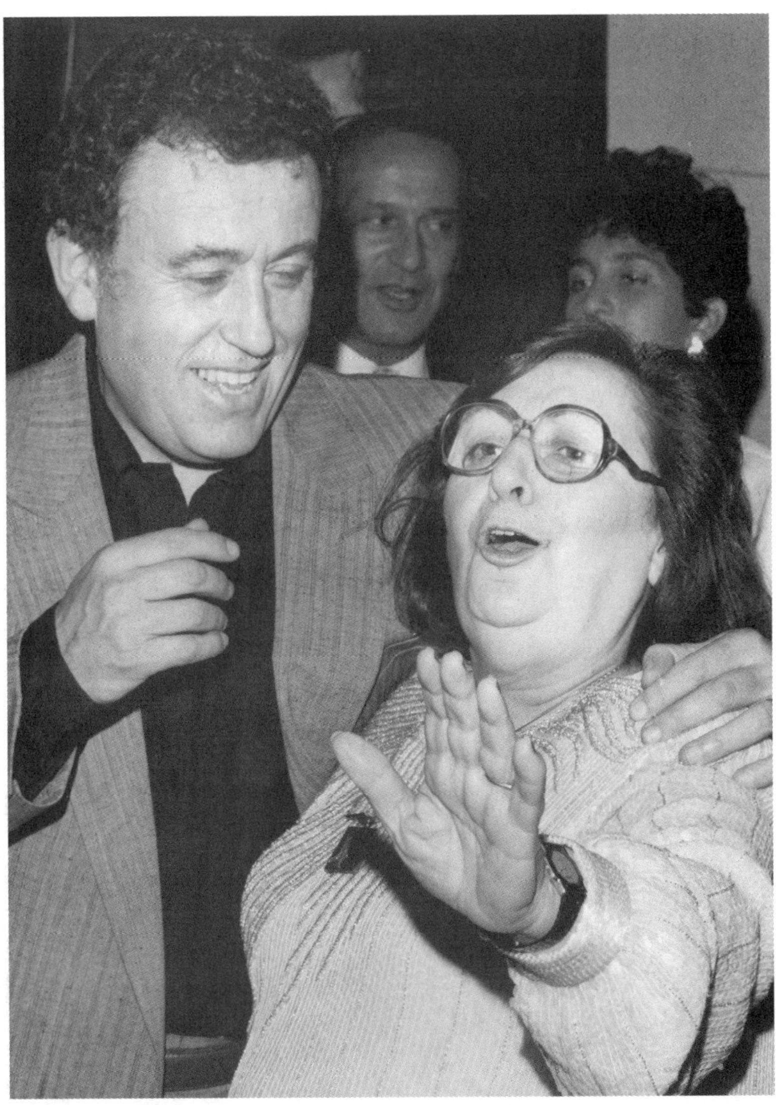

Fishel with mentor Dora Wasserman. Montreal, 1987. Photo courtesy of Ron Diamond.

1

2

1 Fishel and his wife, Lorna. Montreal, circa 1990s.

2 The Goldig children and grandchildren. Montreal, 2011.

1

2

3

1 The only photo Fishel has of his rescuer, Nikolai Kravchuk. Date and place unknown.

2 Maria and Vladimir, grandchildren of the Kukurudza family, at the ceremony for the Righteous Among the Nations. Kiev, 2009.

3 Fishel's cousin Eva Andermann (right) with the daughters of Nikolai and Yulia Kravchuk, Yaroslava (left) and Irina (centre), at the Righteous Among the Nations ceremony. Kiev, 2009.

1

2

1 Irina (second from right) and Yaroslava (far right) with their family members before receiving the honour of Righteous Among the Nations. Kiev, 2009.

2 Members of the Ukrainian families at a restaurant after the Righteous Among the Nations ceremony. Kiev, 2009.

1

2

1 Fishel and Lorna with cousins Eva and Fred Andermann and their extended Ukrainian family at the Babi Yar memorial. Kiev, 2009.

2 Fishel at Yad Vashem indicating the names of the Kravchuk and Kukurudza families on the Wall of the Righteous. Jerusalem, Israel, 2011.

Fishel Goldig, 2019.

More Stories of Rescue

The thirteen stories featured in this section are excerpted from some of the many Holocaust survivor memoirs published by the Azrieli Foundation. Each narrative expresses important aspects of the experience of rescue and survival, and adds to the diversity of experiences in different countries during the Holocaust. At great personal risk, those who sheltered and helped Jews did so for various motivations and lengths of time, and the relationships between survivor and rescuer also varied after the war — some stayed in touch, connecting as family members, while others lost contact. For some survivors, especially child survivors, finding their rescuers after the war was impossible; and for some rescuers, especially those living in Communist countries after the war, staying in touch with people who had moved to Western countries was complicated. Lastly, as some of these stories show, not all rescuers were honoured as Righteous Among the Nations, for a wide variety of factors: lack of the documentation required by Yad Vashem, disinterest on the part of rescuer or survivor, or the survivor's inability to find those who had helped them during the war. All together, these memoir excerpts present a record of rescue and survival during the Holocaust, giving the authors and readers a way to honour and remember the actions taken by rescuers.

Tenuous Threads
Judy Abrams

Judy Abrams was born in Budapest, Hungary, in 1937. Nazi Germany occupied Hungary in March 1944, and two months later, Hungarian Jews outside of Budapest began to be rounded up and sent to Auschwitz-Birkenau and other Nazi camps. By April 1944, Judy's father had obtained false identity documents for Judy so that she could pass as an "Aryan" Catholic girl, Ilona Papp, and Judy hid under this identity in a convent with Ursuline nuns in a village near Budapest. The persecution of Jews escalated in the city of Budapest that summer, with Jews forced into segregated Jewish houses; that fall, members of the new Arrow Cross Party government[1] perpetrated anti-Jewish violence, killing thousands. As violence and deportations increased, even the convent was no longer considered safe. Mária Babar, a non-Jewish friend of Judy's parents who had helped place Judy at the convent, arrived at the convent to help.

---

1 The Arrow Cross Party were far-right extremists who assumed control of Hungary from October 15, 1944, to March 28, 1945, with assistance from the Nazis. The Arrow Cross regime confined approximately 70,000 Jews in a ghetto in Budapest and instigated the murder of tens of thousands of others through violent roundups, forced labour, shootings, deportations and death marches.

It was fall when my daily penitent pilgrimages on the red gravel paths of the convent garden came to an end with the sudden arrival of Mária. My parents had entrusted me to her care when they left Budapest on a journey that eventually led them to the Bergen-Belsen concentration camp. Mother Superior had contacted Mária and asked her to take me with her to Budapest, where I would be safer. The German SS, Hitler's black-uniformed security force, had been alerted to the presence of Jews in convents and monasteries. They were committing atrocities against the Jews they discovered and brutally punishing those who dared to shelter them. We were to return to Budapest by train the next day, packing only a small suitcase with the most essential belongings and my smiling celluloid doll, Anikó. Whatever else my parents had given to the nuns on my behalf would be lost forever.

I regretted leaving the convent and the familiar garden surrounded by lush green fields and orchards. I would miss the white stucco house with its narrow corridors where the nuns whooshed by in their dark habits, the wooden beads of their rosaries clicking at every hurried step. I would no longer sit in awe in the chapel on Sunday mornings, lulled by the music of the liturgy, admiring the intricate embroidery on the back of the cassock of the priest officiating at the altar, inhaling the perfume of incense wafted in silver censers by the village boys whose white smocks were bordered in lace like the tablecloths of the home I had to forget.

The train ride to Budapest was very different from the one that had brought me to the country. Then, I had sat comfortably in a compartment accompanied by the sister who elicited a respectful "Praised be Jesus Christ!" from passengers and officials alike as they made the sign of the cross, touching their foreheads and shoulders in the form of a cross. Now, we stood in the aisle among peasant women in ample gathered skirts of many colours. Everyone carried some luggage. There were bulging suitcases fastened with string and baskets of food containing fat rods of salami and giant wheels of country bread wrapped in checkered cloth. There were even chickens and geese, their feet tied, tucked in baskets, clucking and quacking all the way to the city. I held onto Mária's hand with my left hand and clutched the beads of my rosary in my right, secure in the earthly protection of one woman and the heavenly intervention of the other.

It was late 1944 and World War II was drawing to a close, but Hungary continued to support the losing German army. Ferenc Szálasi, the fascist dictator of the country, was still enthusiastically helping the effort to eradicate the Jews of Europe. His loyal troops, the Arrow Cross brigade (Nyilas), assisted the German SS in rounding up Jews and sending most of them on death marches into Greater Germany. The brigade, a haven for easily influenced young men, roamed the streets of Budapest arresting Jews who transgressed the imposed curfew, failed to wear the compulsory yellow star or possessed false "Aryan" documents. They relished wielding their power over women, children and old people, proudly sporting their emblem — an armband marked with intersecting arrows that formed the arrow cross — as a symbol of allegiance to Szálasi, Hitler and death.

By the time Mária and I took the train from Pincehely to Budapest nearly all the Jews in the Hungarian countryside had been deported and Budapest was the only capital in Europe with any considerable Jewish population. These Jews managed to exist in buildings designated as Jewish houses, marked with Stars of David. The apartments were shared by several families, mostly made up of women, children and the elderly since able-bodied men had already been sent in special *Munkaszolgálat*, forced labour detachments to assist the army at the Eastern Front of the war.

How much did I know about all this? Probably very little, perhaps some fragments I had overheard. As Mária and I stood in the cramped train, I was also ignorant of the fate of my parents, now in Bergen-Belsen, the concentration camp in Germany where Anne Frank had spent her last days. I was fortunate to be sheltered by Mária, my grandmother, Nagyi, and my mother's sister, Aunt Marika, who were already in Mária's tiny studio apartment when we arrived. Mária had rescued them when the woman who had agreed (for a price) to shelter them in her home on the outskirts of Budapest became frightened and made them leave her house in the middle of the night.

In the crowded apartment Mária surrounded me with love and even playfulness that made up for my grandmother's stern silence and Aunt Marika's quiet sadness. I don't remember what their new names were, but they too had written proof attesting to their "Aryan" origin. We never talked of the past but lived in a present fraught with dangerous secrets. My grandmother tried to uphold high standards of behaviour, order and cleanliness. War and persecution didn't lessen her expectations. She still reminded me firmly not to use a dishtowel to wipe my hands when hand towels were available.

It was Mária I loved best. She was affectionate and funny and took me to church with her on Sundays at the bottom of Naphegy (Sun Mountain), where we lived. I had grown to relish the perfumed incense and the melodic refrains of the Latin mass. My grandmother frowned on the daily Rosary sessions I shared with Mária. Outward manifestation of any faith seemed to her to be in bad taste, the transgression of a personal code of conduct. This included my holy beads. She held them at arm's length if I left them lying around, as though they were not quite clean.

While hiding in the apartment of their family friend Mária, Judy continued to be at risk. She was in the middle of a war zone where groups of Arrow Cross members were still searching for and murdering Jews. During this time, Judy, her family members and Mária took shelter in the basement of the building they were hiding in.

From Christmas 1944 until mid-February 1945 we seldom emerged, miraculously safe while the building fell to pieces above us. In the basement, Auntie Superintendent and I had become great friends. She was a reliable dispenser of hard candy, even during the Siege of

Budapest. Years later history would testify that World War II was drawing to a close at that time. I later found out that Naphegy, where we lived, was the last hold-out of the German and Hungarian forces against the Soviet Red Army. As the Soviets closed in, the sound of their arrival was deafening. Electricity had failed almost as soon as we entered the cellar, where we lived mostly by the light of candles and petroleum lamps. The glass chimneys set above round containers of petroleum protected the flickering flames of felt wicks and channelled smoke and foul smells up toward the exposed beams of the ceiling.

I recall two memorable occasions when we climbed the stairs into the light of day from the dimly lit cellar. The first must have been in mid-January. The dirty snow was littered with rubble and fragments of broken glass from the shattered house. We stood with our backs to the stucco building, which by then had been battered by cannon, bombs and grenades. My eyes — and those of the frightened collection of men and women obliged to leave the dubious safety of our shelter — were riveted on a small group of young men facing us menacingly. Somebody had reported that there were Jews in the building, hidden by some of the tenants. It was their purpose to find them.

The men did not wear uniforms. I don't remember if they carried weapons, but the dreaded Arrow Cross armbands were intimidating enough. Numerous accounts confirm that even while the Soviet troops approached Budapest to finally defeat the Germans, while the city lay in ruins and the bridges spanning the Danube were destroyed, these gangs still roamed the streets to capture any remaining Jews. In the winter of 1944, Jewish victims were lined up on the banks of the Danube and machine gunned until they disappeared into the icy waters. The trains carrying Jews to foreign concentration camps were no longer rumbling, yet the Arrow Cross continued to enact their own version of the "Final Solution to the Jewish Question."

In spite of my recently acquired faith and firm belief in my new identity, there must have been a sudden apprehension that somewhere underneath Ilona Papp was a different and endangered person. I felt the terror of my grandmother and my aunt, and the anger of Mária who hovered close to us. In spite of their proximity, I remember standing alone in my grey winter coat with its blue lined hood. I had inherited it from my cousin Zsuzsa, who always looked particularly well-dressed and never wore out her clothes. The occasional hand-me-downs from her were very special. I loved the grey coat, but suddenly felt awkward in its bulk. I felt clumsy and vulnerable as the young men ("hoodlums" Mária called them in secret) examined the papers that were supposed to prove our "Aryan" origin. Slowly, one by one. My aunt and grandmother were given long, piercing stares as their new names were verified. A sigh of relief, when the documents were handed back without comment. My grandmother's icy blue eyes and my aunt's elegant profile aroused no suspicion. It was my turn.

"This birth certificate seems very new," one of them commented.

"Of course," my grandmother spoke up with authority born out of habit and desperation, "in other times, we did not have to carry around our documents to prove who we were…." (Did she add, "to every stranger"?) One of the men looked at me too carefully and conferred with his colleagues.

"The child looks Jewish," he pronounced with disdain.

The lump of dread in the pit of my stomach is a clear memory. I remember standing very still and separate, waiting…. And then, Auntie Superintendent's voice boomed over the sporadic gunfire around us.

"Shame on you! This child is a devout Catholic. She prays more than you, you punk!"

In spite of the sounds of battle, silence descended on the panic-stricken band of survivors from the shelter. (I later found out that most of them were Jews in hiding.) There was a long, long silence until my papers were wordlessly handed back to Nagyi. I was saved by the beads.

Many decades later, after her mother's death in 1984, Judy thinks back to her mother's sacrifice.

I know she did love me when I was small. "Before you were born, I knew you'd be a girl, a Judit," she'd say. She copied my first words in a scrapbook that survived the war in Hungary and accompanied us to Canada. She also kept the poems she had written to me during the year we were separated, she in Bergen-Belsen and I first in the convent and later in Mária's apartment. She often told me about the cold night in Bergen-Belsen when she gave up her blanket to a little girl whose name was Judit like mine, offering it in the hope that others would give me, who was then so far from her, a warm cover when I needed one. Her sacrifice seemed to work; thanks to the nuns and our friend Mária, I did survive. I often wondered whether I'd have been ready to do what she had.

Mária Babar-Kennedy was honoured as Righteous Among the Nations in 1994.

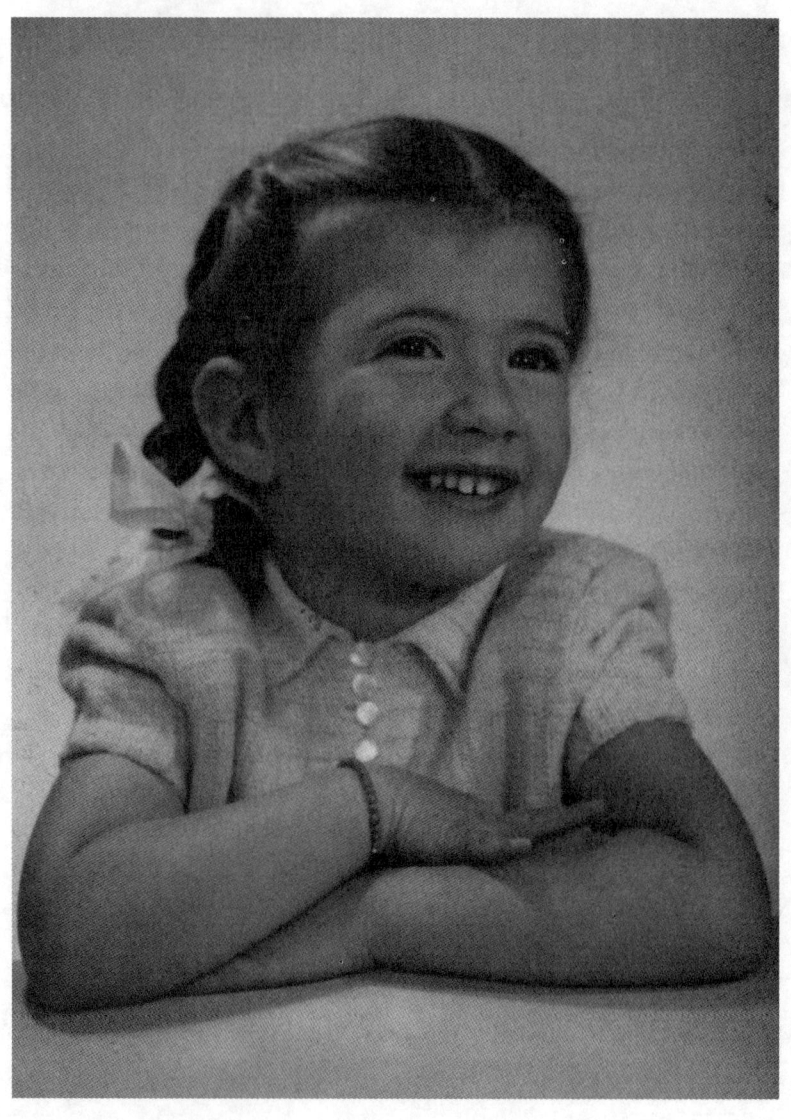

Judy at five years old. Budapest, Hungary, 1942.

1 Judy (centre) sitting beside Mária Babar (second from the right), who helped her hide at the Ursuline convent in Pincehely, Hungary, in 1944.

2 Judy, standing second from the right, with Mária and other girls at the convent in Pincehely, 1944.

3 Judy and the Mother Superior of the convent. Pincehely, 1944.

4 Judy (right) with Mária, now Mária Babar-Kennedy, on the day that Mária was honoured as Righteous Among the Nations by Yad Vashem. California, 1994.

The Hidden Package
Claire Baum

Claire Baum was born in Rotterdam, the Netherlands, in 1936. During the Nazi occupation of the Netherlands, Claire's parents decided that Claire and her younger sister, Ollie, needed to be hidden with non-Jewish families to be kept safe from the roundups and deportations of Dutch Jews. Pauw Wielaard, a friend of Claire's father, was active in the Dutch Resistance and tried to find safe families for the sisters to stay with. The sisters were first sent to live with the Duchene family, until the family decided that hiding the girls was too risky because neighbours were suspicious that the girls were Jewish. They were then sent to a woman named Nel Van Woudenberg, whom they called Tante (aunt) Nel. Claire and Ollie lived with Tante Nel for two years.

In the spring of 1943, it was extremely difficult and dangerous to find us another home to hide in. Most Jewish people were either already hiding in Christian homes or had been sent to a concentration camp. Oom (uncle) Pauw didn't know where he could take us. Out of desperation, he thought of his sister, Nel. She was twenty-eight years old, her husband was working in Germany, and she had no children, so he was hoping she could look after us for a few days until he could find us another place. When he asked her, she did not hesitate, saying, "Of course, I don't have a choice; how could I let these two little children die?" Oom Pauw told us that Nel was looking forward to meeting us and was very happy to have us stay with her. We were back on the train, going back to our birthplace of Rotterdam, but to another home. Although Oom Pauw told us not to be afraid and that we'd be staying with his sister, we didn't know what to expect. When we arrived, we were greeted by a very pretty lady whom we were to call Tante Nel. In a way, she resembled Mam, which was strange because now she was going to be our new mother/caregiver. She welcomed us with such warmth that our fears dissolved.

Tante Nel lived in a basement apartment. She led us into the front room of her three-room apartment, the living room, where we saw two mattresses on the floor, one for me to sleep on and one for Ollie. That first night while we were supposed to be sleeping, I was awake all night from the sound of the clock on the mantle, which chimed every hour. I wondered if this room was to be our permanent bedroom and secretly hoped that we did not have to sleep on the floor in this room forever.

After a few days, Tante Nel gave us the middle room. She realized that it was difficult for us to sleep on her living room floor. Jan, Tante Nel's youngest brother, had cleared out the furniture in the middle room, which was just large enough for a double bed. However, there stood only a single bed for Ollie and me to share. We couldn't lie side by side. We had to sleep head to foot together in this little bed.

In Soestduinen, before we came to Tante Nel, we each had a single bed, so to share one was very different. We weren't used to it, but we didn't care. We knew we were going to be happy with Tante Nel. At first, Oom Pauw said that we could only stay at Tante Nel's for a few days but she was such a very special, kind lady that we were hoping we could stay longer — we didn't want to leave again. The way she looked after us, it was hard for us to believe that she had no children.

Oom Pauw tried once more to find us somewhere else to hide, but it was impossible. It was 1943 — no one was willing to take us in. We had to stay with Tante Nel. Although she could never have replaced our real parents, Mam and Pap, we didn't mind living with her. When her brother told her that he was not able to find us another home, Tante Nel let us stay in the middle room. It became our bedroom with a double bed to share. She knew that we would not be able to sleep head to foot in such a little bed forever.

It was the beginning of April when we arrived at Tante Nel's home and since April 7 was Pap's birthday, Tante Nel asked us to make him a birthday card. We were surprised that Tante knew it was Pap's birthday. She showed us that on her bathroom wall hung a birthday calendar with everyone's birthdays on it, even Mam and Pap's. To Tante Nel, birthdays were always very important and very special. Even after the war, none of our birthdays were ever forgotten.

When I asked Ollie if she could make Pap a birthday card and colour it in while I wrote the birthday greeting, she insisted that she write to Pap also. Tante Nel knew that it would make Mam and Pap very happy. We promised Tante Nel that we would always write to Mam and Pap, even if it was not for a birthday.

Once our letters were written, they were given to Oom Pauw, Tante Nel's brother, to deliver to our parents. He knew where they were hiding; he was the only stranger we could trust. Tante Nel couldn't know where my parents were and my parents didn't know where we were, should either one of us be questioned by a collaborator, or worse, arrested. During the war you couldn't trust anyone, not even your best friend, the corner grocery store clerk or your neighbour. Holland had many collaborators.

Tante Nel knew the risk she was taking, just as Claire and her sister knew — even at such a young age — the risks to their lives as well.

For another distraction, Tante gave us a cardboard box to play house with. Most of the time I pretended to be Mam and Ollie was Pap, but we took turns. Every night before we went to bed, we imagined we were going on a special trip and we always picked a different destination. At least we had each other and our imagination. The Nazis could never have taken that away from us. We had to stay indoors until 4:00 p.m. when school ended, and then we were allowed to go outside and play with the neighbourhood children. Our friends in the neighbourhood were curious where we went to school since they never saw us during the day, so we told them that our school was quite far away. We knew we had to pretend that we had been in school, so we carefully listened to what our friends had learned that day and compared our day with theirs. They really believed we had been at another school.

For three years we lived a life of pretense and a constant lie. We realized our lives were in danger and knew we had to lie in order to protect each other, to survive. We knew what hiding meant: to hide our religion; to always be quiet; to never fight or argue with each other. Our parents were hiding somewhere else and even our toys were hidden. We also knew that we had to find a hiding place in our house or next door, in case our house was searched by the Nazis. These random searches were called *razzias* and it was during one of these searches that we almost lost our lives for the second time.

One day, we were surprised by a lunchtime raid — most house searches took place during the evening. After Oma and Opa's house was searched, Nel knew our turn was going to be next. She told us not to worry and to quietly go to our secret hiding place in the cupboard behind the couch. When Nel looked outside, she couldn't believe that the Nazi soldiers had decided to sit on our doorstep to eat their lunch. They were laughing and joking while they were eating. Ollie and I were so scared. Tante Nel told us to run out the back door to Oma and Opa's house and hide in their backyard. We ran as fast as we could and arrived, trembling. Then, Oma took us into the chicken coop. There was another secret hiding place in Oma and Opa's house, behind the broken glass that was stored in large garbage cans in their basement, but there was no time to hide there; it was safer to stay in the coop. We waited there patiently, hoping they hadn't seen us.

Nel knew that once the soldiers had finished their lunch and stopped laughing, it would have been our turn to have our house searched. Nel stayed at home, unafraid, knowing we were safe with her parents. To Tante Nel's surprise, after their lunch, the soldiers left, moving on to search the next house. They must have forgotten and thought, mistakenly, that our house had already been searched! It was a miracle we had escaped for the second time.

Claire and Ollie were liberated by the Canadian army and then reunited with their parents in May 1945. Claire, Ollie and Tante Nel stayed close for the rest of their lives, writing letters to one another, visiting regularly and celebrating important life moments together.

In 1979, Nel was awarded the righteous designation. Nel told me that she was awestruck, feeling that she did not deserve the honour, but was so grateful to our family.

In 1995, Ollie and her daughter Jennifer visited Nel as a surprise. And once a year, for many years, my husband, Seymour, and I went to visit. After Nel's daughter Paula passed away and could no longer act as a Dutch translator for Seymour, I continued to visit on my own, as Nel could not speak or understand English too well and it would have been too difficult for me to translate all our conversations. Nel told me that it was the highlight of her life to reminisce and spend time with both me and Ollie.

In 2002, on the occasion of her granddaughter Yolanda's upcoming wedding, Nel sent invitations to us, her "family" in Canada, with whom she had such a special bond. Ollie was unable to go at that time so my daughter Dianne and I made the trip. Dianne was so pleased to be able to meet this very special and humble family and take part in their celebration.

A few years later, Nel moved into a retirement home. When Ollie and her husband, Warner, visited her, they saw that the plaque that Pap had made so long ago was, even there, hanging on the wall of her room. They knew Nel would never forget us. Unfortunately, it was the very last visit. In 2006, at age ninety-three, Nel passed away. Ollie and I had stayed in touch with her for sixty years and it was an unbelievable loss; we felt as though we had lost our lifeline, our special caregiver and our other mother. We had never been able to repay her for saving our lives.

We knew that she was grateful we had always stayed in touch. We will never forget her and will always remember her as our definition of a hero: it was she, an ordinary person, who under very difficult circumstances had done an extraordinary deed. She had not only saved two little girls, but she had also saved their future generations.

1

2

3

4

1 Claire (left) and her sister, Ollie, soon after arriving at their new hiding place at Tante Nel's. Rotterdam, the Netherlands, 1943.

2 Claire (left) and Ollie with Tante Nel. Rotterdam, circa 1944.

3 Nel and her husband, Koos, in Toronto for the bar mitzvah of Claire's son, Jeffrey. June 1974.

4 Claire visiting Nel on the occasion of the wedding of Nel's granddaughter Yolanda. Rotterdam, 2002.

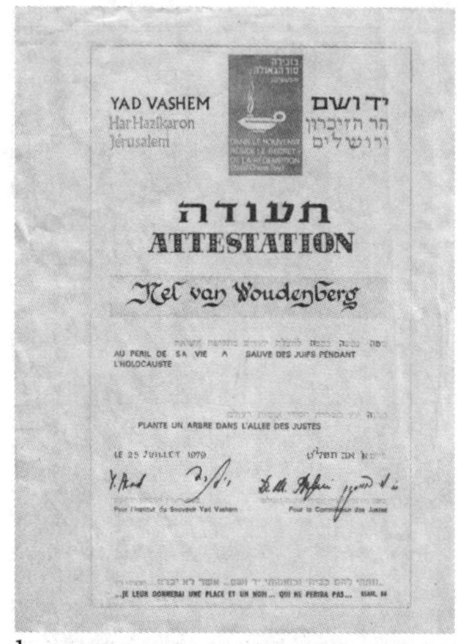

YAD VASHEM
Har Hazikaron
Jérusalem

יד ושם
הר הזיכרון
ירושלים

תעודה
ATTESTATION

Nel van Woudenberg

AU PERIL DE SA VIE A SAUVE DES JUIFS PENDANT L'HOLOCAUSTE

PLANTE UN ARBRE DANS L'ALLEE DES JUSTES

LE 25 JUILLET 1979

Pour l'Institut du Souvenir Yad Vashem

Pour la Commission des Justes

...JE LEUR DONNERAI UNE PLACE ET UN NOM... QUI NE PERIRA PAS...

1

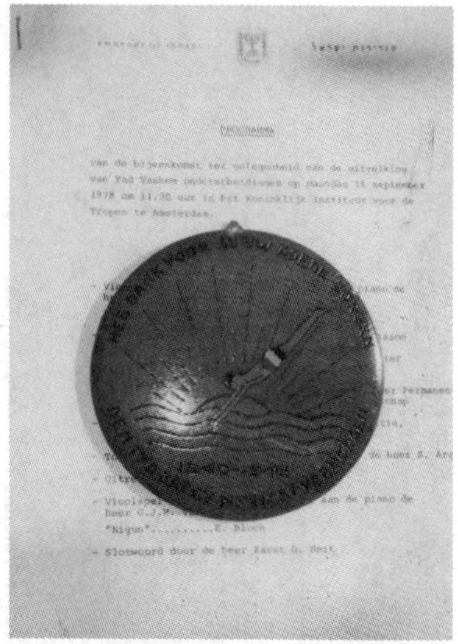

2

3

1 The certificate from Yad Vashem recognizing Nel Van Woudenberg as Righteous Among the Nations. Jerusalem, July 25, 1979.

2 The plaque that Claire's father made for Tante Nel while he was in hiding, thanking her for keeping Claire and Ollie safe during the war.

3 Nel's plaque on the Avenue of the Righteous at Yad Vashem, Jerusalem.

Joy Runs Deeper
Bronia Beker

Bronia Beker was born in the small town of Kozowa, Poland (now Kozova, Ukraine), in 1920. She met Joseph (Josio), who was also born in Kozowa and would later become her husband, before the war. After living under Soviet occupation for two years, Bronia's hometown came under the control of Germany in the summer of 1941. Not long after, Bronia and her family were forced into the town's ghetto.

Throughout 1942 the Germans killed and deported Jews. The ghetto became smaller. We all lived in one room with my eldest half-brother and two of his daughters. He, his wife and all three daughters had been caught and loaded onto a train to a concentration camp, but my brother and his two older daughters managed to jump off the train and come home. My other brother's wife and their three children also lived in the same room. The situation was so bad that we saw no hope of surviving.

Rumours circulated that the Nazis would very soon come to kill us all, and so we started building better bunkers. Josio came to help us build, or rather dig, our bunker. Also helping us were some other young men still left in the ghetto. In our cellar, we dug a hole about six feet long, four feet wide and six feet deep. We covered it with boards and earth so that it looked like the rest of the cellar, but we left a square hole big enough for a person to go through. We then fitted a wooden box full of earth to cover that opening. Wires were put through the side of the box for use as handles, and when we went down into the bunker we pulled the wires down. The opening was covered and it was impossible to see the entrance to the bunker. Even if one looked hard, nobody would have suspected that a bunker was there.

One day in April 1943, a few days before Passover, the Germans surrounded the ghetto. Always on the lookout, we saw what was happening. In general, we slept very little, walked around at night on alert, and never got undressed to go to sleep. That day, we all ran down to the bunker, where we had food already prepared and cots to lie on. On a previous occasion, we had stayed there for two days and the Germans had gone through the house without finding anybody. On that day in April, ten of us went down: me, my father and sister, my half-brother with his two daughters, and my sister-in-law and her three children. After about six hours, we heard heavy boots running down the steps to our cellar. They were looking for us, digging.

We held our breath and didn't move for about half an hour, until they left without finding our bunker. But the pipes through which we got air must have gotten covered during their digging. We couldn't breathe. I was the weakest of all of us because of the typhus that I had just barely recovered from. I remember seeing my father sitting on the floor in his prayer shawl, praying, and my brother with a hammer in his hand trying to open the entrance to the bunker. Then I fell down and everything went black.

When I woke up or, rather, when the doctor brought me out of my unconsciousness, I opened my eyes and saw many people around the bed in which I was lying. My cousin Cyla was beside me. The first thing I asked was, "Where is my sister Sarah?" When I saw the looks on their faces, I understood that she was gone. Everybody in that bunker except for me, all nine of them, had suffocated. I was alone.

I became wild with grief. When the doctor tried to give me an injection to calm down I grabbed him by the throat, wanting to kill him for bringing me back to life. I had felt so peaceful while sleeping, and it seemed to me that I had been woken from a good, sound sleep to face a dreadful life, alone and terrified.

When Josio came into my room he was stunned. I will never forget the look on his face — he could not believe that I was alive. I couldn't understand it myself. I believe it was fate. From then on, Josio took care of me. I was completely helpless and couldn't walk because of my sore leg. I would never have survived on my own and didn't care at all. On that horrible April day it felt as though I had lost everybody. Only Josio had survived. He told me that the Germans had caught a thousand people, told them to dig their own graves, and then killed them all. Then the Nazis made the ghetto smaller yet again.

As I lay in bed, watching the peasants come into the house to take what they wanted, I thought how dear every little item had been to my mother, how she had collected those things over the years, how she had kept everything. It was a horrible experience, lying there in bed wanting to die, to go to sleep and not wake up. But Josio wanted me to live, so I did. He still had his mother, brother and sister, and their house remained within the new border of the ghetto. He gave me a small room at the back of his house and I moved in, taking the bare necessities and leaving the rest.

I could not figure out why he wanted me. He was so handsome, so good, so everything. He was all a girl could dream of. He could have had his pick of the most beautiful girls in town — there were still a few left — but he wanted me. He took such good care of me, better than a mother would. I lived in that little room in Josio's house for a month. Life was unbearable, but I thought, I can't keep crying and being a burden to Josio, so I told myself that I was away from home on a vacation and would soon be together with my family. Really, I saw no way out, no way of living through that hell. But Josio could get out of the worst situations, and he never gave up. One day, Josio came running into the house. "The Germans are back in town!" He quickly picked me up and ran, his mother and sister following. We reached the fields outside the village and stayed there the entire night. In the end, we found out that it had been a false alarm, and came back. It was nevertheless clear that we just couldn't live like that anymore. Josio started to look for farmers who would take his mother, brother and sister. He found a few who were willing, but he couldn't trust just anybody. Finally, he found a very nice man, someone he had known for years, who was willing to keep them in a hiding place in his house. Josio and his brother then bought two bullets, thinking that if they were caught they would shoot one German and leave a bullet for themselves.

In the meantime, life in the ghetto became even more unbearable. The Nazis came to town more often, making all kinds of demands. We could tell that the end of the war was near and they were getting desperate. I didn't worry at all. I was not afraid anymore because I just didn't care what happened to me. But Josio did. Josio was making plans with his close friend Kawalek, a dentist, who still had a fair bit of money. The two were very fond of each other. Kawalek had a Protestant friend named Gnidula, who had once said to him, "If things go really badly, come to me and I will keep you hidden in my house."

One day, in the middle of May, Josio and Kawalek took Gnidula up on his offer. They went to Gnidula's farm to build a bunker in his barn for us to hide in. They worked for two days, building the bunker under a chicken coop, and then came home. We stayed in the ghetto for two more weeks and then heard an announcement that it was to be liquidated. After June 1, 1943, no one would remain. The Germans were coming to take everybody away. After that date, anyone seen would be shot. We knew that the time had come to leave. Whoever had a place to go, left, and the rest remained, waiting....

I will never forget the exodus from Kozowa. I was leaving everything behind and yet, we were lucky to have a place to go. We sneaked out in the middle of the night so no one would see us. We feared not only the Germans, but also the Ukrainians who lived all around us — they were our greatest enemies after the Germans. Some of them were always ready to point a finger at us, catch us, or even kill us themselves.

We left the house and everything in it, leaving the door open. All I took with me was a sheet, a skirt, a coat and pyjamas. We walked for a long time, reaching our destination before sunrise. When Gnidula saw me and Kawalek's wife he was furious. He wanted to take just the men, not the women, and it took a lot of persuasion before he finally agreed to let us stay. I thought that we were in heaven — Gnidula's house stood all alone in the middle of a beautiful field with green grass all around. He was a gardener and he had a strawberry field nearby. It was so very peaceful, a lovely day in June. The sun was shining, everything was green, and I could have stood there forever. But all that beauty was not for me. I had to hide, bury myself somewhere. When I crawled into our bunker I felt safe. I didn't think that perhaps I was seeing daylight for the last time in my life, or that maybe I would never be able to feel sunshine again or breathe fresh air. It's hard to believe that I was actually happy to be there in the bunker, yet I was. I was thankful to be hidden from the eyes of evil men and to be together with Josio.

The bunker was a dark hole in the ground with an entrance through a camouflaged opening from the chicken coop. In the barn, there was a wall with wheat stacked against it, so when someone came into the barn, only the wheat was visible. We spent our nights in a narrow spot in the barn and moved around a bit in the morning, exercising before going to spend the day in the bunker, where we could only sit or kneel. At night we covered our feet with blankets and for light used a small bottle filled with kerosene and a wick. We played cards to pass the time. Gnidula came once a day to bring us food and tell us the news. He brought me a notebook and a pencil so I could write my thoughts and feelings. He wanted to know what it felt like, being buried alive. I wrote little poems for him, which he always enjoyed reading. I also knitted him a sweater. Every day he left a pail of water in the barn. We washed ourselves even on the very cold days when the water froze. Somehow, despite the ice water, none of us ever caught a cold.

We stayed in Gnidula's bunker for nine months, never raising our voice above a whisper and learning how to sneeze without making a sound so that no one would know we were there. We had to be careful that people who walked by the barn didn't suspect anything because some of them wouldn't have hesitated to call on the Germans. Gnidula kept us well informed about the events of the war. The front lines kept moving closer to us and we had high hopes of surviving. In March 1944, about thirty kilometres from us, the front stopped and remained in one place for a whole month.

We kept waiting for the Soviets to liberate us, but sometimes we couldn't stand it any longer. We felt disgusted, angry and nervous, and we started to fight amongst ourselves. On calmer days we would tell each other our dreams and wishes. I wished that I could go over to a well and drink as much water as I wanted and walk with the wind blowing through my hair. Josio wished that he could cut a piece of bread from a whole loaf. Kawalek wished to drink from a clean, shiny glass. We kept making wishes and playing games and hoping that someday this would all end. When our spirits were low we prayed not to wake up. It would be so easy just to stay asleep forever without thinking.

On the night of March 17, 1944, we heard noises outside Gnidula's barn. We sat in the bunker and held our breath, like we usually did when someone was near. We heard a knock on the door of Gnidula's house and heard men asking directions. After a few minutes, we heard a gunshot and people running away. Immediately, Gnidula's wife came to the barn and told us that Gnidula had been shot. She asked us to come to the house, hoping that we could still help him. Josio went with her, but it was too late. Gnidula was dead. His killers were Banderowcy, Ukrainian revolutionaries who were anti-Soviet.[2] Gnidula was a communist and had been telling those Ukrainians that the Soviets would return and everybody would pay for their crimes. When the Banderowcy saw that the Soviets were near and the Germans were backing out, they figured that Gnidula might report them and put them in danger. After they killed him, they told his wife to take their three-year-old son and leave. She told us that we better get out too. It's impossible to imagine how we felt — we hadn't walked for nine months and we had nowhere to go, but we had no choice but to leave our hiding place. As long as it was still dark, we had a chance to escape without being noticed. We put on our clothes and shoes and walked out into a dark, cold night. The snow had just melted and the roads were muddy. The Ukrainian killers were out there somewhere, probably on these same roads. Josio more or less knew his way around, so we planned to go back to our hometown. We hoped that one of our Christian friends would give us shelter.

With much difficulty, and often under threats of betrayal and denunciation, Bronia and Josio managed to find shelter with different acquaintances for the next several months. They were liberated in the summer of 1944.

---

2 The Banderowcy were bands of Ukrainian nationalists who used the German occupation to pursue their own program of killing, often targeting Jews, with the aim of creating what they saw as an ethnically pure independent Ukraine.

Bronia and Joseph (Josio) Beker after the war. Lodz, Poland, 1945.

Always Remember Who You Are
Anita Ekstein

Anita Ekstein was born in 1934 and raised by her parents, Edzia and Fischel Helfgott, in their small hometown of Synowódzko Wyżne, Poland (now Verkhnie Synovydne, Ukraine). In September 1939, the area Anita lived in came under Soviet occupation. In the summer of 1941, Germany invaded the Soviet-held areas, and in the fall, Anita and her parents were forced into a nearby ghetto in a larger town called Skole. On October 18, 1942, Anita's mother was caught in an Aktion, a roundup, and deported to a Nazi camp.

My father seemed to have lost his will to live but became desperate to protect me, his only child. He knew that if I remained in the ghetto, I would be caught in the next *Aktion*. He did not know exactly what had happened to those who were taken, but he understood that they were not coming back. We heard that the transports from our region were taken to a camp in the small town of Bełżec. The rumours that circulated about the mass murders underway there were terrifying. My father no longer kept any secrets from me. Since he was desperately trying to save me, he told me exactly what was going on. I trusted my father and knew that he would do everything in his power to keep me safe.

Once the Germans realized how valuable my father's accounting skills were, they moved him into the office hut in our hometown permanently. There he came into contact with non-Jews, who were permitted to live outside the ghetto walls. My father quickly befriended a Polish Catholic man, Josef Matusiewicz, who had been brought from his town to serve as the stock-keeper.

Before the war, Josef had served as an officer in the Polish army. He was a very well-educated, intelligent man with a huge heart. Both he and my father spoke several languages and engaged in long conversations. Eventually, my father confided in Josef that he had an eight-year-old daughter. I was later told that during their conversations my father expressed an interest in Catholicism and an inclination to convert from Judaism after the war. My father asked this man, practically a stranger, to try to save my life and raise me as a Catholic. While I do not believe for a heartbeat that my father wanted to convert to a different religion, I understand fully why he might have made this declaration. My father was appealing to Josef's deep faith and would have said anything to save my life.

My father did not know where to turn or what to do after the loss of my mother. He was scared of the day when he would come home from work to find that I, too, had disappeared. But asking Josef to help me was a dangerous proposal. In German-occupied Poland, strict laws prohibited people from helping Jews in any way, including providing food rations or hiding Jews in their homes. Any person caught or even accused of helping a Jew risked their own life, as well as the lives of their family and, sometimes, communities.

When he agreed to take me, Josef knew he was violating Nazi law. Josef had not been a family friend, and I did not know him. Many years later, I learned about the night Josef told his wife that he wanted to bring a little Jewish girl into their home. He explained the situation and what he had been asked to do. Josef's adopted daughter Lusia told me that her mother, Paulina, was dismayed by the request: "Are you crazy? You're going to bring a little Jewish girl into our house? You're going to endanger our lives, you cannot do that!" I believe that Josef was an extremely courageous man and responded that God would help. They were a very religious family and fervently believed that

God would help them protect me. Josef saw my father's desperation and could not look away. At tremendous personal risk, the decision was made to take me in.

My father tried to prepare me for another major change. He explained that it was very important that I understood that he could not keep me safe. Every day in the ghetto was dangerous for me. I knew that being Jewish was dangerous. My mother was already gone. I did not want to lose him, too. My father reassured me that I would live with people who would be good to me and care about me. Life would be much better for me there than it was in the ghetto. Before we had come to the ghetto, I was terribly spoiled, an only child. Needless to say, after a year in the ghetto, I was not spoiled any longer. I did not want to go. But my father made it absolutely clear that I had no choice in the matter. I had to go. Otherwise, he told me, I might die. And I had seen death in the ghetto. I am not sure if I understood at the age of eight what it meant to die, but I knew that it was final.

My father assured me that he would be fine, and that we would be together shortly. "It won't take long. Everything will be fine. I'll come and see you and I'll take you home...." He promised me everything a parent would promise an eight-year-old child. And so, when Josef Matusiewicz came to get me, I went along with him. I was petrified because I didn't really know this man, whom I had met only a handful of times. I didn't want to leave my father.

Josef Matusiewicz's position granted him special access to the otherwise restricted ghetto, and one night he was able to get into the ghetto to collect me. I had to say goodbye to my father. I clung to him and did not want to let go. When we could no longer delay the inevitable, Josef put me in a large bag and carried me out of the ghetto like I was a sack of potatoes. I was cautioned not to make any noise, not to move, not to draw any attention to myself. Years later I learned that there was a police station located right next to where we left the ghetto. I don't know how Josef managed to take me out. It really was a miracle that we were not caught.

Josef carried me in the bag some distance outside the ghetto to where he had a horse-drawn wagon waiting. He placed me in the bottom of the wagon and covered me with straw. He then drove the wagon for what seemed a long time until we arrived at our destination. Josef had brought me to his home in a neighbouring town called Rozdół, which is now Rozdil, Ukraine. Josef shared his home with his wife, Paulina, and an eighteen-year-old adopted niece, Emilia. The couple never had children of their own. They adopted Emilia, or Lusia as everyone called her, at birth along with two other orphans, a niece and a nephew. All three children were raised as their own. By 1942, the elder niece was married, and the nephew was a priest. Lusia was the only child living in the family home.

Josef and his wife were middle-class people and owned a little house. It was a one-storey home with a kitchen and three rooms that opened into one another. Paulina and Josef slept in one room, which I never saw; there was a living/dining room; and there was Lusia's bedroom. She graciously shared her room, and her bed, with me. The bed was raised high off the floor, and I was barely tall enough to climb up onto it. Although the indoor kitchen had running water and electricity, it lacked hot water. Whenever somebody wanted to take a bath, they had to drag a big tub into the kitchen and heat water on the stove. The outdoor bathroom was located close to the barn where the cow was kept. Although food was scarce for all Poles during the war, the Matusiewiczes grew their own food and had fresh milk from the cow. I arrived during the winter, so I didn't see the garden, but I heard about it.

I arrived in Rozdół shortly before Christmas 1942 with only a handful of possessions: the clothes I was wearing, a coat, a change of clothes and lace-up shoes. At some point, my rescuer approached our landlord in Synowódzko Wyżne to try to collect some of the clothing we had left behind. But despite having once saved our lives, the landlord refused to release my worthless belongings. He was a very complicated human being. The only item I had that I cared about was a small amulet in a pouch, which had once belonged to my mother. I do not know what was on the amulet, but I wore it around my neck to feel close to my mother — it was all I had left of her. Paulina took the amulet away from me, saying that it could identify me as Jewish. I already had so little, and the loss of the amulet was devastating. But there was nothing I could do about it. Many years later I saw something similar to the amulet at a synagogue museum in Krakow and thought of my mother.

Although I was upset, I had to move on. I focused on adapting to my new situation and family. That first day in my new home, there was a large Christmas tree, its branches decorated with real candles and little ornaments. For an eight-year-old child who had spent a year in the ghetto, this was like a fairy tale, a wonderful sight. All of the preparations for Christmas were very exciting. On the one hand, I didn't know what was going on and why, and I was afraid of everything. On the other hand, this was a different experience for me. I was terribly hungry, and my rescuers fed me food that I had not had in a long time. Then they put me to bed. Physically and mentally exhausted, and longing for my father, I fell asleep.

Christmas Eve was a few days later. Straw was placed in the corners of the main room and under the tablecloth to represent the manger that Jesus was born in. Wonderful cooking smells came from the kitchen. Carolers were singing outside. Snow was falling. During that time, I was so busy taking everything in that I was distracted a bit from thinking about how much I missed my mother and father. Lusia told me years later that I would get into bed every night, cover myself completely with blankets and cry. I did not want anyone to hear me, but they obviously did.

It was very important that I pass as a gentile child. The family called me Haneczka. I did not have any papers at this time to verify my identity. The story offered to neighbours was that I was another niece whose parents had died in an influenza epidemic. Since the couple had already raised three orphans, this was not a strange notion. I had to assume a completely new identity and forget who I had been. And the family immediately began to teach me how to be a Catholic.

Paulina Matusiewicz was an extremely devout religious woman who went to church every day. I was a very good child but deeply afraid of her. I think I feared that they would not keep me if I misbehaved. Since meeting other hidden children over the years, I have learned that this was a common experience: we were all very well behaved because we were afraid of being sent away (and possibly having our true identities as Jews revealed).

When I arrived in Rozdół, I did not know anything about the Catholic religion. I barely knew anything about the Jewish religion for that matter, only what I had seen at home. Before the Matusiewiczes could let me be seen by people, they had to teach me about being a Catholic. These lessons were supposed to protect me from accidentally revealing the fact that I was Jewish. Everyone was a potential enemy.

Worried about my true identity being discovered, Josef and Paulina did not allow me to leave the house, and if they expected visitors or heard anyone approaching, I was instructed to disappear and hide in another room or under a bed. Even though the neighbours believed that I was an orphaned niece, the family discouraged any contact between me and the outside world.

I was never outside by myself, and I spent almost all of my time in the house. The only exception was when my rescuers took me to church for Midnight Mass. Josef simply announced, "We're going to church." I was surprised they would allow anyone to see me. I can perfectly remember the snow crunching under my feet as we walked to church. It was so nice to be outside. The inside of the church was beautiful and decorated with flowers even though it was the dead of winter. The space was larger than the *shtibel* where my family used to attend holiday services, and it was filled with people. I didn't understand the proceedings at Mass, but though foreign to me, they were very interesting. I had never seen anything like this at synagogue services. The priest in his vestments went up and down the aisles with incense — I remember the powerful smell — and people went up to the front to take Communion. There was a manger with baby Jesus in it, and I wanted desperately to look at those little figurines. Josef hovered over me throughout Mass and prevented anyone from speaking with me. He was probably concerned they would ask me a question about the service that I, as a little Jewish girl, would be unable to answer. I was well behaved and saved all of my questions for later.

My feelings toward the Matusiewiczes, whom I referred to as Aunt and Uncle, were complicated during the war. I was mature enough to understand that they were trying to save my life, but for the devout Paulina, everything I did was a sin. She was very, very strict. She would accuse me of vanity and say that I was showing off if I combed my hair the wrong way. During my time there, Paulina never touched me. A tall and thin woman, she was completely unapproachable, and I was always afraid of getting in trouble with her. This was an unfamiliar feeling. My parents had adored me, and I had received many hugs and kisses from them, but Paulina was a much colder person. I missed my father very much. But there was nothing I could do about it. That's just how it was.

Lusia, on the other hand, was good to me. She was an absolute doll. She was very pretty and tall. Though, of course, I was little, so everyone seemed tall. Always smiling, she exuded kindness, although she also never hugged me or showed physical affection. I supposed this was just the family's way. Lusia was in school, training to be a teacher. I was her first pupil, and she showed a genuine interest in me. Since I had never been allowed to attend school, she taught me how to read and, to a lesser extent, write, in the evenings. The lessons kept my head occupied and distracted. She wasn't terribly religious at the time and was far less intimidating than her aunt.

I spent most of my days sitting in silence, eating meals that Paulina prepared for me and waiting for my reading lessons. Josef only came home on the odd weekend. His visits were always special. He was a wonderful, warm human being, and more nurturing than his wife. First of all, he spent time with me. I would sit on his lap as he told me news from my father, sometimes reading a letter from him aloud. I was always so excited to hear from my father and know that he was all right, and I was counting down the days until we could be together again.

Life continued on like this for more than a month. Then, one day in early February 1943, my world was shaken again. Lusia and I were sitting in the living room having a reading lesson when, through the window, we saw two Ukrainian policemen with rifles over their shoulders walking toward the porch. The police were coming to get me. A neighbour must have denounced me and told the Gestapo that the family was harbouring a Jew. And now they were coming to take me.

Without stopping to think, Lusia picked me up and ran with me to the back of the house. She opened a window, pushed me out into the snow and told me to run. It was a very cold winter and there was a lot of snow. I was not dressed for the outdoors and was wearing slippers on my feet. I was terrified. Where was I to go? There was an outhouse behind the house, and I ran toward it and locked the door. I stayed in there in the freezing cold for five hours, afraid to come out.

While I hid in the outhouse, I heard a repetitive noise in the distance. I had no idea what it was. Later, I found out that, on that day, the Germans and their Ukrainian helpers rounded up all the Jews left in Rozdół. The group was marched to the cemetery, lined up and shot. From my hiding space, I was hearing gunshots. Had the police found me, I would have been one of those shot. In the meantime, the policemen went through the house searching for me. Apparently, they turned the whole place upside down — looking under the beds, in the cupboards, everywhere. My rescuers insisted that I had gone to visit other family members and adamantly denied the claim that I was Jewish. It was a miracle that the police did not look out the window. Had they done so, they would have seen small footsteps in the snow leading to the outhouse.

It's amazing how many escapes I had. I guess I was meant to survive.

I finally crept back to the house when it was dark and quiet. Everyone was surprised to see me. They thought that the police had caught me. It turned out that a neighbour had indeed gone to the police with the suspicion that the Matusiewiczes' orphaned niece was actually Jewish. He or she had seen me in and around the house, or perhaps at Christmas Mass. Denouncers received rewards like a pound of sugar or a bottle of alcohol in exchange for information. Imagine a world where a pound of supplies is valued more than a human life.

It was impossible for the family to keep me after this. They were rightfully afraid that the policemen would come back and that, the next time, nobody would escape. Much later, I learned that the police did in fact return several times. Paulina contacted her husband and told him to move me quickly. Because of his position, Josef had access to the Hochtief compound, where my father was, and he returned me to my father in the same wagon we had used to escape the ghetto.

Anita hid in a small wardrobe in her father's room in the Hochtief labour camp for seven weeks while Josef tried to find another place for her to hide. He managed to obtain a false identity document so that Anita could "pass" as a gentile Catholic girl and travel under the new name of Anna Jaworska. In the spring of 1943, Josef smuggled Anita out of the camp and took her to the village of Liczkowce (now Lychkivtsi, Ukraine), where his nephew, Father Michal, was a parish priest. Anita lived a quiet, lonely life with the priest and his housekeeper until the area was liberated in March 1944, during which time she became a devout Catholic. After the Matusiewicz family sent for her, she lived with them for more than a year until she was reunited with her aunt, who had survived the Holocaust. Anita's parents did not survive. Anita eventually readjusted to life after the war, and after some time had passed, she reclaimed her Jewish identity. She kept in contact with Josef Matusiewicz and his family, corresponding with them by letter, and in 1955, Josef sent her the falsified birth certificate that helped her to survive:

Dear Haneczka,

Your letters make us happy. It seems that your heart has not changed toward us.

We are very happy that when there is an important event in your life, you let us know. It shows that between us is a bond, more than that of family — when family could not help you in those tragic days when you were faced with death, God sent you a family who saved you. How difficult this was only God knows, but this passed, and you together with us are alive and are not in the same grave. We are very moved by the news of your marriage.

When we speak about you, we remember a little girl, like a bird, who flew to us, finding safety under our roof from those who wanted to take [her] life. She stayed a while, rested a little, and again flew into the world, far over seas and mountains to find a new life, to find a friend and husband to go through life with.

We wish you on your new path of life health and happiness and blessings from God in every step and luck in everything.

Dear Haneczka, we too are sending you a wedding present. Take good care of it…like a talisman [and] souvenir for the future. It is only a small paper card, but how important it was for you. If not for it, there would not be Haneczka today and family and everyone else would have forgotten about her.

Today, I am sure you will understand how important this birth certificate was for you in those times. Everything was done the Christian way, not for payment. God helped us in this work. I am sure you can remember when they [the police] came for you. It's as if God put an invisible cover on you, and I was able to take you to Liczkowce because of that piece of paper.

With this birth certificate you were legally registered as a cousin of the priest, and you lived legally until you left. It is easy to write this, but living through those times cost us our health. I have problems with my nerves and my liver. When we sometimes think about your survival, we think your parents must have had great help from God and must have prayed for your life.

To end, we are sending you the birth certificate and sending you and wishing the young couple once again good luck in your new life journey.

J. Matusiewicz with the entire family

In the 1990s, after visiting the areas in Poland and Ukraine where she had grown up and survived, Anita reflected on her past.

These trips reminded me of where I came from and how I survived when my parents did not. It was of utmost importance to my family and me to officially recognize the Matusiewicz family's courage and selflessness during the war. Josef, Paulina and Lusia risked their own lives to save me, a little Jewish girl — they deserved to be honoured, even posthumously. I began the process of honouring my rescuers as Righteous Among the Nations through Yad Vashem in the mid-1990s. The first step involved documenting my entire Holocaust narrative and my relationship with my rescuers. It was challenging to corroborate my story — a necessity for the honour to be bestowed — since most of the witnesses to my survival were dead. By this time, Josef, Paulina and Father Michal had already been dead for many years. Father Michal died of a heart attack when he was only in his late forties or fifties. Lusia Młot was the only one in the family still living at that time. Fortunately, my cousin Stefan had met with Josef in Katowice after Aunt Sally found me in Kluczbork, and Stefan provided a letter of attestation, detailing the conditions of my rescue.

The nomination package included the letters from my late father, letters Josef wrote to me, my false birth certificate and photographs from my time at Father Michal's parish. For a long time, Lusia was reluctant to receive the title Righteous Among the Nations. She and I had remained in close contact all those years, and she felt it was unnecessary to receive formal recognition. Under Communism, there was an added fear of repercussions for her family's wartime activities. After the fall of the Iron Curtain, I convinced the very modest Lusia to write to Yad Vashem about her and her aunt and uncle's efforts in saving me. Everyone was thrilled when my nomination was approved.

The Righteous Among the Nations ceremony took place at the Israeli embassy in Warsaw on July 14, 1998. The Israeli emissary in Toronto arranged for the ceremony to coincide with my family's visit to Poland. Lusia, her two daughters and two granddaughters travelled to Warsaw for the ceremony. Her son did not come. Frank, Rick and Lillian, and my granddaughters Stephanie and Michelle accompanied me. Thank God Lusia was still alive to receive the Yad Vashem medal and certificate of recognition from the Israeli ambassador to Poland. I was immensely happy to honour my rescuers in this way. Frank told Lusia the ancient Jewish saying: "When you save one life, you save the world." Lusia was a devout woman, and I think this made her happy. It was a very emotional ceremony, and I was filled with gratitude. Lusia died in 2005 after a long life and passed along her medal to Marysia. Today I have warm relationships with Marysia and Marta Kornacka, who recently completed her medical studies in Poland. I communicate with mother and daughter by email and phone and try to get together with them whenever I travel to Poland. They are very important people in my life and part of the extended Ekstein family.

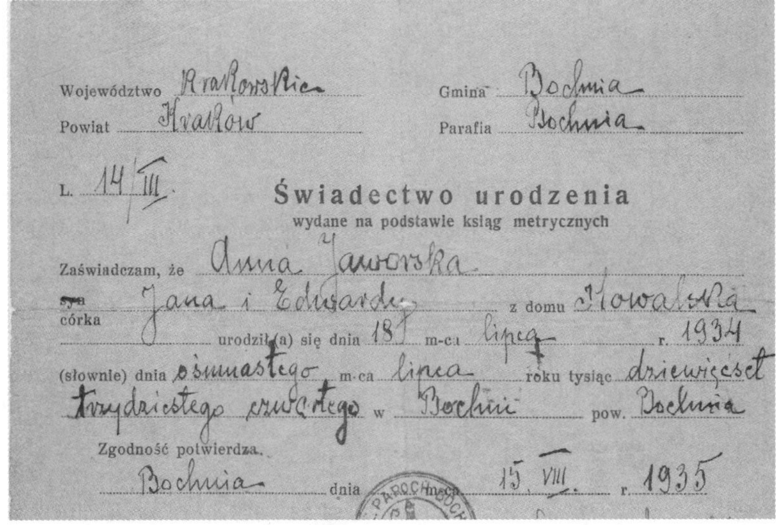

Województwo Krakowskie Gmina Bochnia

Powiat Kraków Parafia Bochnia

L. 14/III.

Świadectwo urodzenia

wydane na podstawie ksiąg metrycznych

Zaświadczam, że Anna Jaworska

~~syn~~ córka Jana i Edwardy z domu Kowalska

urodził(a) się dnia 18 m-ca lipca r. 1934

(słownie) dnia ośmnastego m-ca lipca roku tysiąc dziewięćset trzydziestego czwartego w Bochni pow. Bochnia

Zgodność potwierdza.

Bochnia dnia 15. VIII. r. 1935

1

2

1 The forged birth certificate that Josef Matusiewicz commissioned to identify Anita as a Polish Catholic girl named Anna Jaworska.

2 Anita (front, centre) with Father Michal (centre, with glasses) and members of the Liczkowce parish. Liczkowce, Poland, 1943–1944.

1

2

3

1 Anita (left) with Lusia, Josef and Paulina's daughter. Kluczbork, Poland, 1946.

2 Anita (front, centre) with the Matusiewicz family. From left to right: Paulina, Lusia (standing) and Josef. In front (left to right): Josef's great-niece Ola, Anita and his great-niece Basia. Poland, 1946.

3 The ceremony honouring the Matusiewicz family as Righteous Among the Nations in the Israeli embassy in Poland. From left to right: Anita's daughter-in-law Lillian; Anita's grandchildren Stephanie and Michelle; Anita; the Israeli ambassador, Yigal Antebi, and his wife; Lusia Młot; Anita's son Rick; and Anita's husband, Frank. Warsaw, Poland, 1998.

Daring to Hope
Rachel Lisogurski and Chana Broder

Rachel Lisogurski was born in Grodzisk, Poland, in 1911. She and her husband, Avrumeh (Abraham), lived in his hometown of Siemiatycze, Poland, where their daughter, Chana (Chanale), was born in 1938. At the start of the war, their town was under Soviet occupation. In the summer of 1941, the Germans arrived, and one year later the Jewish population of Siemiatycze was forced into a ghetto. In the fall of 1942, as rumours about the impending liquidation of the ghetto increased, Rachel understood that they would be deported to a death camp. That November, as soldiers arrived to round up the Jews for deportation, Rachel and Avrumeh escaped from the ghetto with their young daughter, Chana, as did a few other members of their family. Desperate for refuge, they wandered the countryside, hiding in forests and barns, hoping for help from their closest friends. Turned away and denied support and assistance, they eventually managed to find shelter with acquaintances, usually in exchange for their last remaining possessions. But as their possessions ran thin and the danger in the area increased as Germans searched and found other Jews in hiding, they were forced out, on the run once again. In the spring of 1943, Rachel, Avrumeh, Chana and her maternal grandmother, Rivka, arrived at the barn of the Krynski family, who had agreed to hide them.

The Krynskis greeted us warmly and gave us a corner in a loft of a shabby barn. They were poor people but very well-known in the district for their honesty. They had three children — a daughter named Gienia, who was married and lived in the village and didn't know about us or the other Jews who had been coming and going; a son in his twenties, Heniek, and a twelve-year-old daughter, Krysia. The girl would come up to the loft after school; we helped her with her homework and then she played with Chanale. There, too, Mother and I knitted sweaters and sewed shirts by hand, trying to be useful.

At the end of the two weeks, old Krynski told us that they didn't have the heart to make us leave. They were all very religious and believed that if we had lived until now and had come to them, they shouldn't be the ones to throw us out.

"Besides," he said, "I was a prisoner in Germany during World War I, and I know what hunger means. You are facing death without ever having committed a crime. Who should we help? The Germans who grabbed our country and are destroying it? Or you? You don't know me, but after I got out of the German prison, I was poor, and your father used to lend me salt and fuel."

He told us about a time when he was in our store and wasn't able to pay, but didn't have the nerve to ask for something before he had paid for the items he had bought earlier. My father told him not to be shy and said, "We are only human. No one knows what will happen to himself the next day. Maybe someday I'll be poor, and I'll need your help." I suppose that Father wanted to make him feel better. He knew Krynski was an honest man and would pay us as soon as he had some money.

"Maybe God made your father be good to me," Krynski said, "so that I would help you now." So we remained there beyond the two promised weeks.

The Krynskis didn't have much to eat. But in the evenings, if a few hungry Jews came by when Krynski was about to take a pail of potatoes to feed his pigs, he would let the Jews have the potatoes and would let the pigs go hungry for a night. None of those Jews had anything to give him in exchange, nor did he ask anything of them.

When we had arrived, Krynski hadn't asked what he would get for hiding us. In the beginning, he hid us as a way of repaying my father's kindness. But then, he and his family just didn't have the heart to turn us out. They were always satisfied with what my brother Shieh gave them and never bargained. They always said, "The war isn't over yet. Make sure you have enough to help you to the end." I was very moved by Krynski's behaviour and his warm feelings for every living person, no matter their religion. He always said, "We are not here to judge and condemn people for what they believe. One thing I know — in every religion, killing is a crime." That simple uneducated farmer had more humanity and feeling for what was right than the whole German "master race"!

The summer months passed quickly and soon the fall winds started to blow into the loft. The nights were cold. We didn't have anything to cover ourselves with, and the Krynskis had nothing to spare. At Shieh's suggestion, Heniek Krynski, with Avrumeh's help, dug out a shelter for us under the stable. They put wood on top of it to make a floor, and they piled wheat and the rest of their harvest for the winter on top. A wooden shack stood next to the barn, and there the Krynskis kept the wood they had chopped for their stoves. In the floor of the shack, next to the wall of the barn, was an opening, big enough for one person to get through and slide into our new shelter. The opening to our hiding place was covered by a trap door made of a large wooden board with pieces of chopped wood nailed onto it. It looked like a real wood pile and we were able to cover ourselves without leaving any sign that we were there.

We felt safer there, and the Krynskis felt surer that they would be able to protect us till the end of the war. We promised they would get the reward they deserved for all their trouble and fear. There were many times when I felt sorry for them. Why should these kind, gentle people get involved in our tragedy? But on the other hand, how could

I save my child if not with their help? There was only one answer — if even one of us lived through the war, we would never forget them. We kept reminding ourselves of this. Every day at sunset, when Krynski milked the cow, he would come to the little shack, cough twice as a signal, and give Chanale a glass of milk. Every time he did that, Mother urged me always to remember his kindness.

The hiding place under the shack, which I called our "palace," was big enough for five people to lie down in — four places for us and one for Shieh when he visited — and high enough to sit in. It was pitch black. After a few weeks, Shieh brought us a lamp so that we could do some handiwork. The Krynskis didn't have enough for us to eat, so Shieh brought me wool to knit sweaters, which he then exchanged for food. He, Chaim and Chazkel were with Henia and her family at the shelter she had found, which was about two kilometres away in Krynki-Sobole.

I called our new shelter a palace because we felt more secure there, but Mother called it being buried alive. We often had to open the wooden trap door a crack just to give us enough air to breathe. And because there wasn't enough air, we couldn't light the lamp whenever we wanted to either. But the tremendous will to live through the war — or was it the will to keep my child alive? — made me thankful for every hour that passed, because each one brought us nearer to the end of the war.

Krynski brought us newspapers whenever he could get them. We knew that the Germans were retreating. We were full of hope. But one day in October 1943, he came with the news that on a farm in Krynki-Sobole there had been another hunt for Jews, and that a boy of seventeen had been shot by a Polish youth. Krynki-Sobole was not only so close by, but also where the rest of our family was hiding, and we were shocked. The Krynskis were scared. But we felt even worse when, a few evenings later, Shieh told us that it was my mother's nephew, Shimon Goldshtern, who had been killed — and by whom? By a boy our cousin had gone to school with in Grodzisk!

Mother couldn't stop crying about Shimon — to be shot by a schoolmate after eleven months of torture and suffering! "If no one survives," she said, "how will the world know what has happened to us? There won't be anyone left to tell what the Germans and our Polish friends did to us." Mother didn't know yet that even if we did survive, very few would care to listen to our tragedy.

The days passed in sorrow and grief. We heard that the Soviets were moving forward, and we waited anxiously to see if they would cross the old Polish-Russian border, terribly afraid they would stop there. We had no hope that anyone else would liberate us. As Mother kept saying, "The whole world has become deaf to our suffering."

The Krynskis sheltered the Lisogurski family throughout increasingly dangerous situations — the threat of Germans in the area who were searching for Jews and killing both the Jews in hiding and the families who sheltered them, and Polish nationalist groups who also perpetrated violence against Jews. The Krynskis, though nervous and scared throughout this time, and at one point even assaulted and robbed by men who accused them of hiding Jews, continued to protect the Lisogurski family. They were liberated by Soviet soldiers in the summer of 1944.

After the war, Rachel, Avrumeh and Chana immigrated to Canada, and Rachel kept in touch with the Krynskis, sending them packages, until she received a letter from the son, Heniek, asking that she stop writing. As Chana wrote in her memoir, continuing the story from her perspective, "It was not clear to us whether receiving letters from Canada was getting him into trouble with the Communist authorities or whether he did not want his neighbours to know about their correspondence. In any case, my mother stopped writing to him and we lost contact." In 1997, Chana returned to Siemiatycze, Poland, and managed to find Heniek Krynski. After an emotional reunion, they once again kept in touch.

After that, I would send Heniek money every Christmas, and he would write me beautiful letters, thanking me profusely and explaining that his only other income was a meagre government pension, so the money I sent him, which came to a huge sum in Polish zloty, made his life easier. The woman who translated the letters for me told me that for a man who had grown up on a farm and presumably had no higher education, Heniek's written Polish was very elegant, and I could see for myself that his handwriting was very delicate.

When I returned from Poland, I told my mother about my trip. It had been intense, meaningful and just good for our family members to be together, to laugh and cry together, and to fill in bits of the story that is our family's heritage. I said to her that we should apply to Yad Vashem, Israel's museum and memorial to the victims of the Holocaust, to name Heniek and his parents as Righteous Among the Nations. Yad Vashem recognizes and honours gentiles who, at personal risk and without a financial or evangelistic motive, chose to save their Jewish neighbours from the ongoing genocide. My mother replied, "You do it after I am gone." I think that she did not want to be forced to delve into her memories of the war.

After Heniek passed away in 2005, Chana once again had no way of keeping in touch with the family, as she did not know of any family descendants. In 2013, Chana was surprised to receive an email from a young woman named Izabella Wierzbicka, who explained that she was the granddaughter of Krystina (Krysia) Krynska, and that she had been trying to locate Chana and her family. Chana was finally able to embark on her mission to have the family awarded the righteous designation.

The ceremony was set for May 24, 2016, in Siemiatycze. The title of Righteous Among the Nations would be granted by Yad Vashem to Konstanty and Bronislawa Krynski and their children, Henryk (Heniek) and Krystina (Krysia) and awarded by the Ambassador of Israel to Poland. Since the Krynskis had passed away, the award would be accepted on their behalf by their eldest granddaughter, Zdzislawa Chlebowska, who came home from Brussels especially for the ceremony.

I went to Siemiatycze with my daughter Pnina, her husband, Navot, and their son Ohad, my son David, his wife, Carmel, and their daughter Mika, and my younger daughter Shlomit, who lives in Toronto. Her partner, Michal, stayed home to care for their three young children, Amit, Alma and Noam. My husband, Tashie, who was not well, was not able to make the trip. My two other Israeli grandsons, Eitan and Yonatan, were also not able to come with us.

Late one morning, one day before the ceremony, we arrived in Siemiatycze. Because I had been there in 1997, I was able to show my family where I had lived with my parents before the war and the street where my father's family had lived.

We had arranged to meet at Zdzislawa's home. Although she and her family had agreed to receive the award, and I knew that fourteen of their family members would attend, we did not know how they would receive us. We were totally amazed when they greeted us outside with hugs and kisses (three kisses on the cheeks) and some of the men even kissed the ladies' hands, European style. Izabella's aunt Zdzislawa, a spunky woman, was very enthusiastic.

As we walked into the house, they lined up and sang *Sto Lat*, which is sung on festive occasions and means "A Hundred Years." We responded with the festive song *Hevenu Shalom Aleichem*, which means "We Brought Peace to You." The table was set and we partook of herring, devilled eggs, latkes and cakes. None of our party spoke Polish, so our driver was the interpreter and Izabella had also hired a translator from Siemiatycze. Izabella also understood English and spoke it haltingly, so we managed some kind of conversation.

From there, we went to the Jewish cemetery where my grandfather Ephraim Kejles is buried. From my visit in 1997, I knew that only a large, flat gravestone remained over the mass grave. I had originally thought that this would be a private visit, but before we left Israel, I received word that the Chief Rabbi of Poland, Michael Schudrich, and the Israeli Ambassador to Poland, Anna Azari, would be there. It turned out that representatives of both churches, Catholic and Eastern Orthodox, the mayor of the town and other officials were also there, and the descendants of the Krynski family also came along. We were surprised to see that a police car had closed off the street. There were lots of still and video cameras.

I explained briefly who was buried there, and we lit two memorial candles, one for my grandfather and one for all the others. Then the rabbi read *Tehillim* (Psalms) and sang *El Maleh Rachamim*, the memorial prayer for the souls of those who have passed. My three children and I said Kaddish. It was a very meaningful and emotional experience for me and the children.

Following this, we went to the cultural centre, formerly the synagogue, where the Righteous Among the Nations ceremony was to take place. How symbolic! In the building where my parents and grandparents had once prayed, those who had saved our lives during the Holocaust were going to be honoured.

After a few greetings, Emil, the young man who organized the ceremony for the embassy, explained why we were there and introduced me. I had prepared a speech at home and someone in my son's office had translated it into Polish. Now I read one paragraph in English, and Emil was able to read it immediately in Polish.

I told them that I was there to fulfill a long-overdue duty, to honour the saintly family that had saved my life, the lives of my parents, Rachela and Abraham Lisogurski, and that of my grandmother Rivka Kejles. I briefly recounted how we had escaped from the ghetto on the night of November 2, 1942, and thus avoided being sent to the Treblinka death camp. I explained how we had come to the Krynskis in May of 1943. I told them that Pan Krynski had agreed to keep us on a trial basis for two weeks, but that when the two weeks were up, he did not have the heart to send us away.

I was very young at the time, I told them, but my parents had later told me that the Krynskis had helped many Jewish people before us. Nobody had lived there permanently, but Jews would stop in their house to rest, to get something to eat or perhaps to sleep over in the barn.

By sheltering us, I told the audience, the Krynskis had taken a terrible risk. If Polish people were caught helping Jews their whole family would be killed. It was an extremely courageous step to take, to put oneself and one's children in danger in order to help strangers. And yet, the Krynskis had taken this compassionate step.

I told them about our liberation, our move to Canada and then Israel, and how my mother had corresponded with both Panie Krynska and Heniek for a time. I also told them about our 1997 visit to Poland and my emotional reunion with Heniek, and our subsequent correspondence until his death in 2005. Because Heniek had not told me that Krysia had children, I hadn't known there were other family members I could have been in contact with.

I gave credit to Izabella Wierzbicka for doing the research and finding me on the internet, which was not easy. We have been corresponding by email since then and I feel that we are almost family. Thanks to her, we were able to grant the honour to the Krynski family, which they so richly deserve and which took so many years to come to fruition.

I introduced the members of my family who had come with me to this ceremony. I stressed the fact that if the Krynskis had not saved me, many of these people would not have been born.

Finally, I told them that when I wrote my story to Izabella, she responded that I had used very beautiful words to describe her great-grandparents. I responded that there were no words in any language beautiful enough to describe what her family had done for us. They risked their lives and the lives of their children to save us. What could be more beautiful than that? They were truly righteous people because they did what they believed to be right. I expressed the wish that their memory be blessed.

When I finished, I noticed that some members of the Krynski family were wiping tears from their eyes. Then both the ambassador and Zdzislawa were called to the stage and the medal and the certificate were given to her. She was very excited and spoke a few words of thanks. She and other family members repeatedly told us that they were thrilled that we had not forgotten what their forebears had done for us. We then hugged and kissed and posed for many pictures.

Next, we climbed into our van and they climbed into their cars, and they took us to the place in Morze where the Krynski house had stood and where the barn and the bunker in which we'd hidden had been. Nothing was left but an empty field. But this was still very exciting for me because I had not been there on my first trip back. We continued on to the Catholic cemetery, where their family is buried, side by side, and lit memorial candles for the people who had saved our lives. Finally, at my daughter Pnina's request, we drove through Grodzisk, the village where my mother was born and grew up, the place she used to tell Pnina about when she was little.

In the evening, we had a dinner for both families in Siemiatycze's main hotel. There was a lot of conversation with the help of the translators. Finally, we said goodbye in the parking lot amid a lot of hugs and kisses and promises to keep in touch and mutual invitations to visit.

It was a very emotional day, a magical day, above and beyond all our expectations. I feel a great sense of satisfaction that I accomplished this morally necessary deed.

1 Rachel Kejles before the war. Poland, date unknown.

2 Passport photo of Rachel Lisogurski taken in Cremona, Italy, in preparation for the family's departure for Canada. May 7, 1947.

3 Chana Lisogurski, age eight, in the Cremona displaced persons camp after the war. Italy, 1946.

4 Chana's passport photo. Cremona, 1947.

1

2

3

1 Chana Broder reuniting with Henryk (Heniek) Krynski, son of Konstanty and Bronislawa Krynski, who saved Chana and her family during the war. Morze, Poland, 1997.

2 Chana with Izabella Wierzbicka, granddaughter of Krysia Krynski. Izabella had researched her great-grandparents' wartime story of saving a Jewish family and located Chana, who was motivated to nominate the family for the honour of Righteous Among the Nations. Siemiatycze, Poland, May 2016.

3 Chana (centre) with Zdzislawa Chlebowska (Krysia's oldest daughter, left) accepting the award on behalf of the Krynski family. On the right is Israeli Ambassador to Poland Anna Azari. Siemiatycze, May 24, 2016.

Where Courage Lives
Muguette Myers

Muguette Myers was born in Paris, France, in 1931. In September 1939, at the onset of the war, Muguette and her family were evacuated from Paris due to the perceived danger of air raids. Muguette was sent to a small town called Sens while her mother, older brother, aunt and grandmother were sent to the village of Champlost, about one hundred and fifty kilometres southeast of Paris. Muguette eventually reunited with her family in Champlost, where the mayor considered her mother an "honorary citizen" because she had protected a resident's property from thievery. Muguette and her family returned to Paris at the end of the summer of 1940, after the German occupation. Persecution began to be felt that fall, with Jews being forced to register their addresses; in June 1942, anti-Jewish laws escalated, with all Jews having to wear a yellow star; and one month later, Muguette and her mother barely escaped a roundup. Muguette's mother recalled the mayor of Champlost saying that if she needed shelter at any time, she would always be welcome in the village. By 1943, Muguette and her family were living together in Champlost under false identities, protected by the townspeople.

Where We Lived

In Champlost, there was — and still is — a *place*, the village square where in happier times the circuses pitched their tents and villagers danced on Bastille Day. Champlost had a baker, two grocery stores, a butcher and two cafés. It had two schools — one for boys and one for girls — a town hall, which also housed the boys' school, a post office and, of course, a church. Champlost also had neighbouring hamlets that depended upon it for all the necessities provided by the above conveniences. Not all of Champlost's inhabitants were farmers. There were the teachers, Monsieur and Madame Bérault, who came from a very distinguished family in Villeneuve-sur-Yonne, an important town thirty or so kilometres away. Then there was the postmistress Madame Barré, whose daughter Thérèse was my best friend. Madame Barré and her two daughters, Thérèse and Jacqueline, came to Champlost to be with family in 1942. Monsieur Barré was being held as a prisoner of war. Two villagers owned the two cafés, two ladies worked at the two grocery stores, and there was the baker and the butcher. There were also other families who were not farmers, among them a refugee like us, although not Jewish, who was a retired professor originally from Algeria. His daughter, Marie-Josée, was a renowned singer heard daily on the radio. There was another refugee family, Poles and also not Jewish, the Pollack family. They had two children, a son, Taddeck, and a daughter, Lili, who was my best friend — before Thérèse came to Champlost — and one of the best students in the class.

The radio station we most listened to at that time was Radio Andorre. Andorra, a small principality between France and Spain, had the highest transmitter in Europe, on the Pyrenees Mountains; consequently, its reception was excellent. Every evening at about 8:00 p.m. they played requests. We eagerly awaited the hour and the call sign in Spanish, "Aquí Radio Andorra." We heard old and new songs by singers like Tino Rossi, Rina Ketty and Lys Gauty. We often heard Marie-Josée on Radio Andorre, and we were all proud that her father lived in Champlost. She herself seldom visited. I remember seeing her only once, and that was after the war.

My Religious Education

Growing up in Champlost, a Catholic village, we of course celebrated Christmas. We went to midnight mass at 8:00 p.m. in order to save electricity and to morning mass on Christmas day. However, the gifts were given out not at Christmas but on New Year's Day. That day, we children went from farm to farm not only to wish the farmers a Happy New Year but also to collect presents. We knocked at the door and when it was opened we said in unison, "Je vous souhaite une bonne année, une bonne santé et le paradis à la fin de vos jours." (I wish you a Happy New Year, good health and paradise at the end of your days.) The good farmers wished us the same and always gave us either a few francs or some toys they had. That occupied us for most of New Year's Day because there were about forty houses in the village. In case of an inspection by the Germans, I was sent to church and to catechism, in order to be like the other children. I loved those lessons, which really spoke to a child's imagination: a baby born in a manger, the wise men, the shepherds. It was like a fairy tale and I rapidly became the best in my catechism class of six girls. And on Sundays at mass, the priest l'Abbé Tallard, a saintly man, read my name out loud as being first in catechism.

When we first arrived back in Champlost, Monsieur l'Abbé came to visit Maman. He suggested that we change our last name (the very foreign and very Jewish-sounding Szpajzer) and he gave us new names under which we were inscribed in his registers and in the town hall's. Maman's first name, Bella, became our family name. He gave Maman a new first name: Isabelle. He said that Muguette was not a saint's name, and since he had no little Marie in his catechism class, I became Marie Bella. He had no problem with my brother's name, which is Joseph. I was as proud as a peacock when on Sundays he announced from the pulpit, "First in catechism, Marie Bella."

The priest came to our house quite often because Maman, a seamstress, often had to repair his threadbare cassocks. He sat and made conversation. Maman, self-taught, was a very knowledgeable lady and quite a conversationalist. Whenever he came, he asked Maman the same sempiternal question: "Alors Madame Bella, quand est-ce-qu'on la baptise votre petite Marie?" (Madame Bella, when are we going to baptize Marie?) "All her friends in catechism will soon be doing their First Communion, and if Marie is not baptized she won't be able to do it with them." He then proceeded to tell Maman that people in Champlost were ready to donate the complete outfit — dress, veil, shoes, rosary, white prayer book — for me to be received in style to the bosom of the Catholic Church.

Maman, knowing she was indebted to Champlost for hiding us, didn't know how to refuse. She really didn't want us to lose our deeply-held Jewish identity, even though we were not observant. She hit upon the idea of pretending that Ignace, Uncle Yidele's friend, was her brother.

Maman told the good priest that for such a momentous occasion, she would like to wait for her "brother" Ignace to come home. Monsieur l'Abbé understood. But Maman also had to contend with me. I wanted to be baptized. Now that I think about it, I realize that it was mostly not to be different from all my friends.

Once, one of the girls brought a song sheet to catechism class; it was quite a naughty song, I remember. We were passing it delightfully around when Monsieur l'Abbé looked up. Naturally, I was the one holding the song at that time. He marched over to me and yanked the sheet of paper out of my hand. After looking at it he crumpled the paper and with the voice he sometimes used in pulpit in order to get his point across, he thundered, "Marie, si vous continuez comme ça, je ne vous baptiserai pas!" (If you don't behave, I shall not baptize you!) I dissolved into tears. No punishment could have been worse as far as I was concerned.

The BBC

Monsieur Basile was a wise, generous and very learned man. He had at one time been mayor of Champlost. His witticisms were legendary throughout the village, and heaven help the intolerant. He had no patience for them. I was told that there were some, but I never met any. Many years after the war, when I returned to the village, I learned that Monsieur Basile had been to see the villagers and warned them that no harm had better come to us because of them or they would have to answer to him. He was a big, tall, very imposing man and no one dared cross him. I also learned, on my return, that the wartime mayor, Marcel Thierry, sat at night by his fireplace smoking his pipe, reading letters of denunciation — accusations of who was Jewish, or who had betrayed the regime — that had been delivered to him that morning and casually tossing them into the fire. This I learned from my friend Jacques Delagneau, husband of Lucette Petit. Jacques used to go to the Thierry household to help his daughter Yvonne with her homework and he witnessed the above. The mayor willingly told the two children why he was burning the letters. Everyone in Champlost had a hand in hiding us.

Monsieur Basile, an ardent Frenchman and patriot, listened to the BBC (British Broadcasting Corporation) every night. Amid the fiendishly parasitical German interference, we could hear the four notes of Beethoven's "Fifth Symphony" and the eagerly awaited words: "Ici Londres. Les Français parlent aux Français!" (This is London. Frenchmen are speaking to Frenchmen!) The radio turned very low, we strained to hear every word. Monsieur Basile was convinced that only through London could we hear the truth about the war. When one listened, sometimes just for laughs, to Radio Paris, the German-controlled French radio station, all we heard were Third Reich victories and the German army's forward push everywhere; this continued up to 1944. London had a song for Radio Paris, sung to the tune of "La Cucaracha": "Radio-Paris ment, Radio-Paris ment, Radio-Paris est allemande." (Radio Paris lies, Radio Paris is German.) I think that it was London's station that always ended its broadcast with Handel's "Water Music," and whenever I hear it, I am carried back fifty years and more.

Madame Nizier

Madame Nizier, our landlady, was a wonderfully gentle person and very pious. She went to church every morning, and on Sundays she went to vespers and compline as well. On Thursdays, which was not a school day in France, Maman sometimes asked her if I could stay with her for part of the day. Madame Nizier never refused. She and her husband hadn't had children and I think she was eager to pass on what she knew. She showed me how to mend socks and how to knit, which I must admit I never had any aptitude for. While we were busy, she taught me songs that her grandmother had sung to her. I always loved singing and quickly learned songs in every language I heard. She also told me stories, often religious ones. She had a supply of old almanacs — the most famous almanac in France, *Almanach Vermot*, so well-known with its blood-red cover. This almanac, with a page and a cartoon for each day, also had all kinds of stories, most of them humorous, and I used to read them to Maman at night while she was cooking or sewing. *Almanach Vermot* has been published each year since 1886, excluding the four years of war from 1943–1946. Madame Nizier also lent me a small book of the gospels, meant for children. I was fascinated by the stories.

Epilogue

During the war, the people of Champlost hid a Jewish family — my mother, Bella, my brother, Joseph, and me — from 1942 to 1945. On June 8, 2005, I went back to Champlost for a ceremony to honour our protectors. According to Mr. Victor Kuperminc, delegate of the French committee for Yad Vashem, Israel's Holocaust museum and memorial, the honour of Righteous Among the Nations is the highest distinction given by the State of Israel other than military medals. Yad Vashem posthumously awarded the medals and certificates of the Righteous Among the Nations to Monsieur Désiré and Madame Marie Nizier, on whose property my mother and I had lived, and to Monsieur Basile and Madame Léonide Roy, on whose farm my brother had resided. In Champlost, emotions ran high. Every inhabitant of the village was there, and the teachers came with their students. My old schoolmates were there, too. The mayor, Monsieur Michel Delagneau, spoke. "This is an important moment," he said. "It rewards two families, Monsieur Désiré and Madame Marie Nizier, as well as Monsieur Basile and Madame Léonide Roy, who did not hesitate to put their lives in jeopardy in order to save Jews." Madame Rina Sorek, delegate from the Israeli Embassy in Paris, said, "Whoever saves one person, saves the world." The medals and the certificates of the Righteous were then awarded. The mayor accepted on behalf of the two families.

After this, I stood up and said the Hebrew blessing, "Shehecheyanu vekiyemanu…" (Blessed are you, our God…who has brought us to this moment) and Monsieur l'Abbé Benoit, priest of Champlost, said a blessing in Latin and French. Then I recounted my stay in Champlost, which inspired me to write this memoir.

1 Muguette during the war, wearing the obligatory yellow Star of David. Paris, France, 1942.

2 The Roy family, who sheltered both Muguette and her brother, Jojo, during the war. From left to right: Marcel, Monsieur Basile, Madame Léonide and Maurice. Champlost, France, circa 1940.

3 Désiré and Marie Nizier, the friends and landlords who lived downstairs from Muguette and her mother in Champlost. Date unknown.

4 Muguette speaking at the ceremony honouring the Roy and Nizier families as Righteous Among the Nations. Champlost, 2005.

W Hour
Arthur Ney

Arthur Ney was born in Warsaw, Poland, in 1930. Under the German occupation, Arthur and his family were forced into the Warsaw ghetto in the fall of 1940. Arthur became a smuggler, escaping the ghetto and bribing the guards at the gate so he could go into what was known as the "Aryan" side of the city to barter for food to bring back to his family. Outside the ghetto, he often found shelter and advice at the home of the Serafinowicz family. In the spring of 1943, Arthur was outside of the ghetto when the Warsaw Ghetto Uprising — a large resistance effort by the Jews in the ghetto — began, and he was trapped on the outside. Arthur, alone, would have to pass as a gentile to survive the war. He left Warsaw to try to work as a farmhand in the countryside.

Clutching the ticket that I hoped would at last take me to safety, I boarded the train. It departed on time and, momentarily forgetting my troubles, I enjoyed looking through the window at the passing countryside. We stopped once or twice at small stations to pick up other travellers. Then the conductor announced that the next stop would be Piaseczno — I remember well the nervous excitement that shook my body. My mouth was dry and I couldn't concentrate on the next stage of my plan; I had no one to count on but myself. As I was getting off the train, I was almost knocked over by a unit of German soldiers, armed to the teeth, who were boarding the train heading back to Warsaw. I overheard the soldiers say that they were going to Warsaw to reinforce the German soldiers who were liquidating the ghetto. Some of them made comments that were, astonishingly, in praise of the Jews for standing up heroically to the Germans. These remarks were said in muted voices to avoid their being overheard by other Germans or their collaborators.

As had been true in Otwock, there were no farms in sight in Piaseczno, so I knew that I would have to leave the town as soon as possible. I didn't know the name of a nearby farming village to ask directions to and, what was worse, I didn't even know how to recognize a farming village. I finally decided to follow the railway tracks in the direction that would take me farther away from Warsaw. Sooner or later, I felt, I would see a farm with cows, horses and other animals. After walking for what I thought was hours, I found myself surrounded by fields, trees and occasional rows of small houses with thatched roofs. I didn't see any animals near the houses, though, so I assumed that the real farms were still farther away.

It was almost dusk and I was just becoming afraid that I would have to spend the night outside when I spotted a tiny group of houses that looked more like a small town than a farming village. The sight of this little town made me feel hopeful and I decided to try my luck there so I left the train tracks and cut across the fields. My heart was beating wildly as I walked to the far end of the town, silently rehearsing my obligatory greeting. I don't know why I chose one house over another, but I found myself knocking at a door, trembling with fear.

A thin man opened the door and looked at me questioningly. I greeted him faultlessly and the standard reply came without hesitation. The smoothness of the ritual put me at ease and I began to tell a variation on my well-rehearsed story. The man seemed to be satisfied and invited me inside, asking me if I would like to eat something. I accepted gratefully and crossed myself before eating the piece of Easter cake he put in front of me.

After I had finished, he asked me about events in Warsaw. The fires were visible even at this distance and everyone who passed through told a different story about the ghetto uprising. Managing to sound detached (which was a miracle in itself), I gave him a version of these events that would not identify me as a sympathizer, much less as a Jew. After hearing me out, he asked me why I had come to the countryside. Without naming Mr. Serafinowicz, I told him that people in Warsaw had suggested that a young boy's best chance of finding a job in the summer season would be as a shepherd. The man told me that he couldn't employ me because he didn't have animals that needed tending, but that one of his relatives, Franciszek Puchała, lived nearby in the village of Runów. Franciszek, he said, was the richest farmer in the village, with thirty morguens (measures of land), six cows, two horses, chickens and pigs, and surely needed help for the summer. I felt better right away and later, when I lay down to sleep on a cot that my host had kindly made for me, I fantasized about riding horses and milking cows. The next morning, after having a breakfast of black bread with jam and a cup of black ersatz coffee with sugar, as I took my leave, my kind host said, "May you go with God," to which I replied, "Amen."

The morning was beautiful as I walked west along the train tracks. With every passing minute, the rising sun spread more warmth until I felt as if I were being wrapped in an invisible blanket. I saw small green leaves, harbingers of the approaching summer, and little creatures coming out of hibernation. Above my head, many different sizes and colours of birds were flying and singing to each other in a discordant yet beautiful symphony. I thought back to the wonderful summers I had spent at my grandmother's house in Tomaszów, with its lovely orchard and vegetable garden.

I was awoken from my reverie by changes on the horizon — in the distance were a group of thatched-roofed huts on either side of a sandy road. In the background, I could see a dense evergreen forest. The whole scene looked like one of the paintings I had seen on family visits to the museums in Warsaw. I forced myself back into reality as I entered the village and approached the first house. To my delight, the first and last names of the occupant were on the fence surrounding each hut, usually carved into a log.

I soon came to a spacious house with the name Franciszek Puchała painted on the fence. I saw two horses drinking from a trough, chickens noisily strutting around in the courtyard and could hear the grunting of a pig. I didn't see any cows — I later learned that when the cows were not in the pasture, they were chained up in the barn with containers of hay and plant cuttings.

Before I could knock on the door, a watchdog jumped out of his doghouse, barking at me menacingly. I froze, but fortunately the dog was stopped in his tracks at the end of his long chain. In response to my knock, the door was opened by a man who, as far as I could tell, looked like a typical farmer. After exchanging the required religious greetings, I launched into a condensed version of my story. When I finished, the man motioned for me to sit on a big bench against the wall. The room was without doubt the main one in the house — there was a long narrow table, with a bed on either side, and four or five chairs on which guests sat eating, drinking, smoking and talking in a kind of Polish that I could only partly understand. I listened intently to the conversation, trying to anticipate when I would have to start answering questions. The man whom everyone called Franciszek gave me a piece of cake and a large cup of ersatz coffee. I accepted the cake and coffee with sincere gratitude, crossed myself and said grace. Then it happened — I heard the word "Jew" several times in the conversation. I couldn't understand the exact context, but luckily they didn't pursue the subject. Not long after, people started to leave and I soon realized that the only people left were those who lived there. It seemed I had been given the job!

The mother, whose first name I never learned, must have been in her sixties and I realize now that she must have been in the early stages of dementia. She was a massive woman who spent most of her day in bed sleeping, or complaining and criticizing everyone around her. All through these tirades, she talked to herself, which is why everyone called her crazy. When her children asked her to do something specific such as peeling potatoes, she did it. But she refused to milk the cows.

Her eldest son, Wawżyniec, who had been sitting across from me talking to himself, suffered from a head injury he had gotten in World War I. Though harmless and willing to do anything asked of him, he never took any initiative in carrying out the many tasks required on the farm. Like his mother, he talked to himself constantly, telling himself stories, some of which made sense.

Franciszek, who was in charge of the farm, was next in age. He didn't smoke, drink or gamble, and I never saw him with women — he worked hard from sunrise to sunset. He had a highly developed sense of humour that he shared with everyone. I never heard religion discussed in his house, nor did I hear any of the Puchałas use any kind of profanity, unlike their neighbours. They all prayed before retiring for the night and crossed themselves before each meal. Franciszek went to church on most Sundays.

Next came Czesiek, a colourful character. His broken nose was the subject of many wild stories revolving around everything from differences of opinion to fights over women. He smoked and drank, though moderately. His Saturday nights were his great outlet. He would put on his best shirt, his knee-high leather boots and set out for a neighbouring village where young people gathered. Although he crossed himself before meals and prayed at night like the others, he did not attend Sunday mass as often as Franciszek or their sister, Helen.

Helen was the only daughter in the family. In my eyes, she was not as plain as many of the other peasant women; her features were delicate and complemented her expressive eyes, which she unconsciously used in every conversation. She had a great sense of humour and a remarkable voice that sometimes sounded arrogant and sometimes seemed to invite further conversation. She was curious and thirsty for knowledge, never too shy to encourage people whom she met — including me — to share what they knew with her. Like her brothers, she had barely finished elementary school, but she loved to read the newspapers that Franciszek brought home from the market. Helen was religious and went to mass every Sunday, dressed in her best clothes, a sight that must have turned the heads of all the village men. She loved organ music and admitted that it often brought tears to her eyes. Helen was married to a farmer from the same village whose large family did not have an extra room for the couple, so the Puchałas allowed Helen and her husband to use a small bedroom off the kitchen at night. Since they were not able to live together, the anxious husband came over to the Puchała house regularly. He would spend a few minutes exchanging the news of the day with the Puchałas, then retire to the tiny bedroom to join Helen.

Franciszek showed me the stable where he kept the cows and horses and the barn that was used to store wheat, grass, hay and flour. If he hired more people, he noted, the barn would become like a hotel.

When we got to what I realized was the toilet, Franciszek opened the door and told me to be careful not to fall in, especially at night. When I asked where the toilet paper was, he burst out laughing and, when he recovered his composure, told me that I had a whole stable full of hay and straw at my disposal. He assured me that I would get used to living conditions in the country very quickly. Finally, we arrived at the potato cellar that was to be my bedroom. Franciszek went into the house and came back with a plaid blanket and a farmer's sheepskin that was long enough to serve as a duvet. He wished me goodnight and said that he would wake me at 6:00 a.m.

I didn't feel at all sleepy, so, for the first time since my unplanned separation from my family, I began to relive every moment from the time I had said goodbye to my grandmother. I didn't want to think about the last time I had talked to my parents or sister. I also pushed away thoughts about when and how they might have died. I have continued this avoidance for most of my life. Franciszek had left the tiny door to my potato cellar open, which allowed a little of the light from the bright, cloudless, star-filled sky to illuminate my quarters. My bed was a rectangular mound of hay and straw, raised about six inches off the floor, that was big enough to fit the blanket and sheepskin. I covered the hay with the blanket and lay on top of it fully dressed, pulling the sheepskin over me. Within a few minutes, I began to itch everywhere and I suddenly became afraid that creatures could enter through the open door. If I shut the door, I would be plunged into darkness, and I had always been afraid of the dark. Thankfully, I fell asleep much sooner than I imagined and the next thing I remember is Franciszek's voice waking me up.

Although it was only 6:00 a.m., the whole Puchała family was already up. Helen was busy at the stove and her brothers came and went, going between the house, the stable and the barn, letting the cows and horses out of the stable and steering them to their separate troughs. Helen took a basket full of grain out to the courtyard and fed the chickens and geese, imitating their calls as she did so. After all the animals were fed, everyone gathered in the house and ate their breakfast — a large piece of bread with a bit of jam on it, and black ersatz coffee. Franciszek said that it was still too cold to take the cows to the pasture, which was to be my job. In the meantime, I would be taught to perform many other tasks on the farm. Before we brought the cows and horses back to the stable, we would have to put new straw and hay in their stalls. He told me very seriously that animals performed their jobs better if they lived in clean surroundings.

Franciszek sent me to fetch a small pitchfork from the barn so he could teach me how to add hay and straw to the decomposing mass in the animals' stalls. The idea of work in the stalls, knee-deep in manure, made me nauseous. To make matters worse, everyone on the farm walked barefoot. Franciszek was understanding and assured me that I would only feel that way the first few times I did it. I took off my shoes and socks, which by this time were nothing but holes anyway, and jumped into the first stall. I didn't have to roll my pants up above my knees as the others did because I had fled the ghetto wearing shorts. As it turned out, the job wasn't all that unpleasant and, once I got used to the rank smell, I learned to perform it without any problem.

Franciszek and his siblings treated me like a member of the family, which made me more hopeful about my future. I liked them and felt grateful, but it was hard not to miss my own family and wonder what had happened to them. It was barely a week or ten days since the start of the ghetto uprising and, according to the news trickling in from Warsaw, the ghetto was still burning and its fighters were still keeping the German troops at bay. Thinking about the outcome and the fate of its possible survivors kept me from falling asleep at night. One evening, a neighbour came and told us to go outside and watch the flames shooting up from the burning ghetto. As we joined a group of people excitedly pointing at the sight and talking about it, people began to dust off the ashes that had been carried all this way from the burning ghetto. I stooped to pick up a tiny piece of paper with burned edges and saw that it must have come from a Jewish book because the print was in Hebrew. I felt a physical pain and tears came to my eyes. Pretending I needed to go to the toilet, I ran to the outhouse, crumbled the scrap of paper and threw it away. I had to wipe the tears from my eyes before I could rejoin the group of onlookers. This was one of the worst moments during my stay at Franciszek's farm.

Life on the farm was starting to get busier because of the approach of planting season. The trees were blooming in splendid, perfectly matched colours. Birds were flying from branch to branch, searching for the best place to build their nests and lay their eggs. Franciszek also began preparing me for the job I had been hired to do: being a shepherd. It had been a month or so since I had arrived and the whole village was busy preparing for the coming summer. Farmers were out in the fields, ploughing, fertilizing and seeding, and all around one could feel the controlled nervousness associated with the unpredictable outcome of their work. This mood seemed to be picked up by the animals as well. Cows were continually mooing in protest at being kept on chains in the stables, and were demanding to be taken to the pasture.

We used a common pasture for Runów and the surrounding villages, so I had the company of other shepherd boys. We did what other boys did in the countryside — pushing and shoving each other, telling tall tales and, later in the summer, swimming in the stream. In the fall, we made fires and roasted frogs, apples, potatoes and anything else edible that we could take from adjacent fields.

At the beginning of the summer, we wore cut-off pants in the water, but later, when the boys started swimming naked, I had two problems. The first was that I didn't know how to swim and the second was, of course, that I was worried about letting the other boys see me naked.[3] I told them that I was from a very religious family, that it was against my beliefs to appear naked even in front of males, but that I would go in wearing my underpants. I also told them that I was willing to take swimming lessons from anyone who wanted to teach me. My explanation seemed to satisfy the boys. Although I was out of danger for the moment, I knew that this would not be the end of the story.

As usual, Czesiek woke me up when it was time to go back to work. This time, however, instead of waking me and leaving the barn immediately, I heard him waiting at ground level near the door. This alarmed me and my mouth became dry. I slid down the haystack and walked toward the door, pretending that I found everything as usual. Chewing on a piece of straw, Czesiek demanded, "Show it to me." I

3 Arthur was concerned that the boys would notice that he was circumcised. Circumcision, removal of the foreskin of the penis, is a common practice in Judaism.

felt a tremendous weight on my chest, but I didn't cry. Was it possible that my experiences in the past few months had built up my ability to feel horrendous pain inside without tears? I didn't obey the order but instead told Czesiek that I was Jewish. I don't know why I chose to admit that rather than do as I was told. After a moment, he almost gently told me to go to the house and ask Helen for bread and jam. I'm sure that this was Czesiek's way of comforting me. I had no idea who had found me out. It may have been that one of my shepherd companions had told his parents about my not wanting to swim in the nude and a naturally suspicious farmer had talked to Czesiek. After my confrontation with him, though, I was overwhelmed with insecurity and fear. It took a long time for me to feel safe again.

In the high summer I could see all around me the growing crops and other signs of nature taking its course. I was fascinated by the appearance of little calves and colts shadowing their mothers and trying without success to reach their teats. Unfortunately for the newborns, as soon as they could graze in the pasture, the mothers gradually withdrew from nursing and pushed the more aggressive ones away with a gentle nudge. I loved watching this young generation of animals frolicking, playing tug-of-war and sniffing everything they encountered for the first time.

One day during this pleasurable time, I was very surprised to see Helen running across the pasture toward me. My first thought was that she shouldn't be running because she was pregnant. When she reached me, trying to catch her breath and control her emotions, she looked around to make sure no one was near enough to overhear her. Putting her hand on my shoulder she said quietly, "The Germans are looking for Jews."

According to Helen, there were apparently two Jewish girls in an adjacent village who were, from what people were saying, paying for their upkeep with their bodies. Someone had denounced them to the Germans and they were now conducting a house-to-house, village-to-village search for other Jews. The Puchała family had heard about it from a peasant who was on his way to the market from one of the villages that had been searched. Helen and her brothers had decided to give me a chance to escape rather than just wait to see whether the Germans would find me. I was very frightened and couldn't focus on what I should do. Helen told me to run to the forest, gathering whatever fruit and vegetables I could find in passing, and hide there for two days. She would stay in the pasture with the cows and tell the neighbours that I had gone to the next village to help another farmer.

I took off immediately for the forest, crouching, zigzagging and hiding behind trees, bushes and the high wheat near its harvest time. In the end, I only stayed out one night. I decided to come home on the second evening when I saw German trucks filled with soldiers driving along the road toward Warsaw. I found out later that the two Jewish girls from the next village were the only victims of the hunt and that the German soldiers had taken them away.

Arthur eventually had to leave the farm and return to Warsaw. He continued to hide his Jewish identity while sheltered in a Roman Catholic orphanage run by the Salesian order, and also passed as a gentile during his time in the Polish resistance effort, when he took part in the Warsaw city revolt of 1944. Even after the war, back at the orphanage, Arthur maintained his non-Jewish identity until he reunited with his only surviving relatives.

1

2

3

1 Arthur (in front) with his family before the war. From left to right: Arthur's father, Jerzy Ney, his sister, Eugenia, his mother, Pola Ney-Holcman, and his paternal grandmother, Henia Ney. Poland, 1936.

2 Arthur (left) at the Eiffel Tower with his only surviving relatives, his aunt Ronia and uncle Józiek, after the war. Paris, 1947.

3 Arthur's reunion with Franciszek Puchała, the farmer who sheltered Arthur in Runów in 1943. Poland, 1988.

In Hiding
Marguerite Élias Quddus

Marguerite Élias Quddus was born in Paris, France, in 1936. After the Nazis occupied France in 1940, they passed anti-Jewish decrees, confiscating property and prohibiting Jews from holding jobs. This persecution increased, and eventually French collaborating officials rounded up Jews to be deported to Nazi camps. Marguerite's father was arrested and taken away, and her mother was later arrested as well, although she was released. Young Marguerite and her sister, Henriette, needed a place to hide, and their mother made a plan to save them with the help of non-Jewish friends and acquaintances.

Mama has a long conversation with us. She explains how she was freed thanks to Madame Graziani. Then she says that Henriette and I have to leave home without her. The government is arresting all the Jews in Paris, even the ones who are French. We can't stay here anymore. She reminds us of when we went away to Fontainebleau, the time we spent without her in the country with the lady who brought us back on her bicycle because the concierge had informed on us, and of Hélène's arrest. She tells us the story of the Virgin and baby Jesus because we are going to pretend to be Catholics. We will have to pretend until the war ends and Papa comes back. We have to hide separately from her. I listen closely without understanding. While she speaks, she cuts the threads from the stars and removes them from our clothes. I take them and throw them in the air, laughing. "They fly, Mama! Look at my shooting stars!"

I'm happy. We laugh for a minute and then she takes us in her arms and kisses us tenderly. She looks at the time and says, "Time to go to bed, girls. It's midnight. I have a lot of things to get ready." We go to bed sadly. How is the separation going to happen? She says goodnight and turns off the light.

"Leave the door open, please!" Henriette begs her.

What did Mama mean? It's keeping me awake. Where will we go? Who will take us? We get out of our beds and tiptoe over to watch her. She fills her hatbox with the best merchandise. She puts our clothes in our suitcase and then changes some of them for others. She places some photographs and all sorts of papers inside the big picture frame that she's taken down from the wall. She throws a lot of things in the garbage. She wraps her big gold spoon in a black cloth and puts it in the bottom of her shoulder bag. Nobody must know that I went with her to the jeweller's to have her rings and necklace and our chains and bracelets melted down. Then she sits down at the corner of the table where she used to eat with Papa and puts her face down on her arms, wailing, "Oy vey iz mir..." Without a word to each other, my sister and I go back to our beds. The sandman comes and I fall asleep.

We wake up at dawn. There's no hot water for us to wash but it doesn't matter — we don't have time. We put on our best outfits, white fur coats and hats. My sister brings her violin. I bring my baby doll, which is the least heavy of my dolls. I can't bring the stroller or my pedal car or any other toys.

"Are you ready, girls?" asks Mama tearfully from the kitchen. She hasn't stopped wailing and shouting. Now, she opens the sideboard and takes out some crystal glasses. She throws them against the wall we share with the neighbours, saying something I don't understand. Crash, bang! The neighbour answers by knocking on the wall with her crutch, once, twice, three times. "Stop it, Mama! Stop!" begs my sister. Everything is so painful right now.

A short woman arrives. "She's a dwarf," my sister whispers in my ear with a mischievous smile. She's going to take us to her daughter who has a dry cleaner's shop and is a friend of Madame Binet.

Mama hugs us to her and says, "Listen to me, children, this is important. If anyone asks you where your parents are, don't forget that you have to say Papa is a soldier and he's gone to the front. Me, you don't know. Say as little as possible about the things that have happened here in the last little while — the telephones, the radio, the arrests, the informers — not a word! You're Catholic, right, Marguerite? Henriette is responsible for the two of you. She'll be able to explain better." She turns to the woman and says, "Be careful, make sure no one notices you. Are you able to carry their suitcase?"

"I'm small, but I'm agile. Look!" She gets up on the table and then jumps to the ground. After that little demonstration, she says, "Let's get going. I left the downstairs door open. Everything will be fine. Let's go!" She takes charge, just like our maid Georgette... I wonder where she is. I'd rather go away with her, she's twice as big.

I pat Choukette and then I pack my schoolbag. I'm ready, but I'm overcome with sadness. Mama hugs us and kisses us, and then we go outside, where it's still dark. "Goodbye, children! Go, and don't look back. We'll see each other soon," she murmurs, and I hear her blow her nose several times. "Goodbye, Mama," I say, my heart filled with sorrow. The dwarf pulls me behind her.

Marguerite and her sister were soon helped by an organization called Œuvre de secours aux enfants (Children's Relief Agency), through whose network the children were placed with Catholic families on farms and hidden in convents, secretly escorted from one place to another, with false identification papers in case they were questioned. Marguerite became accustomed to being moved to new hiding places. Eventually, the sisters arrived in the village of Vatilieu, at the farm of Antoinette and Robert Chatenay — where they would live for two years.

A lady comes to get us, as usual. This one is called Colette Morel. She carries our suitcase.

Who will I be with tomorrow? "Quickly, young ladies, we have to take the train," she announces cheerfully. I've taken it so many times that it doesn't have any effect on me. This is all supposed to be for our own good. Henriette reads a magazine with lots of pictures. I watch the countryside go by.

We finally get off and then walk for a long time, a very long time. I have to keep changing my schoolbag from one hand to the other. A bell rings. In the building opposite us, boys and girls come out, jostling each other. That must be the teacher standing at the door. Maybe she's waiting for us. We stay there for a moment and then go on.

A little bit further and we're there. "Here's your new home," says Colette Morel. My head is itching. I see cows and horses. I can smell manure from the stable. We are introduced to the farmers, the Chatenays. Our guide is in a hurry. She hands them our suitcase, says goodbye to us and leaves. The man, Robert, smiles and jokes and seems very jolly. The grandmother knitting in a corner is his Mama. There's another woman, Antoinette, who's the lady of the house. She seems more severe than her husband and she's also taller. She gives the orders: "Come here!" "Put that there!" "Do this!" "Do that!"

After a delicious snack — I still have my eye on the cake that's left — she shows us around. They have a grocery store. I see blocks of butter, cream cheese, barrels of wine, and several kinds of bread and milk. I won't die of hunger.

We go upstairs and Madame Chatenay shows us our room. My sister and I will sleep together in the double bed, under the crucifix on the wall. "Careful not to dirty my bedspread," she says with a scowl, noticing traces of earth.

We scratch ourselves constantly. "Get your clothes off now! You need a good shower." She pushes us toward the bathroom and gathers up our clothes, examines them and takes them away, as they did at the convent. To make sure we're clean, she scrubs us all over. Then she dries us. Then she picks up a brush and starts to do our hair. "Holy Mary, mother of Jesus! You're full of lice! We'll have to get rid of those dirty bugs!" she exclaims, throwing each of us a towel.

We go downstairs and she leads us outside. She brings out two chairs from the kitchen, a big basin and a pitcher of hot water. She shampoos Henriette's hair first. Without worrying about the neighbours who are watching, she soaps her hair. If only I could stick my tongue out at them! She rinses Henriette's hair and pours a bottle of gasoline on it. "Ow, it burns!" yells my poor sister, who seems to have it in her ears. The lady wraps her head in the towel and sits her down. Then, pointing a finger at me, she says, "Now it's your turn."

Henriette has spoken to me seriously about the Chatenays. It's been over a year that we've been living with them. She proposed that we call them Papa and Mama for good and asked what I thought about that.

How can she burden me with this? What about our real Papa and our real Mama? I don't understand her. I agree that we should do it in front of people — but not for good. All my hopes are dashed. I don't feel like answering her.

"Yes or no?" she insists. I don't like her tone of voice or the way she orders me around just because she's the older one. If I say no, she'll get mad and if I say yes, I'll feel like a traitor. What will my parents think when they come back? She looks me in the eye and I'm thinking of them. She says, "Imagine, Marguerite! They'd be so happy. Why are you being such an idiot? You know they want to adopt us. We'll be baptized. And one day, you'll have your first communion in a long white dress like all the other girls. So, is it yes? Can we start tomorrow?" I don't answer, but she repeats, "Is it yes?" She shakes me so hard that I say, "Okay, do what you want, it doesn't matter to me."

"We'll both do it, when I give the signal."

At breakfast, torn between my shame and her pride, we lie, saying, "Thank you, Mama."

The next day, I go picking apples with Robert. I gather poppies and avoid addressing him. I listen to the sound of our steps and the creaking of the wheelbarrow. I think of my sister's words and of my love for Papa. I walk softly along the grass-lined path, wondering whether I have to give up the true to gain the false. I see myself far away from here, on our street in Paris before the war, in our shop near Monsieur Bieder's tailor shop, and I compare it with what I have now. I wish I could be elsewhere, at the age I was when my father would hold me and read me lovely stories in a low voice while turning the pages. I'd nestle my head in the hollow of his shoulder, and everything would be all right.

"Are you coming, child?" asks Papa Robert.

"My name is Marguerite!" I cry, upset.

As the German occupation of France draws to a close, Marguerite is eventually reunited with her mother, at first for a brief visit and then permanently.

In a caustic tone of voice, Antoinette declares, "Listen to me, girls. Your mother — yes, Madame Élias, in person — called me on the phone. After nearly two years' total absence, after never answering my letters, back she comes, just when I was thinking of adopting you. And not only that, I discover that she's not crazy, contrary to what they had told me." She looks at the two of us with an expression that's both scornful and sad. Henriette has her head down. I'm upset by all this and I need to move around. Madame Chatenay looks at the clock. "Hurry, girls, in an hour, you have an appointment to meet her at Notre-Dame-de-l'Osier, across from my sister's house. My niece, Cécile, will go with you, I don't have the desire or the courage to go myself. To think that I kept you and took care of you as if you were my own daughters. In spite of the risks. And this is my thanks!"

"Look, here she comes! She's coming out. I see her! Mama! Mama!" she shouts, loud enough to wake the dead. She can't stand still, she's jumping up and down. I don't move. Mama didn't have a hairdo like that. She really does look crazy. Who is this person?

She throws off her cape, spreading her arms like Jesus Christ on the cross, and says with her accent, "My little girls! My dear little girls!" Her model daughter rushes to her and throws her arms around her neck, talking non-stop and kissing her again and again. They don't need me and I don't care. They collapse onto the grass. Finally, she calls me, "Margueritaleh! Margueritaleh!" I'm irritated and hesitate, then I run to her. She takes me onto her lap, moving the big one aside. "Come, mayneh beybeleh, you too, come and kiss dayneh mamaleh. You've grown! Don't you recognize me?" It's when she hugs me that I feel it's my mother. She has the same accent as Auntie. They can't speak French properly. But the more I hear her, the less it bothers me.

She takes some chocolate-covered shortbread cookies out of her shoulder bag and offers them to us, as many as we want. We laugh until we cry and we cry for joy. She gives her favourite a beautiful watch. Doesn't she realize I also know how to tell time? I weep with jealousy. She slips a package into my pocket: it's a tiny baby-doll wrapped in fabric. I don't want it but I thank her grudgingly. She explains that she had bought us beautiful chain bracelets engraved with our names. She wrapped them up in a handkerchief with her big gold spoon, her papers and her jewellery, but there was a *rafle* (roundup) in Lyon when she was at the grocery store and she had to run, leaving her bag of food on the counter. When she went back ten minutes later, it was gone. "Thieves! Bandits!" she says angrily. But it was a close call. She could have been picked up and sent to the camps with all the other Jews. She cries into her handkerchief and I'm upset. Henriette is talking so much I can't get a word in, but everything she's saying is false. She talks about her life with the Chatenays and she makes it sound like she's Cinderella. As usual, she's exaggerating.

At the Vinay train station, they [the Chatenays] kept gazing lovingly at us. "So much has happened in the two years we've taken care of you. We got to know each other. Do you understand, girls? You were family!" I felt so uncomfortable that when they kissed me, I couldn't even wipe their tears from my face. I wanted to scream with rage, but I cried. I was upset and sad, and I didn't know what to think. With my nose against the window of our compartment, I watch them disappear. I don't say anything. We don't need them anymore. From this moment on, they're no longer our parents. We must forget Vatilieu. Seated comfortably in our corner of the train, we can see the train driver not far from us. I'm facing my sister, who's looking out at the mountains. Goodbye, Chatenays! We're never coming back.

1

2

3

1 Marguerite and Henriette with the Chatenay family during the war. From left to right: Antoinette, Marguerite, Robert, Henriette and Robert's mother. Vatilieu, France, 1943.

2 Marguerite (left) and Henriette reuniting with their mother in the spring of 1945. Notre-Dame-de-l'Osier (Isère), France.

3 Marguerite and her son, Michael, visiting Antoinette and Robert Chatenay. Vatilieu, 1980.

Behind the Red Curtain
Maya Rakitova

Maya Rakitova was born in Smolensk, Russia, in 1931. When the war broke out, Maya, her mother and her older brother were living in Vinnitsa, Ukraine. Nazi Germany occupied Vinnitsa in 1941, and Maya quickly learned how important it was to hide her Jewish identity. Nazi roundups of the Jews in Vinnitsa began, followed by mass murders in the forests nearby. Maya and her mother only avoided becoming victims of these roundups and massacres by hiding with Nyusya, a non-Jewish woman who was staying in their home, and Maria Khomichuk, a family friend.

The situation in town grew more and more tense. At dawn one morning in mid-September 1941, a neighbour raised the alarm, informing us that screams had been heard at the boundary streets of the Old Town. The Germans were seen going from door to door, taking Jews. We thought they were taking young men and women to work, as they had done the week before. My mother asked Nyusya to take me to her rooms and rushed to the garden with Grandfather and Adya, Aunt Sonya's husband. Aunt Sonya stayed at home with her granddaughters because everybody thought that the Germans would not take old people and children for work. Nyusya put me in the same bed where her three children were sleeping. At that moment, the Germans came in, accompanied by a Ukrainian policeman. They asked Nyusya what nationality she was. Frightened to death, with her hands shaking, she showed them her Ukrainian passport. As the Germans pointed to the children Nyusya told them, "These are my children." With that decisive statement, this brave woman saved my life. The Germans left, heading to the house extension where Aunt Sonya and her granddaughters were. In a few minutes, they were brought out. I could see through the window that they hadn't been allowed to put on proper clothes. Sonya carried the younger girl, Vita, who was wearing only a short nightgown.

That day, Nyusya took her children and me and we all moved to her mother's house. Knowing nothing about my mother's fate, I stayed with Nyusya for two or three days more. Meanwhile, the news spread across Vinnitsa that the Germans had taken at least ten thousand Jews out of town to the nearest forest, where a huge trench was dug; all of them were executed there. There were many wounded, as well as children, who were thrown in the trench alive, buried together with the dead. People said that for several days it looked like the earth was moving.

After two days, Nyusya made it clear to me that she was afraid to keep me any longer. The only thing I could do was try to find my mother. I decided to look for her at the homes of her close friends. First I went to Maria Khomichuk, who lived in the Old Town. When I asked her if my mother was there, she looked frightened and answered that she knew nothing about her whereabouts. I headed further into the Old Town, going into many houses, but all my efforts were worthless. As I passed through almost all the streets of Vinnitsa, it was getting dark and I was scared. In spite of my young age, I understood why Nyusya refused to keep me any longer, but I had no idea where else to go. Walking down the street toward the bridge leading to the Old Town, I stopped near the park and began to cry in despair. When complete darkness fell, I got so frightened that I had no choice but to go back to Nyusya. To my great joy, my mother was waiting for me there! She was very worried about me because she knew I had left the house in the morning. I found out that my mother had been at

Maria's but that Maria had been afraid to tell me because she did not want to let Mother's whereabouts become known to anyone. What a horrific time it was!

Late that night, my mother took me by the hand and we returned to Maria Khomichuk's house. We spent only a few days there. Maria had two children and didn't want to take the risk of hiding us in her house. I don't remember if the Germans had already announced that they would execute anyone trying to save Jews, but everybody knew of the executions near Vinnitsa and nobody doubted that they would pay with their lives for helping Jews. It was dangerous to stay in Maria's house, so every night Mother and I went to the forest. Since it was already October, nights were cold and my mother covered me with the dark blue shawl she had taken with her at dawn when the first raid had begun. My mother understood that we wouldn't be able to remain this way for long and that we needed some shelter. She found another friend in the Old Town, a woman who agreed to take us in. This woman had a six-year-old child, who could easily reveal to the neighbours who we were, so she placed us in a dark corridor where nobody usually walked. I remember lying on the floor of that corridor all day long, listening to the voices of children playing in the yard. I had a strong wish to play with them, but at age ten I understood very well why we had to hide. Two or three weeks later, her child discovered us and we had to leave again. I didn't want to leave this very uncomfortable place because I knew that our every movement was associated with mortal danger — in the Old Town, everybody knew us.

Since we had nowhere else to go in Vinnitsa, we had to leave. It was too dangerous for my mother to show up on the town's streets, where anybody could recognize her. We needed papers to move to another town, which meant that Mother had to have a passport with a record confirming that her nationality was Russian. Some people advised my mother to apply at the police station and claim that just before the beginning of the war she had given in her passport to be exchanged for a new one, which she had never received. Such cases were not unusual, but five witnesses were required. Three people were found at once — Maria Khomichuk, Olga and her niece. After a while, Mother found another two; I suspect she simply paid them.

Using their false identity documents, Maya and her mother moved from city to city in search of safety, finding themselves in Vapniarka (then part of Transnistria, now in Ukraine) in spring 1942, where they met a woman named Anna Mikheyeva. She sympathized with their struggle to hide their Jewish identities in an area occupied by Romania, an ally of Nazi Germany, and realized it would be difficult for Maya and her mother to survive in hiding together. Anna offered to take Maya with her back to Odessa to keep her safe. Maya lived with Anna — under a false name, using a document she was able to get after being baptized at age eleven — into 1944, until it was clear the Soviets were winning the war against the Nazis.

I have often asked myself, What did our neighbours think of me? I lived at Anna's openly and everybody knew that I was not her daughter. I don't remember what kind of history was presented to our neighbours, but I do remember one episode from that time. One day, a woman who lived in the same house came to us, asking Anna to help her kill a live hen for dinner. Anna answered that she was not able to do it but that her Marusya (that was me) would. I was horrified but couldn't refuse. Luckily, I had once seen how women did this, so I took that miserable hen to the shed and cut her throat. When the woman left, Anna explained to me why she had insisted that I kill the hen. Doing this job, she said, would dispel suspicions that I was a Jewish child. I believe such rumours and suspicions were circulating but nobody betrayed me; on the contrary, everybody treated me well.

In the autumn of 1943, Anna decided to enroll me in the Gymnasium where she worked. Undoubtedly, this decision was made with my mother's consent. Nobody knew what was more dangerous — staying at home would prompt the question of why I wasn't attending classes while Anna worked at the Gymnasium, and attending classes would expose my face to many people.

I was enrolled in the first class, which required four years of primary school. I had only three years but had never had a problem with school. Besides, I was so happy to go to school again and to be together with other children that it gave me a strong motivation for learning. My favourite subject was religion, maybe because it was new for me.

Unfortunately, the fact that I had started to live openly made my life more dangerous. One day, a young friend of Anna's, a former student who had become an artist, approached Anna with the idea of drawing me; since she was painting a canvas representing a religious episode, she needed Jewish faces and considered my face quite appropriate. We were all horrified and tried to persuade her to give up this bad idea. To make sure our refusal would not cause any unwarranted suspicions, Anna's good friend, a doctor, placed me in a hospital for three weeks.

Maya credits two women with her survival during the war years, and many decades later — although she was not able to trace the women or any descendants — she made sure they were recognized for their efforts.

I worked for seventeen years and retired at age seventy-two. Having more time available, I started to look into having both my mother's friend Maria Khomichuk and Anna Mikheyeva named as Righteous Among the Nations. This is an award that Yad Vashem, Israel's Holocaust museum and memorial, gives to non-Jews who helped Jews during the war. It took some time to gather the evidence needed to be able to have them recognized, and in this I received help from Igor Komarovsky, a researcher who did some work for the World-Wide Club of Odessites. Thanks to his wonderful research, Maria and Anna were recognized posthumously by Yad Vashem in August 2009.

1 Maya with her mother, Zinaida. Smolensk, Russia, circa 1933.

2 Maya at age five. Smolensk, 1936.

3 Maya's mother, Zinaida. Leningrad, the Soviet Union (now Saint Petersburg, Russia), 1950s.

4 Maya Rakitova. Montreal, 2005.

Traces of What Was

Steve Rotschild

Steve Rotschild was born in Vilna, Lithuania, in 1933. Vilna, under Soviet occupation in September 1939, was invaded by Nazi Germany in June 1941.

At the end of June 1941, when I returned home from Popishok after spending the week there with my grandparents, Vilna was under German occupation: for the Jews the war had begun in earnest. Anti-Jewish edicts were issued daily and posted on buildings all over town. A yellow six-pointed star had to be sewn on the chest and on the back of each article of clothing worn by a Jew, young or old. Jews were forbidden to walk on the sidewalk and had to walk in the gutter on the right-hand side of the road. Jewish property was confiscated.

Lithuanians, who did all the dirty work for the Germans, began what were called *hapunes*, abductions of Jewish men. They would cordon off a street and go from house to house, searching out and taking away any Jewish men they found. Once captured, the men were taken to a prison and from there to the Ponary forest and killed. Five thousand Jewish men were thus murdered in the first month of the occupation.

One early morning, the Lithuanian militia came to search the homes on our street. We lived in an apartment that had been built in the back of a large wood-frame house belonging to a middle-aged

Lithuanian couple. There were flower beds in the front yard and, in the large backyard, vegetables and tall sunflower plants grew. There was also a clean, roomy outhouse to which a large tom turkey was tied by one leg with a string. It would try to attack me each time I used the outhouse. One day, standing safely out of his reach, I pissed on him.

The landlady, who was a very decent person and had befriended my mother, came to warn us of the approaching danger. My father, a short, slim, dark man with a shock of curly black hair on his head, could never pass for an Aryan. My mother, on the other hand, was a tall, beautiful woman with long blond hair made up in two braids and pinned up on top of her head, encircling her very Slavic-looking face.

My mother never panicked or despaired; she kept her composure in the face of mortal danger, always looking for an escape, no matter how hopeless a situation seemed. She quickly led Father to the back garden where there was a pile of lumber left over from when they had built on the addition to the house, had him lie down against the wall and covered him with the wood. She took my baby brother in her arms and me by the hand and came out into the front yard just as two Lithuanian soldiers with rifles came through the gate, asking where the Jews were. The landlady, who was standing on the porch, told them there were no Jews here. One of them went inside the house to have a look; the other went to the back, looked in the outhouse, went slowly through the garden and came back. My mother sat calmly on the steps of the front porch playing with the blond baby in her lap and a seven-year-old boy in short pants with ash blond hair and grey-green eyes, his face a mirror image of his mother's, sitting next to her. The older, taller one of the soldiers excused himself for disturbing us, but someone had told them that there were Jews living here, obviously a mistake, and they left.

By the first week of September 1941, the Germans were ready to herd the Jews of Vilna into two ghettos. With typical Prussian efficiency and the willing help of the Lithuanians, they first emptied an area of several blocks in the oldest part of the city, which was by then one thousand years old, and split the area into a "large" and "small" ghetto. The district was a maze of twisting, narrow cobblestone streets where the Jews of Vilna had lived, worked and prayed in dozens of tiny synagogues for hundreds of years. Most of the people who had lived there were already resting in mass graves in the pits in the Ponary forest. The remaining Jews, numbering by then about 20,000, still the size of the population of a small town, were to be squeezed into the ghettos.

On the fine, sunny day in September that the Jews of Vilna were ordered to move to the ghettos, a Lithuanian soldier, holding his rifle in both hands, came into the front yard where our family was already packed and waiting. He told us to get moving and gave Father a push with the steel-clad butt of the rifle. This time there was nowhere to hide. The announcements posted on the walls and lampposts all over the city warned the population that anyone found hiding a Jew would be hung from the nearest lamppost along with the rest of his family. This was not an empty threat. Germans were known to keep their word.

Mother carried Monik and a valise; Father carried two large valises; and I carried a bag stuffed with some clothes slung over my shoulder. All our other possessions were given for safekeeping to our kind landlady, who was wiping away tears as we left. When we came out of our side street to the main road leading to the old town, we saw that it was filled with families carrying all sorts of baggage, all trudging in the same direction.

It was a sad and silent procession, the only sound being the shuffle of feet on the cobblestones and the heavy breathing of people burdened with heavy loads. There were no guards with dogs, just the occasional soldier standing on the sidewalk, watching. There was no place to run.

By my eighth birthday, November 10, 1941, I spoke fluent Russian without a trace of an accent. I'd been living outside the ghetto with the Fiodorov family for several weeks. The family consisted of Mr. and Mrs. Fiodor Fiodorov, his spinster sister and their three children — a girl my age, Galia, Kolia, a boy a year older, and the eldest, Fedka, whose full name was Fiodor Fiodorovich Fiodorov. To understand how I came to spend that winter with a Russian family, I must go back to the first week of September when we arrived in the ghetto. Upon arrival we were assigned a small space in the attic of a three-storey building. It was a true attic, not an attic apartment, the roof sloping down from above the door to the bottom of the wall opposite at a distance of no more than three metres. Over the next few days every man in the ghetto was issued a *Schein*, an identification certificate. The men useful to the war effort were issued yellow *Scheine*. All others were issued white *Scheine*.

On Yom Kippur, when most Jewish men would be found praying in the synagogue, the Germans carried out the first *Aktion* in the ghetto. They sealed off the exits to every synagogue and arrested and removed anyone who didn't have a yellow *Schein*. Again, very efficient — the Germans saved time and effort by not trudging up and down stairs searching dark closets and cramped attics for Jewish men.

My father had a white *Schein*, but he wasn't religious and so we were not in the synagogue. However, it was only a matter of time before we would be caught and taken away, so my parents decided to take a chance on the outside. My baby brother, Monik, was left with Fruma and Shmuelitzik Katz and their three children, my mother's cousins and our best friends. Shmuelitzik had been a carpenter in his youth and so had the life-saving yellow *Schein*.

Leaving the ghetto was not difficult. Every morning at daybreak, parties of workers would leave through only one gate, as all other exits were sealed. My parents joined a large group of workers and I was smuggled out hidden among them. The Jews in the ghetto were like the inmates in a Mississippi prison I once saw in a movie. The prisoners were kept in open barracks in the midst of alligator and snake-infested swamps. You could run but there was nowhere to escape to.

My parents found work in a warehouse where items of value looted from Jewish homes were stored, sorted, cleaned and sent to Germany. The manager, a decent older German, pretended he didn't know that my parents didn't return to the ghetto each night, as was required; instead, they spent the nights hiding in the warehouse.

Mother took me to the Dzeviatnikovs, the people who owned the house where we once lived and where I was born. Because people living close by knew me as a Jewish child, they couldn't keep me and so Mrs. Dzeviatnikov arranged for me to stay with her sister, Mrs. Fiodorov, which is how I came to spend the next six months with this Russian family. My story was that I was the son of Mr. Fiodorov's brother whose wife had died recently.

Life outside the ghetto was harsh. What work Mr. Fiodorov could get was not enough to support his family of six. That winter we ate three things: homemade black bread, cabbage and potatoes. These three foods were served for breakfast, lunch and dinner, the potatoes and cabbage boiled or fried with onions, or made into a soup. There was tea but no sugar, honey or any kind of sweets.

The Fiodorov house, which stood on an acre of land at the very edge of town, was small and primitive. The only entrance, through the kitchen, faced a large brick oven; straight ahead was the door to the living room and on the left, a door to the bedrooms, rooms I never saw during the time I was there. Facing the oven was a long wood table with benches on each side. On the wall over the table was a dark painting of Christ. At the entrance stood a basin filled with water and a bar of soap.

Mrs. Fiodorov was very strict. Before every meal we had to wash our hands and genuflect to the picture on the wall. We ate from metal plates using either a spoon or our hands because there weren't any forks or knives at the table. The children ate as fast as possible. The outhouse in the far corner of the yard had only one seat and no one wanted to be the last in line, waiting in the bitter cold. The first one in also had the luxury of a relatively stink-free environment.

There was no running water in the house. I don't know how the women bathed, but the men occasionally went to a public bathhouse in the city. The first time I went with them, I was scared that I would be found out to be Jewish because of my circumcised penis, but the bathhouse was full of men and boys of all ages and no one seemed to notice my difference.

These public bath visits were an absolute necessity because of the lice. The long-sleeved cotton nightshirts we slept in were worn during the day as undershirts and the little parasites made their nests and laid their eggs in the seams under the arms. This provided the children with a sporting activity. On Sunday mornings all the kids would congregate in their nightshirts in the living room — where I slept on a board laid between two chairs — and destroy as many of the pests as quickly as possible. The winner was the one who killed the most in the agreed-upon time.

The two boys didn't usually play with me but Galia, who was closer to my age, spent her after-school hours with me. She was a pretty, blond girl with dimples in her cheeks. Among the books in the living room was a medical encyclopedia, where she showed me diagrams of the male and female genitals, which was very exciting for me. We had a lot of fun with that.

The week of the Russian Orthodox Christmas, the priest and his assistant came to visit. The priest was old, with a bushy grey beard, and dressed in a long black cassock. His assistant, who was dressed the same way, was young, with a black beard. We all went into the living room, where in the far corner was an icon of the holy mother and baby Jesus. Mrs. Fiodorov had told me to do as the other children were doing. Each of us genuflected in front of the icon, then stood in a row for the priest's blessing. The old priest blessed each of us in turn by putting his hands on our heads and murmuring a blessing. I was the last and when my turn came, he didn't put his hand on my head, but instead, with his finger under my chin, tilted my face up, looked into my eyes for a long while, then asked whose child I was. I said nothing. Mrs. Fiodorov explained. He looked at me again, smiled and blessed me as well. I think he was a kind man.

Eventually, Steve's parents had heard that the ghetto was safe enough — that there had been no further roundups — and they returned to live there together. Throughout spring 1942 and part of 1943, "life in the ghetto went on." But soon after Steve's father passed away from an illness in the spring of 1943, rumours of the liquidation of the ghetto were rampant. Steve's mother arranged for them to escape, and led him through the darkness. They spent a night at the Fiodorovs but could not stay because the family was already hiding another Jewish family. Ultimately, with no other option, Steve and his mother joined the only place she thought survival would be possible — a forced labour camp called HKP, *where their cousin Noah Katz was, and where Steve's younger brother, Monik, had been living with family members. Through the rest of the year and into the next, Steve and Monik often had to stay hidden. In the summer of 1944, "word spread that the SS were coming to liquidate the camp. The Soviet front was approaching, the Germans were retreating and the Jews in the camp were no longer needed." Steve and his family hid in a tiny space, only emerging during the silence. Decades later, Steve found out who had helped warn them of the liquidation.*

In the summer of 2005 I received a phone call from my cousin Yaffa, who lives with her husband and three children in Jerusalem. She is the daughter of Noah Katz, who in his late teens, after his father was killed by the Germans in 1943, took over as head of the family and helped his mother, his two sisters, my mother, brother and me to survive. Yaffa asked if I was coming to Israel next month to attend the ceremony at Yad Vashem, the Holocaust museum and memorial, for the induction of Major Karl Plagge, the commandant of HKP, into the ranks of the Righteous Among the Nations, a designation given to gentiles who saved Jews at great risk to themselves. This was a surprise but then, as more information became available to me about this German officer, I began to realize that our survival in the labour camp was due to a large extent to this commandant, a decent German with a conscience and courage.

I was not completely surprised. As a child of nine or ten I met, or rather was near, when he happened to walk by, an older man with greying hair at the temples and a small moustache, walking with a slight limp, dressed in the grey uniform, black boots and long coat of a German officer. I remember that I felt no fear when he glanced at me as he passed by. Young children, like dogs, can instinctively recognize danger emanating from someone. Quite likely I must have heard from the adults that he was a decent and friendly man who tried to make life bearable for the people who helped him do his job. I later found out that before the camp's liquidation, he managed to warn the Jews that the SS were coming, allowing hundreds to go into hiding.

After the ceremony in Jerusalem, which was attended by several of the survivors from HKP and some of Plagge's relatives (he died in Germany in 1957), I spoke to Yaffa again and she gave me the phone number of a man from Toronto she met at the ceremony. His name is Lazar Greisdorf and he also survived the camp as a young child with his parents and brother.

When we were liberated by the Soviets in 1944, I had imagined that the only survivors from the camp were our family and a few others. Now, after all these years, it turns out that about a quarter of the Jews, about 250 out of approximately 1,000 imprisoned in the camp, survived. Considering that only about 2,000 of the 60,000 Vilna Jews remained alive by the time the Nazis were chased out, the number of Jews who survived the camp seems out of proportion. And so it turns out that the commandant, Major Plagge, was instrumental in saving my life as well as the others.

1

2

1 Steve and his mother with the Dzeviatnikov family before the war. Standing in back are Mr. and Mrs. Dzeviatnikov; in front, left to right, are Steve; Luba Dzeviatnikov; Steve's mother, Esther Galerkin; and Georgic Dzeviatnikov. Vilna, Lithuania, 1938.

2 Steve and his mother after liberation. Vilna, 1946.

The Violin
Rachel Shtibel

Rachel Shtibel, born in 1935, grew up on her family's farm in the village of Turka, fourteen kilometres from the city of Kołomyja in the southeastern section of Poland called Galicia. The area surrounding Kołomyja was occupied by the Soviet Union after the onset of the war in September 1939, and was occupied by Nazi Germany in the summer of 1941. As was the pattern with many ghettos established by the Nazis in Poland, the first stage toward the creation of the ghetto was the forcible resettlement of the population from nearby rural areas. Rachel and her family were forced to move to Kołomyja in November 1941. The Kołomyja ghetto was officially established and fully closed off from the rest of the city in late March 1942.

Life in the ghetto was very difficult. Our living space was quickly permeated with horrible smells from trash and human waste. The few clothes that we had were dirty and torn. We could not bathe. Our shoeless feet were soiled and swollen and covered with blisters. Men and women who were young and strong were sent out of the ghetto to do hard labour, like building and repairing roadways. Some had to carry large, heavy rocks, while others had to cut the large rocks into smaller pieces by hand. The work was very hard and was done under the strict, watchful eyes of the guards. There was constant change inside the ghetto, with Jews arriving from surrounding cities, towns and villages as others were being sent away by train. At the time we thought they were being sent to work. They never came back. We later found out they were sent to concentration camps.

Each morning, the soldiers rounded up the Jews in the ghetto. Then, they randomly selected who would be tortured and murdered that day. The German police rotated their selections daily, choosing either children of a certain age group, adults, the elderly or the ill and disabled. These murders were carried out in front of us as we stood horrified, imagining ourselves in the place of those poor souls who had been selected. One never knew who would be next. I was in constant fear for my family and for my own life.

It often felt as though chance and fate were playing a larger part in our survival than anything else. Some say that it is the will to live that allows those in danger to survive, but I am not sure. While some people were shot for seemingly no reason at all, others managed to escape such a fate. Why? One bitterly cold morning, I stood beside my mother during a roundup. Shivering with cold and fear, we stood close together as two Gestapo officers moved in our direction. They stopped at a fair distance, called out my mother's name and ordered her to step out of line and walk forward. I may have been little, but I knew what that meant. As she began to move, I quickly reached for her ice-cold hand and walked with her. I was six years old and the thought of my mother dying alone was unimaginable. Frantically, my mother tried to push me back, but I held on tight. We walked slowly and finally came to a stop. I closed my eyes. "How would it feel to die?" I wondered. "Would it be very painful? Where would the bullet hit us?"

As we approached, one of the Gestapo officers asked my mother if she could speak German. When she answered in German that she spoke fluently, they ordered her to follow them. She asked to be allowed to bring her daughter along and we followed the Germans to the ghetto gate and beyond. We came to a stop in front of Jacob's house. Jacob was my mother's cousin who had been a tailor of men's clothing before the war. The Nazis had allowed him to stay in his home in Kołomyja, outside the ghetto, so that he could sew uniforms for the Gestapo officers. Jacob, however, spoke only Polish and Yiddish. He had asked them to bring his cousin Sara Milbauer, who could easily translate for him. And so my mother and I found ourselves living with Jacob. We were saved. For now.

As the situation for Jews in the ghetto worsened, with the risk of death ever-present, Rachel's father hid her and her younger cousin, Luci, in the barracks near the field where he was forced to work.

In the summer of 1942, circumstances began to change for us. The Germans decided to send all the young men and women to the village of Turka to work in the fields. Surprisingly, Bubbie Yetta was included along with my parents. The day before my family was to go to work in the fields, my father and Uncle Moses discussed how to sneak Luci and me out of the ghetto. They feared that if they left us behind they would not find us when they returned. Our parents then prepared us for the dangerous journey. Luci and I were to be put into knapsacks containing farm and garden tools and my father and Moses would carry us on their backs out of the ghetto. Early the next morning, my father packed me into the bag, arranged the tools around me and lifted me onto his shoulder. I tried to shrink myself into a little ball inside the bag. I was afraid and stifled with not enough air to breathe. At the gate, the guard poked at my father's knapsack with his dagger. It hurt, but I did not make a sound and held my breath.

So far, the escape had been successful. When we arrived at the village of Turka, each family got a barracks and a plank bed. My father immediately emptied me out of the bag and sent me under the bed. Moses did the same with Luci. Our parents told us to stay under the beds as long as they were at work. When they returned, we could come out and sleep with them on the plank bed. Early each morning, they sent us into hiding. "Remember," they would tell us, "the

German guards can see you and if they catch you, they will kill you."

The days were long and boring. The beds were so low we could not even sit up under them. And we could not speak out loud, only whisper. The barracks had a little window and from beneath the bed we could see the sun shining a little in the room. After several weeks of this hidden life we had both had enough. We were hungry and terribly bored. We decided that it would be fine if we got out from under the bed every day and jumped around a little bit in the room. We did not tell our parents and the plan worked — for a while.

One afternoon, while we were dancing around the room, a German guard spotted us. He came into the barracks like thunder and pointed his gun at us. Shaking and trembling, we both started to cry. All I could think was that our parents would be so angry. I knew that I was older than Luci and should have known better. How could I have not obeyed them? Suddenly, I felt the back of the German soldier's boot as he kicked us both and we flew out the door. We were crying loudly, hoping that someone would hear and help us. The guard looked at me and Luci clinging to each other and, strangely, touched my long blond braids. He had decided not to kill us. He ordered one of the guards to take us to Kołomyja. The guard dumped us onto the street of the ghetto and we just sat there among all the dead bodies, whimpering. I was certain that my parents would never find me. What would they think when they returned not to find us in the barracks? What would happen to us?

The next morning, when my father went to work in the fields, he made contact with a farmer he knew in the adjacent field. Jozef Beck was someone my father had known before the war and he begged him to help. He asked Jozef to go to the ghetto and find us. He asked him to save us if he could and keep us hidden at his farm. Mr. Beck took his horse and carriage and went into the ghetto. He told the guards that he had come to take away some of the corpses. They agreed to let him in. He spotted us, sitting where we had been dumped the day before, in the middle of the street. Luci and I watched as he piled some of the dead bodies on the carriage and then quickly he picked us up and threw us on top, covering us with more dead bodies. When the carriage was full, he drove us out of the ghetto.

Jozef drove to the cemetery and dropped everything onto the ground, including Luci and me. Quickly, he fished us out of the pile and propelled us behind the biggest tombstone he could find. "Tonight," he told us, "my wife, Rozalia, will come to fetch you and take you to our home. You will sit here quietly until it is dark. And do not move. Do you promise?" We promised.

Alone and petrified, crouching behind tombstones and surrounded by corpses, Luci and I waited for Jozef's wife. Every sound of the crackling leaves and the howling wind sounded like footsteps. From time to time, I peeked out from behind our tombstone to see if someone was coming, terrified that I was stepping on Bubbie Frida's dead body under my feet. I tried to occupy my mind with other thoughts and resumed my vigil for Rozalia. It seemed as if we had been sitting there forever, huddled behind the tombstone when, finally, we heard someone walking through the darkness. A woman, bundled up and wearing a huge black shawl on her head, made her way toward us carrying blankets. As she approached, she whispered to us that she was Rozalia. She told us not to be afraid. She took us by the hand and led us out of the cemetery to her waiting horse and carriage.

The barn on the Becks' farm was piled high with straw and hay. Rozalia settled us on the upper level on a huge pile of straw and spoke sternly to us. "I have six children," she said, "so no one can know that you are here. If the Germans discover that you are hiding here, we will all be killed. You must be quiet and promise to behave. Don't move! Do you understand?" She gave us each a piece of bread and covered us with a blanket. Weeks passed. The days and nights became indistinguishable. We could hear the Beck children playing in the barn or outside. We longed to join them, but we remained motionless and silent. Luci cried all the time. At seven, a year older than Luci, I felt as though I had to be strong and responsible. I did everything I could to try to calm her. Neglecting and suppressing my own fears in order to stay alive, I invented a game. There was a wooden ledge that held the straw on the upper level of the barn from falling. I told Luci that we were going to spit on the ledge. If our two drops of saliva joined together it would mean that soon our parents would come and get us. If the saliva drops did not join, then we would have to wait longer. It was hard to produce so many drops of saliva and our mouths soon became very dry. The game was not working.

Jozef sought out my father in the fields and told him that to have us on his farm had become too dangerous for his own family. My father would have to come and get us. It was the autumn of 1942 and the work in the fields would soon be over. My father knew that to go back to the ghetto meant certain death. He was sure that within a few months the ghetto would be liquidated and not one Jew would be left alive. He told Jozef he would come get us, and he began to formulate a plan of escape.

It was at this time, in the late autumn of 1942, that my family and Luci's family separated. My parents and I, Shiko, Baruch Ertenstreich and Dr. Nieder went to Vasil and Maria Olehrecky's farm. They were the couple who had worked on my grandfather's farm. They knew us well and were eager to help us. Vasil settled us under the roof in the attic of their barn and brought food and cigarettes. The straw roof was very old and weak. When the wind blew, even softly, pieces of the roof flew off and small spaces of sky took their place. As beautiful as it was to have sunlight and to sometimes be able to see a star through the roof at night, we feared that if the roof fell apart we would be discovered. In vain, Vasil tried to fix the roof several times, but he was not successful. Winter was coming, and we were cold and afraid. Without a proper roof, we feared that the peasants from the village would spot us or that we would freeze to death.

In addition, the barn was infested with mice. Our clothes were torn and very dirty, and our bodies were covered with lice. Uncontrollably, I would scratch my head so hard that my scalp bled. Even if the Germans did not discover us, we all knew that we would not survive the winter in this barn. My father would clasp the gun with the ten bullets he had kept at his side since his escape from German captivity and say, "If we fall into the hands of the Germans, I will shoot each one of you and then myself." We lived in constant fear. How many ways are there to say that? After a time, those words become meaningless and finding new ways to describe how it felt to hide in a barn with a failing roof in the middle of the winter, awaiting certain death, is almost impossible.

Dr. Nieder, who was hiding with us, had a Polish girlfriend, Jadwiga. He ventured out at night from our hiding place to meet her in the fields. He never told her where he was hiding, but he received newspapers and reports of the progress of the war from her. We learned that the Germans were now drafting young men in occupied Poland, non-Jews, for work in Germany, young men like Vasil. He knew that he could hide to escape the order as others had done, but that if he did, the Germans would come looking for him and they would find all of us. He decided to report voluntarily to the German authorities.

The night before he left, Vasil came to say goodbye. "I told my wife to take care of you and I will write letters from Germany to see if you are all right," Vasil told my father. "I will refer to you as my brother Peter and I will send you cigarettes. Just try to be hopeful. One day the war will be over and everything will be okay again." My father did not know what to say to this man who was putting himself in harm's way to help us, how to thank him. "I am sorry to have to put you through this. You are young and don't have any children yet. You could hide. Maybe we should find another place." "No! You stay here," Vasil replied curtly. "You do not deserve a life like this. You are decent people and have always been good to my wife and me. If I can save you and you will all be alive when the war is over, this will be my reward." My father and Vasil hugged and cried together.

That night felt very long. Vasil stayed with us in the barn until morning. My father tried to convince him not to go, that we could find another hiding place, but Vasil would not hear of it. He knew that there was no place for us to go. Vasil left, but he kept his word. From Germany, he wrote letters to his wife and his brother "Peter." Maria brought my father the letters and the cigarettes Vasil had sent to him. Vasil risked his marriage, his wife's life and his own life to save ours.

Eventually, Rachel and her parents had to flee to another refuge. They joined family members who were hiding in a barn owned by a couple named Vasil and Paraska Hapiuk, and built a bunker underground to conceal their presence. Rachel and her family lived underground, barely able to move, from early 1943 until early 1944.

Vasil did not have the heart to turn out the Jewish family to die, so he agreed. He promised to bring some food for Luci when he could. "Every Sunday when I go to church," he added, "I pray for you people." Aunt Mina was worried. "Vasil only knows about the four of us, and now there will be ten." My father had a solution. "We must dig a bunker in the ground under the straw that can hold the ten of us." Immediately, the men found some tools in the barn and started digging. They worked through the night and dug what looked like a big grave, three metres by three metres square.

Dark and airless. Our positions were organized in such a way that Uncle Moses could lie near the opening so that Vasil would see only him when he came with food. Five people lay on one side and the other five on the opposite side. We lay foot to foot — toes touching. Aunt Mina and Luci lay beside Moses. I lay with my parents. And there was Bubbie Yetta, Shiko and Baruch. And Dr. Nieder.

In these positions we remained. There was no room for standing or moving. When one person had to turn, all of us would have to turn. The deeper we were inside the bunker, the less air we had. There were strict rules for Luci and me. We were kept apart from each other and were not allowed to use our voices to speak. We could only communicate by moving our lips.

Turn. Whisper. Turn.

Sometimes, the adults took pity on us and gave us something important to do. It was our job to wake someone by touching them if they were snoring in their sleep, and that was usually Bubbie Yetta. When we giggled at the strange sounds she made, we were reprimanded with, "Stop laughing and be quiet. The Germans are coming." The word German was enough to make us stop. We knew all too well what that meant. If it wasn't Bubbie who made us laugh it was something else, and then one of the adults would lie on us. Choke us. So we could not breathe.

Turn. Whisper. Turn.

Rachel and her family were liberated in March 1944. In late 1956, before Rachel and her family left Poland for Israel, Rachel's father went to say goodbye to one of the couples who had helped them survive the war.

I was very upset that my father was not taking me with him on this journey. I also wanted to see my home for the last time, to be again in the surroundings I treasured. I never really knew why he did not take me, whether it was because he thought it would bring back painful memories of the past or because he did not want me to look back, only forward.

When they returned, my father brought back memories of the past. He told us that the village of Turka had not been damaged by the war and was just as we had left it. The orchard was as beautiful as it had always been. He had knocked on the door of our old house and told the peasant woman that this had been his family's house before the war and that he had planted the apple trees. He asked her if he could pick a few apples so he could taste, one last time, the fruits of his past labours. She agreed and, tearfully, he picked his apples.

He had also gone to visit Vasil and Maria Olehrecky, the couple hired to help on my grandparents' farm who had become our saviours during the war. My father found Vasil still living on his farm, but he and Maria had divorced and both had new spouses. My father gave him money and gifts and thanked him again for all he had done for us. Like brothers, they hugged and cried and said their goodbyes. My father went to see Maria and also gave her gifts and money. He told them both that we were immigrating to Israel and that we would never see them again. They both asked that my father not write to them from Israel, as the political situation in the USSR at this time made them afraid they would be accused of having "contacts" with Israel. These visits were very emotional and painful for all of them and brought back the memories of the life we had lived and tragically lost.

1

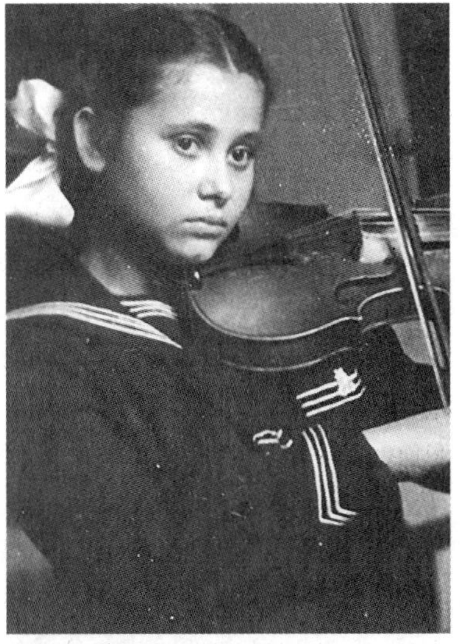

2

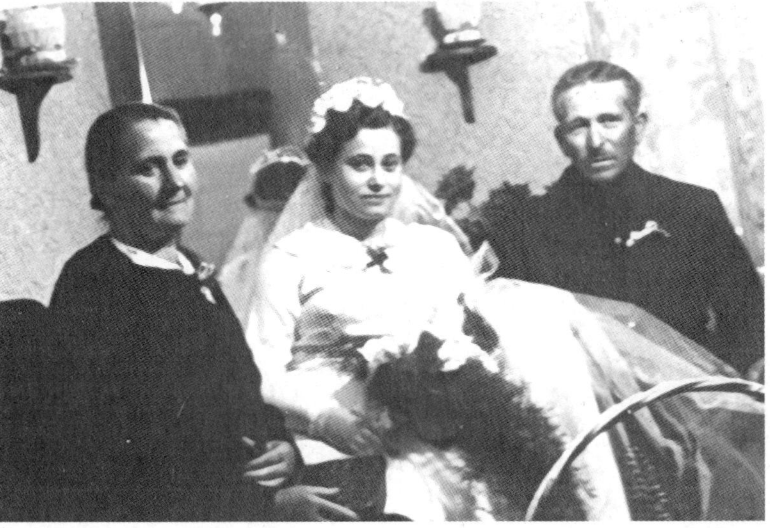

3

1 Rachel at age one. Poland, 1936.

2 Rachel playing the violin after the war. Wrocław, Poland, 1949.

3 Rachel on her wedding day with Rozalia and Jozef Beck, who helped save her family during the war. Wrocław, June 24, 1956.

Chaos to Canvas

Maxwell Smart

Maxwell Smart was born in Buczacz, Poland (now Buchach, Ukraine), in 1930. When the area he lived in came under Nazi occupation in 1941, he witnessed violence and the persecution of his family as the Jews of Poland were forced into ghettos and deported to camps. At his mother's urging, Maxwell escaped while being loaded onto a truck as he and his family were about to be deported. Maxwell managed to reunite with his aunt for a brief time and then, he was on his own.

Meanwhile, my aunt had arranged for me to be hidden on a farm run by a man named Jasko Rudnicki. My auntie, in her anxiety to protect me, hardly knew what she was doing, but she was trying everything possible to keep me alive. For a long time, I thought she had abandoned me; at the time, I was hurt and angry because it felt to me like she did not want me to live with her in hiding. Today I can understand her decision. I'm sure it was hard for my auntie to go into hiding without me, but she had to accept it.

At dawn, we finally arrived at Jasko's place. Jasko had built his little home in the woods, secluded from any neighbour. A dirt road ran through a small settlement of only five homes, all with roofs of straw, and there was a small flourmill next to the small river.

Jasko's home was the first when you entered the settlement and it appeared to be a good place to hide. We were a considerable distance from any traffic, and the dirt road was wide enough for only one wagon at a time. If two wagons approached each other, one had to drive off the road and wait. As time passed, I realized how quiet the area was; there were very seldom visitors, usually only a local farmer going to the flourmill. The mill was powered by water, as there was no electricity in the area. Families had rerouted water from the river, which turned a wooden wheel slowly. The shaft of the wheel had one gear, which turned around a stone and ground a small amount of wheat or corn to produce coarse flour that could then be used for baking bread.

Jasko would become my only link with the outside world. He was twenty-eight; his wife, Kasia, was twenty-two, and they had two little boys. They were poor farmers, living at the edge of the woods. Actually, they were farmers without a farm. He had only a garden plot for growing vegetables such as corn, beets and potatoes for their own use. Jasko would hire himself out to other farmers, working for them during the various seasons: there was a season to cut wheat and a season to harvest potatoes — every plant had a season for cultivating and harvesting. Jasko was not paid with money, but with food.

Jasko's home, called a *lepianka* in Polish, a mud hut, had a single window and one door. The straw roof had a little attic space where I occasionally stayed. Jasko had a stable, one cow, one pig (that he had bought as a piglet, fed during the year and would kill to eat at Christmas time) and a horse. This stable was my home during the cold winter nights.

When I slept in Jasko's attic, it was warm as a result of the heat rising from the main floor. Jasko always had some food for me — mainly black bread and sour milk, which was actually yogurt, in a jug. When I would crawl into the hay in the stable to sleep, Kasia would come in the morning to milk the cow. When I joined her, she would tell me to wait, and she would later give me bread and milk.

Kasia would dress me as a Polish boy in an outfit worn in this area: white pants made by hand from jute and a shirt embroidered with colourful cotton threads. As for my new Polish name, Jasko decided to call me Staszek, which was Kasia's little brother's name.

It was a fairly comfortable time for me. I was known in the small village as Jasko's "Zydek," his "Jew." Nobody bothered me and I was safe, I thought. Unfortunately, the happy times did not last.

One Sunday, Kasia brought me a piece of cloth and asked me to make a cap for her sister's son. While I was sewing the cap, we heard shooting in the distance. An alarmed Jasko told me to hide in the woods behind the house.

I returned in the evening and heard the tragic news: The Banderowcy, Ukrainian nationalists, had caught the family I had travelled with while they were hiding in the forest. For the following few days I ventured into the woods, hoping that some members of the family had survived. On the third day, I found the two brothers, Dolek and Benyick, and they ran over to me and told me that the Banderowcy had indeed captured their parents and sister and dragged them away. The brothers were extremely frightened. A nearby Polish farmer had helped their family, but they were now afraid to go back to the village and to that farmer. I knew that they would need food and would not survive without help and that they must be extremely cautious. Jews were hiding in nearby forests but were endangering themselves daily in the search for food. Many farmers were hostile toward Jews; others were helpful, but wary. The penalty for aiding a Jew was death, not only for the farmer but for the farmer's entire family.

Weeks passed and then one day, without warning, I saw, through the window, Ukrainian policemen walking towards Jasko's farmhouse. Neighbours must have told the police that Jasko was hiding a Jew! I had foolishly thought that I was safe here. I had no time to plan an escape or even to be afraid. I picked up the baby and tried to leave the house, but I could see that many people from the village had gathered in front of Jasko's house. I decided that it was too dangerous to try to flee. Even if I was able to get outside, there were people watching, anticipating my death. There was only one door and one window, and the police were right in front of both.

The police knocked at the door and Jasko answered immediately. The officers took him outside and in front of the crowd declared: "We have been told that you are hiding Jews. If you do not show us where they are and we find them, we will kill the Jews and your entire family." Hearing this, I was frightened beyond belief. My hands were shaking, but luckily, holding the baby hid this from view. I thought, *This is it, I've been caught, I'm going to die.* They had definitely come for me, because they didn't go to anyone else's house. They had probably killed the mother and father of my two friends in the forest, so I thought that certainly they were going to kill me. I had escaped death once, but could I again?

As I stood there, frozen, I heard Jasko quickly and without hesitation say, "I am not hiding any Jews." The police then began an intensive search, scouring the barn, the attic and the small farmhouse. I just stood there, holding the baby. The Ukrainians stuck their bayonets into the empty straw-filled beds and the dirt floor. Throughout this long, stressful search, I was standing in full view, dressed as a Polish boy. I was pretending that I was part of Jasko's family, that I was his son and that the baby and the two-year-old were my brothers. It didn't even enter the Ukrainian policemen's mind that I was not. When the police officers, the well-known brutal killers, had begun their search, I had put the baby down and pretended to help them by lifting a table, moving a chair and searching for "me." The Ukrainian police never dreamed that a young Jewish boy would have the courage to pretend to help them find me, the Jew!

After this incident, Jasko was worried and afraid; he could not believe what he had said to the Ukrainian murderers. He had replied automatically, without thinking of the consequences, and only fully realized after the policemen left how dangerous it was for him and his family. He had saved my life by endangering his own and that of his wife and children. During the war, it meant nothing to kill a Jew, especially if your own family was in danger. Most people, if confronted about hiding a Jew, would have turned us in without hesitation. It is my heartfelt belief that Jasko deserves a medal for saving my life. As I write my memoir now, I still have difficulty believing the huge risk that Jasko took by saying he was not hiding any Jews. I did not realize it fully at that time, as I was quite young, but today I think that he was an angel from heaven. He had saved my life again.

After the police left empty-handed, Jasko did not know what to do because he was afraid that they would return. So Jasko told me not to stay too close to his home in the daytime and to find a place to hide in the woods with the brothers. He was certain that one of his neighbours had reported him to the police. That person might even have been watching the scene unfold, and might not have spoken up about who I was for fear that others would know that they were the rat.

Maxwell left to find refuge in the nearby forest, where he created a shelter. Jasko continued to provide occasional food and support to Maxwell, even if he could not provide lodging. This assistance was crucial to Maxwell's survival.

Jasko still recommended that I stay with my two friends in the woods, as it was too dangerous to be at his home during the day. He told me that I could sleep in the barn at night when it was really cold and that Kasia would bring me some food. Food, I thought to myself. Without food, starving, I will become like a wild animal. I'll lose all awareness of danger and be vulnerable and careless while looking for food. Countless people in hiding were killed because they were searching for food. It was not difficult to hide, but we had to leave our hiding places to feed ourselves. If only I did not need food!

I remember Jasko showing me how to trap a rabbit. He would

tramp into the woods during the winter and set traps in the snow where the animal tracks lay. I often caught rabbits in a trap, but occasionally I would find only half of the rabbit. The other half had obviously provided dinner for someone else, but I was grateful they had left some for me.

Maxwell hid in the forest until the end of 1943, sometimes able to stay in Jasko and Kasia's barn, which was especially critical during the winter, and he received food for himself as well as some food for the friends he was occasionally in hiding with.

Christmas was approaching and Jasko told me that the Ukrainian police had departed and that I could stay in his house again. Months passed. Then one night, he came home drunk and excited, telling me that the Soviet army was in Buczacz and that I was free and didn't have to hide anymore. When I heard the news, tears started to roll down my face, and I kissed him and ran over to Kasia. I hugged her and then asked if it would be possible if Jasko could take me back to Buczacz.

We left for the city at the beginning of April 1944. I was almost fourteen years old, and I was so lucky to be liberated. I had defied the odds and survived and saved myself. I believed that my mother had somehow contributed to my survival.

I can remember sitting on the wagon with Jasko on the front bench, not hidden, like a normal human being, and for the first time in all the years of war, I felt no fear. There were no Germans, no Ukrainian police, no Banderowcy. I was not just a Jew anymore. I was a human being. It was so dramatically different than the way that I had come to Jasko, in the back of the wagon hidden and covered with hay.

My years in hiding had been horrible, nightmarish. As we were driving, I dared to hope that someone in my family was waiting to greet me. I felt so close to freedom now. I told Jasko that if anyone in my family was still alive, they would reward him. But freedom did not happen as I had hoped.

I thanked Jasko for always being so helpful and kind. He had fed me and taken care of me, and I knew that I would not have survived without him. He then told me that he had done it because he liked me, and that many times he wished that I had been his son. We said goodbye and I never saw Jasko again.

When I was free, warm and not hungry, I thought of Jasko many times. If it had not been for Jasko, who had treated me like a son, I would not be alive. I was so thankful that he took care of me without getting paid. He did it from his heart; he wanted the best for me. I survived the war under Jasko's protection. He fed me with whatever little food he had, and he really did not have much. He shared everything with me. It was not as if he ate meat and gave me stale bread; his daily food was the same as mine. As I thought of Jasko, I knew how happy he would be for me if he could see me now, looking so clean and dressed so properly.

Later in life, Maxwell continued to reflect on Jasko's help.

In May 2008, during a visit to the Yad Vashem Holocaust Remembrance Center in Jerusalem, I made a formal submission recommending that Jasko Rudnicki be honoured with the title "Righteous Among the Nations." In spite of the Germans' threat that they would kill anyone who aided Jews, there are more than twenty thousand non-Jews who have been designated as Righteous Among the Nations by Yad Vashem. This figure may represent only a fraction of those who risked everything to help their neighbours. The process for verifying the contributions made on behalf of a nominee require at least two eyewitnesses, and in many instances, no one survived to verify what happened. Although I survived much of the war as a result of Jasko's generosity and compassion, unfortunately I had no documents to prove how he had helped me, and I had no way of finding any of his descendants who could confirm the story. I do still hope to find them one day, and formally recognize Jasko and Kasia's selflessness. I know without a doubt that I never could have survived if not for their care.

1 Sketch of Jasko Rudnicki's house, view from the woods. By Maxwell Smart, circa 2010.

2 Close-up sketch of Jasko's house. By Maxwell Smart, circa 2010.

3 The first photo of Maxwell taken in Canada. Montreal, Quebec, April 18, 1949.

4 Maxwell in front of his painting *Downtown*. Montreal, 2017.

Silent Refuge
Margrit Rosenberg Stenge

Margrit Rosenberg Stenge was born in Cologne, Germany, in 1928. In late 1938, at ten years old, she escaped to Belgium and then in January 1939, she and her family arrived in Oslo, Norway, where her father had found work at a company called Nordiske. After Germany invaded Norway on April 9, 1940, Margrit's family knew they needed to get away from the city and fled to Rogne, a remote Norwegian village. Even in Rogne, the local police officer told them they better hide because the Nazis were tracking down all the Jews in the country. To avoid deportation, Margrit's parents hid on a mountain in a cabin with very little food and no running water. Margrit continued to live in the village during the week so she could go to school and visited her parents on weekends to bring them essential supplies, skiing the long distance across the snowy expanse alone. In the summer of 1942, they realized they needed to escape Nazi-occupied Norway but could not do so without help, which they would receive a few months later.

Two people visited us that summer. An engineer from Nordiske arrived with the usual envelope of money and stayed with us for a few days. He urged us to leave Norway as soon as possible because the Germans had begun escalating the persecution of the Jewish population in Oslo, Bergen and Trondheim. My father told him that we had no connections to the Underground in the area, and without their help, we would not be able to escape. The engineer left with the promise that he would do everything in his power to help us.

The second visitor was Einar Wellén, our neighbour's young nephew. He had the same message as the engineer from Nordiske, and when he heard that we were literally trapped in Rogne, he mentioned that he had a friend in the Norwegian Underground. With this friend's help, Einar hoped to help us escape to Sweden.

During the summer, we rented a furnished house on the outskirts of Rogne. Although it should have been a relief to live in larger quarters and on our own, we were too nervous to appreciate it. I could no longer go to school; my parents believed it was too dangerous, and I made no effort to change their minds. We tried to stay as close to the house as possible, and I was the only one in our family who did the necessary shopping. In the winter, when new ration cards were issued, I travelled quite a distance with our *spark* (a kicksled) to pick them up. With my heart pounding in my chest, I asked for and received the ration cards.

The engineer from Nordiske appeared one day, delivering the terrible news about the deportation of the Norwegian Jews to concentration camps. He promised to be back in January to fetch us and bring us to safety. We had not heard from Einar in a while. My father's depression and violent outbursts became more frequent. We felt caught in a trap with no way out.

My fourteenth birthday on December 27 was like any other day, and when I complained that we did not even have a small celebration, my father lost his temper. I had never seen him that furious and was really frightened when he lifted up a chair and threw it against the wall. My poor father needed an outlet for his feelings of helplessness and frustration, and my complaints triggered this violent outburst.

We had almost given up hope when in the early morning hours of January 14, 1943, there was a knock on the door. Fearing the worst, I opened the door. Relief surged through me when I recognized Einar Wellén. He was with another young man who turned out to be his friend Arne Myhrvold. Both were exhausted and frozen because they had spent the night travelling, the last part of the journey on an open truck bed. The two young men wasted no time in telling us that everything was arranged for our escape and that we would be leaving early the following morning. They advised us how to dress and what to bring in our knapsacks. What I remember best from that day was standing over a kitchen sink dying my hair blond. Much depended on us and how we would be able to handle the situation. We would travel by truck to a small place near Fagernes, where we would board a train headed for Oslo. We would leave the train in a suburb of Oslo. A minister, recognizable by his clerical collar, would meet us at the station and take us to his home, where we would stay until the next transport to Sweden.

This plan sounded easy enough, but we all knew that danger would be lurking in every corner. The truck could easily be stopped for an inspection, and what was even more likely was that we would be asked for identification papers on the train. But these were risks we had to take to save our lives.

While we were preparing to leave, there was another knock on the door. We stared in disbelief at our new visitors, the engineer from Nordiske with a companion. They, too, had come to rescue us. After some discussion, it was decided that we would follow Einar and Arne's plan, since that seemed to be the better one. Arne had been working in the Norwegian Underground for quite some time and had helped many people cross the border into Sweden via the route we were planning to take. It was quite a coincidence that these two pairs of caring individuals arrived the same day.

We left Rogne at dawn the following day. Our truck made it without incident in time for the train to Oslo. Einar and Arne travelled on the same train as us, but in a different compartment, and in fact we did not see them again. My father hid behind a newspaper, and my mother and I tried to look as relaxed as possible. Not one word was spoken among us. By some miracle, we were not asked for identification papers. When we reached the suburb of Oslo where we were to meet the minister, we got off the train and looked anxiously around. To our immense relief, he drove up immediately in a car, and we were off to the minister's home.

It was a lovely house, a home such as I had not seen in a long time, beautifully furnished with paintings on the wall and a piano in the corner of the living room. Coffee and sandwiches were ready for us, and we were shown to a room to rest. The minister told us that we might have to spend the night there, because there might not be a transport to the border that day. This possible delay made us very nervous, but at the end of the day, a message was received that we should leave immediately.

We were driven by car to a farm and shown into the barn, where some other people were sitting in the hay waiting, including an elderly Jewish woman who had been rescued from a hospital. It was there that we found out that the three of us were among the last Jews to leave Norway. When there were about thirty people in the barn, a truck drove up, and the Jewish woman, my parents and I were told to get in first, closest to the cab. Eventually a tarpaulin was stretched across the truck bed and covered with grass. My father immediately realized that he would not be able to stay in such a confined space because he was extremely claustrophobic. He moved slowly to the other end of the truck, where he could see some light through the slits of the tarpaulin, and disappeared from our view.

This was the ultimate agony. Not having my father close to me during those dangerous hours was unthinkable. I called, "Vati, Vati" many times, but there was no reply. I began to imagine that he had gotten off the truck and had been left behind accidentally. The man next to me told me to be quiet, since the noise I was making would endanger everyone on the transport. I was so nervous and upset that my whole body shook, and I could not keep my teeth from chattering. During the next couple of hours, I hardly thought about the danger we were in. All I could think of was whether my father was on the truck and what we would do if he were not.

Suddenly, the truck stopped, and so almost did my heart. Loud voices were heard outside, but soon we were on our way again. We all breathed an audible sigh of relief, but not a word was spoken. The next time the truck came to a stop, we were told that this was the end of our drive and that we would have to walk the rest of the way to the Swedish border. A guide would accompany us. Slowly the truck bed emptied out, and when at last I saw my father and put my hand into his, I was oblivious to the danger we were in. All that mattered was that my father was with us. We walked through the snowy woods, quickly and in absolute silence. Suddenly, a small cabin appeared as if from nowhere with lights blinking through its windows. And then we heard "Welcome to Sweden. Come inside." We then saw the silhouettes of two Swedish soldiers coming toward us.

Our long odyssey, beginning in Oslo on April 8, 1940, had ended.

After immigrating to Canada, Margrit kept in touch with Einar Wellén and even visited him and his family on her trips back to Norway. In the 1990s, she decided she wanted to officially recognize Einar for saving her family and started the process of documenting her personal history. The result was a ceremony in Norway where an entire community, including the Israeli ambassador to Norway, celebrated Einar's selfless rescue of a Jewish family decades earlier.

On December 11, 1995, I received the long-awaited letter from Yad Vashem. Einar would receive a medal, a certificate and the title of "Righteous Among the Nations" for having been instrumental in saving my life during the war. The same day, Marvin, my son, faxed me a letter he had written to Einar to congratulate him and to explain to him the meaning of the honour he was to receive. The thought behind the letter and the letter itself moved me to tears. And if that were not enough for one day, later that afternoon Einar called to say hello. He, too, had received the letter from Yad Vashem. I realized immediately that he did not fully understand the meaning of this honour. He sounded weak and tired at the end of our conversation. Instead of trying to explain the matter to him on the phone, I wrote him another letter that day. As well, the United States Holocaust Memorial Museum in Washington sent him a letter of congratulations, upon my request. The letter was beautifully worded and could not leave any doubt as to the significance of the distinction he would be awarded.

~

At exactly 7:30 p.m., the ceremony began and the hum of many voices died down.

Six candles were lit by survivors, Ambassador Shiloh and a young boy, whose candle represented the children who had perished in the Holocaust. The cantor chanted the prayer for the dead — *El Maleh Rachamim*. The first speaker of the evening was Ambassador Shiloh. He spoke emotionally about the Holocaust — of the children who had died and deprived us of a generation of Jewish lives, of the antisemitism that remains rampant today even in Norway, and of the few who acted to save innocent lives during the war. At the conclusion of his speech, the ambassador presented the medal and the certificate of Righteous Among the Nations to Einar Wellén. No doubt the memory of that moment will be treasured by all those who were present. I, for one, felt only gratitude that this long overdue recognition had come to pass.

Then it was my turn to speak. I did not dare look up from my paper. Since I had read the Norwegian text out loud many times, I managed to get through it almost without stumbling. I knew that I had the attention of the audience. It was quiet except for my own voice. When I returned to my seat, I saw that Marit was visibly moved. And so was Einar. He was the last speaker. He searched for his glasses, found them, put them on, only to take them off again. He began by thanking

Yad Vashem for the honour. Then he spoke of his relationship with my father. I had not realized that Einar had had many conversations with my father, and his speech revealed how fond he had been of him and how much he had looked up to him. He also mentioned his friend Arne Myhrvold. About halfway through his speech, he put away the written text and wandered a bit from his prepared script. Everyone listened with great interest as he spoke of his clandestine work during the war.

Margrit had the chance to visit Einar Wellén one final time before he died in 1998.

Once again, fate had been on my side. I had gone to Oslo just in time to see Einar once more, and he had lived long enough to know that the young girl whose life he had saved had never forgotten him.

1 Margrit (left) with her friend Marta. Buahaugen, Norway, 1941.

2 Einar Wellén (left) and Margrit's son, Marvin (right), standing in front of the Granlis' house where Margrit lived with her family during the war. Rogne, Norway, 1996.

3 Israeli ambassador Michael Shiloh (left) with Einar Wellén (right) at the ceremony honouring Einar as Righteous Among the Nations by Yad Vashem for saving Margrit and her family. Oslo, Norway, April 16, 1996.

4 Margrit and Einar at the reception at the Wellén home after the ceremony honouring Einar as Righteous Among the Nations. Oslo, Norway, April 1996.

Glossary

Agde A camp in southern France established by the French government in 1939 to hold Republican refugees of the Spanish Civil War and later used to house or intern other populations. In 1940, Agde was administered by the French Vichy government and held 6,000 civilian detainees from thirty nationalities, including 1,000 Jewish refugees, mostly from Belgium. Conditions in the camp were harsh, with insufficient clothing supplies and barracks that were ill-maintained with leaky roofs and snow accumulating inside. The camp was divided into four subcamps, and the civilian camp, camp IV, was closed on March 15, 1941; after that period, Agde continued to hold forced labourers and functioned briefly as a transit camp for Jews being deported to Nazi camps and killing centres in 1942. After the Germans occupied the city of Agde on November 13, 1942, the camp was no longer in use.

Aliyah Bet (Hebrew) A clandestine movement established to bring Jewish immigrants without immigration permits to British Mandate Palestine before, during and after World War II. The name, which means "ascent B," differentiates the movement from the immigrants to whom the British granted permits. Aliyah Bet organized ships to pick up Jewish immigrants from different points on the European coast in order to make the perilous journey to Palestine. Many were turned back.

American Jewish Joint Distribution Committee (JDC) Colloquially known as the Joint, the JDC was a charitable organization founded in 1914 to provide humanitarian assistance and relief to Jews all over the world in times of crisis. It provided material support for persecuted Jews in Germany and other Nazi-occupied territories and facilitated their immigration to neutral countries such as Portugal, Turkey and China. Between 1939 and 1944, Joint officials helped close to 81,000 European Jews find asylum in various parts of the world. Between 1944 and 1947, the JDC assisted more than 100,000 refugees living in DP camps by offering retraining programs, cultural activities and financial assistance for emigration.

antisemitism Prejudice, discrimination, persecution or hatred against Jewish people, institutions, culture and symbols.

arizátori (Slovak; pl.; masc. sing., *arizátor*) Slovak gentiles to whom confiscated Jewish businesses and properties were transferred in the process of the so-called Aryanization of Slovakia in the late 1930s and early 1940s. Indicative of how the antisemitic regime in Slovakia modelled itself on Nazi anti-Jewish policies, the word comes from German, related to the words *Arisierer* (Aryanizer) and *Arisierung* (Aryanization).

Auschwitz (German; in Polish, Oświęcim) A Nazi concentration camp complex in German-occupied Poland about 50 kilometres from Krakow, on the outskirts of the town of Oświęcim, built between 1940 and 1942. The largest camp complex established by the Nazis, Auschwitz contained three main camps: Auschwitz I, a concentration camp; Auschwitz II (Birkenau), a death camp that used gas chambers to commit mass murder; and Auschwitz III (also called Monowitz or Buna), which provided slave labour for an industrial complex. In 1942, the Nazis began to deport Jews from almost every country in Europe to Auschwitz-Birkenau, where they were selected for slave labour or for death in the gas chambers. In mid-January 1945, close to 60,000 inmates were sent on a death march, leaving behind only a few thousand inmates who were liberated by the Soviet army on January 27, 1945. It is estimated that 1.1 million people were murdered in Auschwitz, approximately 90 per cent of whom were Jewish; other victims included Polish prisoners, Roma and Soviet prisoners of war.

Bnei Akiva (Hebrew; children of Akiva) A youth movement of Mizrachi, the religious Zionist movement founded in Vilna, Lithuania, in 1902, on the belief that the Torah is central to Zionism and that a Jewish homeland was essential to Jewish life. Mizrachi and Bnei Akiva, and the system of religious schools it established, are still active internationally today.

British Mandate Palestine (also Mandatory Palestine) The area of the Middle East under British rule from 1923 to 1948 comprising present-day Israel, Jordan, the West Bank and the Gaza Strip. The Mandate was established by the League of Nations after World War I and the collapse of the Ottoman Empire; the area was given to the British to administer until a Jewish national home could be established. During this time, Jewish immigration was severely restricted, and Jews and Arabs clashed with the British and each other as they struggled to realize their national interests. The Mandate ended on May 15, 1948, after the United Nations Partition Plan for Palestine was adopted and on the same day that the State of Israel was declared.

cantor (in Hebrew, *chazzan*) A person who leads a synagogue congregation in songful prayer. The cantor might be professionally trained or a member of the congregation.

Chasidic (from the Hebrew word *chasid*; pious person) Relating to Chasidism, a mystical Orthodox Jewish movement founded by Rabbi Israel Baal Shem Tov in eighteenth-century Eastern Europe. Chasidism emphasizes Jewish practice, prayer, an individual's relationship with God and the leadership of a *rebbe* or *tzadik* (rabbi or righteous person).

cheder (Hebrew; room) A traditional Jewish elementary school in which religious studies and Hebrew are taught.

Chumash (Hebrew; from the word *chamesh*, five) The first five books of the Hebrew Bible, or Torah, also known as the Pentateuch or the Five Books of Moses. *See also* Torah.

D-Day The well-known military term used to describe the Allied invasion of Normandy, France, on June 6, 1944, that marked the onset of the liberation of Western Europe during World War II. Nearly 150,000 Allied troops arrived by boat or parachute to participate in this invasion.

de Gaulle, Charles (1890–1970) A French general and statesman who opposed both the Nazi regime and the French collaborationist Vichy government. De Gaulle, a World War I veteran and Brigadier General in World War II, escaped to London after the fall of France in 1940. In London, de Gaulle organized the Free French Forces, a military force that participated in the war effort against Germany alongside the Allied forces and supported the Resistance in France. After the war, de Gaulle served as head of the French provisional government from 1944 to 1946, and as president of France from 1959 to 1969.

displaced persons (DP) camps Facilities set up by the Allied authorities and the United Nations Relief and Rehabilitation Administration (UNRRA) in October 1945 to resolve the refugee crisis that arose at the end of World War II. The camps provided temporary shelter and assistance to the millions of people — not only Jews — who had been displaced from their home countries as a result of the war and helped them prepare for resettlement.

El Maleh Rachamim (Hebrew; God, full of compassion) A prayer for the soul of someone who has died, recited at funeral services, at memorial services held during the year, and to mark the anniversary of the individual's death.

Entr'aide d'hiver du maréchal (The Marshal's Winter Mutual Aid Society) A program within the French government's wartime National Aid (le Secours national) that provided a variety of welfare activities, including seasonal and long-term accommodations for children and youth. Named for the French chief of state, Marshal Philippe Pétain, the program's propaganda campaigns used Pétain's name and image to gain the support of the French population. *See also* Pétain, Philippe.

French Forces of the Interior (FFI) The formal name given to the French resistance fighters after the D-Day landings on June 6, 1944, as they joined other forces participating in the liberation of France. In June 1944, the forces comprised approximately 100,000; by October of that year the numbers had grown to 400,000.

French Resistance The collective term for the French resistance movement that opposed the German occupation and French collaborating regime during World War II. The Resistance published underground newspapers, helped Allied prisoners-of-war escape, sabotaged German war equipment and created intelligence networks that gathered military information in order to gain armament support from Britain. Some groups within the movement were involved in rescuing Jews. In rural areas, the group was known as the Maquis.

Garel network A clandestine network established by OSE (Œuvre de secours aux enfants) to rescue Jewish children in southern France. Named after its director, Georges Garel, the network provided children with false identity papers, organized shelters in institutions or with Christian families, and monitored their safety. The Garel network, which was organized in 1942 and began operating in early 1943, saved approximately fifteen hundred children. *See also* Œuvre de secours aux enfants.

Gemara (Aramaic) The teachings of the Jewish sages of ancient Babylonia and the Land of Israel that discuss and interpret the earlier teachings of the Mishnah. The Gemara and the Mishnah together comprise the Talmud, which is the foundation of rabbinic Jewish law. *See also* Talmud.

Gestapo (German; abbreviation of Geheime Staatspolizei, the Secret

State Police) The Nazi regime's brutal political police that operated without legal constraints to deal with its perceived enemies. The Gestapo was formed in 1933 under Hermann Göring; it was taken over by Heinrich Himmler in 1934 and became a department within the SS in 1939. During the Holocaust, the Gestapo set up offices in Nazi-occupied countries and was responsible for rounding up Jews and sending them to concentration and death camps. They also arrested, tortured and deported those who resisted Nazi policies. A number of Gestapo members also belonged to the Einsatzgruppen, the mobile killing squads responsible for mass shooting operations of Jews in the Soviet Union. In the camp system, Gestapo officials ran the Politische Abteilung (Political Department), which was responsible for prisoner registration, surveillance, investigation and interrogation.

ghetto A confined residential area for Jews. The term originated in Venice, Italy, in 1516 with a law requiring all Jews to live on a segregated, gated island known as Ghetto Nuovo. Throughout the Middle Ages in Europe, Jews were often forcibly confined to gated Jewish neighbourhoods. Beginning in 1939, the Nazis forced Jews to live in crowded and unsanitary conditions in designated areas — usually the poorest ones — of cities and towns in Eastern Europe. Ghettos were often enclosed by walls and gates, and entry and exit from the ghettos were strictly controlled. Family and community life continued to some degree, but starvation and disease were rampant. Starting in 1941, the ghettos were liquidated, and Jews were deported to camps and killing centres.

Hebrew Free Loan Association (also Jewish Free Loan) Organizations that offer interest-free loans to Jews. Local organizations exist around the world, with most being in North America. These non-sectarian Jewish institutions provide an important social service to newcomers. The Montreal organization was established in 1911.

High Holidays (also High Holy Days) The period of time leading up to and including the Jewish autumn holidays of Rosh Hashanah

(New Year) and Yom Kippur (Day of Atonement) that is considered a time for introspection and renewal. Rosh Hashanah is observed with synagogue services, the blowing of the shofar (ram's horn) and festive meals during which sweet foods, such as apples and honey, are eaten to symbolize and celebrate a sweet new year. Yom Kippur, a day of fasting and prayer, occurs eight days after Rosh Hashanah.

Hlinka Guard The paramilitary wing of Hlinka's Slovak People's Party, established in October 1938. Members of the Guard attacked Jews and destroyed property, and later participated in rounding up Jews for deportation. In mid-1944, the German SS took over control of the Guard.

kosher (Hebrew) Fit to eat according to Jewish dietary laws. Observant Jews follow a system of rules known as *kashruth* that regulates what can be eaten, how food is prepared and how animals are slaughtered. Food is kosher when it has been deemed fit for consumption according to this system of rules. There are several foods that are forbidden, most notably pork products and shellfish.

Marcel Marceau (1923–2007) A celebrated French actor well-known around the world for his work as a mime. Born Marcel Mangel to a family of Jewish immigrants from Poland, Marceau was evacuated with his family at the outbreak of World War II from Strasbourg to the South of France, along with other civilians living near the French border with Germany. His father was later sent to Auschwitz, where he was killed. Marceau and his brother joined the French resistance movement; his involvement consisted primarily of creating fake ration cards and helping Jewish children cross the border into Switzerland or get to other safe locations in France. For this work, he was awarded the Wallenberg Medal, named after Raoul Wallenberg, in 2001.

March of the Living An annual two-week program that takes place in Poland and Israel and aims to educate primarily Jewish students and young adults from around the world about the Holocaust and Jewish life before and during World War II. On Holocaust Memorial Day (Yom HaShoah), participants and Holocaust survivors march the three kilometres from Auschwitz to Birkenau to commemorate and honour all who perished in the Holocaust. Afterwards, participants travel to Israel and join in celebrations there for Israel's remembrance and independence days.

mezuzah (Hebrew; doorpost) The small piece of parchment containing the text of the central Jewish prayer, the Shema, which has been handwritten in ink by a scribe. Many Jews place this parchment on the doorposts of their homes, often in decorative cases.

minyan (Hebrew; count, number) The quorum of ten adult Jews, traditionally male, required for certain religious rites. The term can also designate a congregation.

Molotov-Ribbentrop Pact The non-aggression treaty that was signed on August 23, 1939, and was colloquially known as the Molotov-Ribbentrop Pact after the names of its signatories, Soviet foreign minister Vyacheslav Molotov and German foreign minister Joachim von Ribbentrop. The main, public provision of the pact stipulated that the two countries would not go to war with each other for ten years and that they would both remain neutral if either one was attacked by a third party. A secret component of the arrangement was the division of Eastern Europe into Nazi and Soviet areas of occupation. The Nazis breached the pact by launching a major offensive against the Soviet Union on June 22, 1941.

NKVD (acronym for Narodnyi Komissariat Vnutrennikh Del, Russian; People's Commissariat for Internal Affairs) The Soviet Union's security agency, secret police and intelligence agency from 1934 to 1946. The organization's dual purpose was to defend the USSR from external dangers from foreign powers and to protect the Communist Party from perceived dangers within.

Œuvre de secours aux enfants (French; Children's Relief Agency, OSE) A Jewish welfare organization that rescued thousands of Jewish children in France during the Holocaust. The OSE was founded in Russia in 1912 and grew into an international organization based in France. Initially, the French branch of OSE provided health and welfare services to Jews in the 1930s; with the increasing persecution of Jews during the German occupation and the onset of mass deportations in 1942, OSE established an extensive clandestine rescue network.

Passover (in Hebrew, Pesach) An eight-day Jewish festival that takes place in the spring and commemorates the exodus of the Israelite slaves from Egypt. The festival begins with a lavish ritual meal called a seder, during which the story of the Exodus is told through the reading of a Jewish text called the Haggadah. During Passover, Jews refrain from eating any leavened foods. The name of the festival refers to God's "passing over" the houses of the Jews and sparing their lives during the last of the ten plagues, when the first-born sons of Egyptians were killed by God.

Pétain, Philippe (1856–1951) A French general and Maréchal (Marshal) of France who was the chief of state of the French government in Vichy from 1940 to 1944. After the war, Pétain was tried for treason for his collaboration with the Nazis and sentenced to death, which was commuted to life imprisonment. *See also* Vichy.

Resistance *See* French Resistance.

Righteous Among the Nations A title given by Yad Vashem, the World Holocaust Remembrance Center in Jerusalem, to honour non-Jews who risked their lives to help save Jews during the Holocaust. A commission was established in 1963 to award the title. If a person fits certain criteria and the story is carefully checked, the honouree is awarded with a medal and certificate and is commemorated on the Wall of Honour at the Garden of the Righteous in Jerusalem.

Rivesaltes A camp established and administered by the French government located in the South of France that served different functions, most notably as an internment camp. Originally established in 1938 as a military instruction camp, the camp at Rivesaltes became a refugee camp in 1939 for those fleeing the Spanish Civil War, and then an internment camp for refugees from Germany in 1940 during the Vichy regime. Starting on January 14, 1941, the camp became the primary site for interned refugee families, mostly Spanish, Jewish and Roma, who were transferred there from other camps. Although it was a family camp, Jewish men were separated from women and children. With 500 wooden barracks equipped to hold 8,000 people and spread over three kilometres, the camp would see more than 20,000 detainees pass through it between 1940 and 1942. Despite the presence of charitable organizations providing social welfare to the camp population, the living conditions in Rivesaltes were terrible, and dozens of Jewish children died in the camp. During the mass roundups of Jews in the Free Zone in August 1942, Rivesaltes was used as the main collection point for Jews who would be sent to the Drancy transit camp and then to Nazi camps and killing centres in the east. After the Germans occupied southern France in November 1942, the remaining detainees were transported elsewhere and the camp was used by the German military.

Shabbat (Hebrew; Sabbath) The weekly day of rest beginning Friday at sunset and ending Saturday at nightfall, ushered in by the lighting of candles on Friday evening and the recitation of blessings over wine and challah (egg bread). A day of celebration as well as prayer, it is customary to eat three festive meals, attend synagogue services and refrain from doing any work or travelling.

Shema Yisrael (Hebrew; Hear, O Israel) An important Jewish prayer comprising three paragraphs of biblical verses. The prayer starts with the verse "Hear, O Israel: the Lord is our God, the Lord is one." The Shema, or parts of it, is recited in various prayer services. It is considered a fundamental expression of faith in God, and its opening verse is sometimes said by Jews as a prayer of supplication and when facing death.

Slovak National Uprising (August 29, 1944–October 28, 1944) The anti-fascist armed resistance mounted against the pro-Nazi Slovak government by partisans in central Slovakia, which began when Germany occupied the country. The uprising, comprising as many as 72,000 Slovak regular and partisan fighters, including some Jews, was crushed by German forces in two months, although some remnants continued to fight in the Tatra Mountains until liberation by the Soviet army in March 1945. Thousands of casualties resulted from the uprising. In 1945, a square in the city of Banská Bystrica was dedicated to the uprising, and in 1969, a memorial and museum opened to commemorate the uprising.

SS (abbreviation of Schutzstaffel; Defence Corps) The elite police force of the Nazi regime that was responsible for security and for the enforcement of Nazi racial policies, including the implementation of the "Final Solution" — a euphemistic term referring to the Nazis' plan to systematically murder Europe's Jewish population. The SS was established in 1925 as Adolf Hitler's elite bodyguard unit, and under the direction of Heinrich Himmler, its membership grew from 280 in 1929 to 52,000 when the Nazis came to power in 1933, and to nearly a quarter of a million on the eve of World War II. SS recruits were screened for their racial purity and had to prove their "Aryan" lineage. The SS ran the concentration and death camps and also established the Waffen-SS, its own military division that was independent of the German army.

Stalin, Joseph (1878–1953) The leader of the Soviet Union from 1924 until his death in 1953. Born Joseph Vissarionovich Dzhugashvili, he changed his name to Stalin (literally: man of steel) in 1903. He was a staunch supporter of Lenin, taking control of the Communist Party upon Lenin's death. Very soon after acquiring leadership of the Communist Party, Stalin ousted rivals, killed opponents in purges and effectively established himself as a dictator.

Star of David (in Hebrew, *Magen David*) The six-pointed star that is the most recognizable symbol of Judaism. During World War II,

Jews in Nazi-occupied areas were frequently forced to wear a badge or armband with the Star of David on it as an identifying mark of their lesser status and to single them out as targets for persecution.

tallis (Yiddish; pl. *taleisim*; prayer shawl) A four-cornered ritual garment that is draped over the shoulders or head, traditionally worn by Jewish men during morning prayers and on the Day of Atonement (Yom Kippur). Fringes on the four corners of the garment are meant to remind the wearer to fulfill the biblical commandments.

Talmud (Hebrew; study) A collection of ancient rabbinic teachings compiled between the third and sixth centuries that includes explications of scriptural law in a text known as the Mishnah and deliberations about the Mishnah in a text known as the Gemara. The Talmud remains a focus of Jewish study and the basis of traditional Jewish law and practice today. *See also* Gemara.

Tiso, Jozef (1887–1947) A Slovak politician and priest who became head of the pro-fascist Slovak Republic from 1939 to 1945 and led the country down an increasingly antisemitic and pro-Nazi path. Tiso was executed for war crimes after World War II.

Torah (Hebrew; instruction) The first five books of the Hebrew Bible, also known as the Five Books of Moses or Chumash, the content of which is traditionally believed to have been revealed to Moses on Mount Sinai; or, the entire canon of the twenty-four books of the Hebrew Bible, referred to as the Old Testament in Christianity. Torah is also broadly used to refer to all the teachings that were given to the Jewish people through divine revelation or even through rabbinic writings (called the Oral Torah). *See also* Chumash.

Ukrainian Auxiliary Police (in German Ukrainische Hilfspolizei) Ukrainian military units set up by Nazi Germany in 1941, following the Nazi invasion of the Soviet Union, whose role included both assisting German troops in military actions against the Soviets and local policing. Members of these units were active in the persecution of Jews during the Holocaust, including taking part in pogroms, escorting Jews to forced labour sites, guarding ghettos, liquidating ghettos and marching Jews to their deaths.

United Nations Relief and Rehabilitation Administration (UNRRA) An international relief agency created at a 44-nation conference in Washington, DC, on November 9, 1943, to provide economic assistance and basic necessities to war refugees. It was especially active in repatriating and assisting refugees in the formerly Nazi-occupied European nations immediately after World War II.

Vélodrome d'Hiver (Also known as Vél d'Hiv) A sports stadium in Paris that was used as a holding centre for Jews who were rounded up by French police on July 16–17, 1942. Approximately 13,000 mostly foreign Jews living in Paris were arrested, and 7,000 of them were interned in the stadium, where they were kept for days without sufficient food, water or medical care. In the following days and weeks, the vast majority of those rounded up were deported to Auschwitz-Birkenau.

Vichy A resort town in south-central France that was the seat of the government of Maréchal Philippe Pétain in unoccupied France. The Franco-German armistice of June 22, 1940, divided France into two zones: the northern three-fifths to be under German military occupation and most of the remaining southern region, also referred to as the zone libre (Free Zone), to be under French sovereignty. The Vichy administration enacted antisemitic legislation and collaborated with Germany's anti-Jewish policies, including the deportation of Jews to Nazi concentration camps and death camps. *See also* Pétain, Philippe.

Yad Vashem Israel's official Holocaust memorial centre and the world's largest collection of information on the Holocaust, established in 1953. Yad Vashem, the World Holocaust Remembrance Center, is dedicated to commemoration, research, documentation and education about the Holocaust. The Yad Vashem complex in Jerusalem includes museums, sculptures, exhibitions, research centres and the Garden of the Righteous Among the Nations.

yeshiva (Hebrew) A Jewish educational institution in which religious texts such as the Torah and Talmud are studied.

Yiddish A language derived from Middle High German with elements of Hebrew, Aramaic, Romance and Slavic languages, and written in Hebrew characters. Spoken by Jews in east-central Europe for roughly a thousand years, it was the most common language among European Jews before the Holocaust. There are similarities between Yiddish and contemporary German.

Yom Kippur (Hebrew; Day of Atonement) A solemn day of fasting and repentance that comes eight days after Rosh Hashanah, the Jewish New Year, and marks the end of the High Holidays.

Youth Aliyah A child rescue organization founded in Berlin in 1933 by Recha Freier (1892–1984), a teacher, poet and musician. Shortly after the Nazi rise to power, Freier worked to bring Jewish children and teenagers to safety in British Mandate Palestine and Great Britain, where they lived communally and received education and support. After the Holocaust, thousands of young survivors were cared for by this organization. Youth Aliyah continues to operate villages for at-risk children in Israel today.

Zionism A movement promoted by the Viennese Jewish journalist Theodor Herzl, who argued in his 1896 book Der Judenstaat (The Jewish State) that the best way to resolve the problem of antisemitism and persecution of Jews in Europe was to create an independent Jewish state in the historical Jewish homeland of biblical Israel. Zionists also promoted the revival of Hebrew as a Jewish national language.

Index

The Azrieli Foundation was established in 1989 to realize and extend the philanthropic vision of David J. Azrieli, C.M., C.Q., M.Arch. The Foundation's mission is to support a wide spectrum of initiatives in education and research. The Azrieli Foundation is an active supporter of programs in the fields of education, the education of architects, scientific and medical research, and the arts. The Azrieli Foundation's many initiatives include: the Holocaust Survivor Memoirs Program, which collects, preserves, publishes and distributes the written memoirs of survivors in Canada; the Azrieli Institute for Educational Empowerment, an innovative program successfully working to keep at-risk youth in school; the Azrieli Fellows Program, which promotes academic excellence and leadership on the graduate level at Israeli universities; the Azrieli Music Project, which celebrates and fosters the creation of high-quality new Jewish orchestral music; and the Azrieli Neurodevelopmental Research Program, which supports advanced research on neurodevelopmental disorders, particularly Fragile X and Autism Spectrum Disorders.